Celebrating Those Who
Fought for Freedom at the Ballot Box

★ ★ ★

Angela P. Dodson

**CENTER
STREET**

New York ★ Nashville

To my mother, Kira Evelyn Walthall Dodson

Center Street
Hachette Book Group
1290 Avenue of the Americas, New York, NY 10104
centerstreet.com
twitter.com/centerstreet

First Edition: May 2017

Center Street is a division of Hachette Book Group, Inc. The Center Street name and logo are trademarks of Hachette Book Group, Inc.

The publisher is not responsible for websites (or their content) that are not owned by the publisher.

The Hachette Speakers Bureau provides a wide range of authors for speaking events. To find out more, go to www.HachetteSpeakersBureau.com or call (866) 376-6591.

Scriptures noted KJV are taken from the King James Version of the Bible.

Print book interior design by Fearn Cutler de Vicq.

Library of Congress Cataloging-in-Publication Data has been applied for.

ISBNs: 978-1-4555-7093-5 (hardcover), 978-1-4555-7095-9 (ebook)

Printed in the United States of America

LSC-C

10 9 8 7 6 5 4 3 2 1

Contents

Remember
the
Ladies

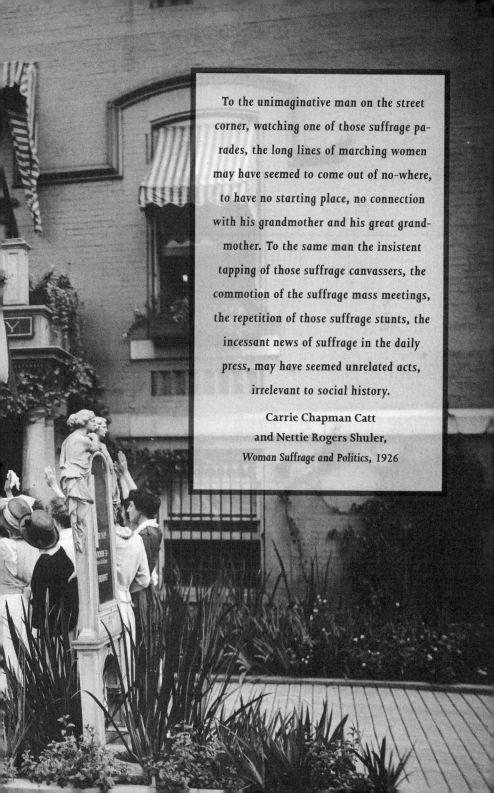

To the unimaginative man on the street corner, watching one of those suffrage parades, the long lines of marching women may have seemed to come out of no-where, to have no starting place, no connection with his grandmother and his great grandmother. To the same man the insistent tapping of those suffrage canvassers, the commotion of the suffrage mass meetings, the repetition of those suffrage stunts, the incessant news of suffrage in the daily press, may have seemed unrelated acts, irrelevant to social history.

Carrie Chapman Catt
and Nettie Rogers Shuler,
Woman Suffrage and Politics, 1926

Overleaf: **Women cheer at National Woman's Party headquarters in Washington, D.C.**
Library of Congress

Hillary Clinton greets the audience
as she accepts the nomination for president of the United States
at the Democratic National Convention, July 2016.

Elizabeth Cady Stanton, seated, and Susan B. Anthony, standing, worked closely together for many years.

Library of Congress

*Carrie Chapman Catt strides down Fifth Avenue
in a suffrage parade in New York City.*

Bettmann / Contributor

Lucy Stone was one of the first American women to graduate from college and to lecture publicly. She founded the American Woman Suffrage Association in 1869.

*Lucretia Mott, a Quaker preacher, was the inspiration
for calling the Seneca Falls Convention.*

Library of Congress

Representative Shirley Chisholm, standing, greets Rosa Parks,
the civil rights heroine.

Library of Congress

Alice Paul toasts the ratification of the Nineteenth Amendment in 1920.

Inez Milholland, dressed in white and astride a horse,
was near the head of the 1913 parade in Washington, D.C.,
the day before the inauguration of President Woodrow Wilson.

Jeannette Rankin was the first woman elected to Congress.

Library of Congress

Section 1

A Long Silence

The history of the past is but one long struggle upward to equality.

Elizabeth Cady Stanton

Cracking the Ceiling

On the day after Hillary Clinton's nomination as the Democratic Party candidate for president in 2016, the mayor of Rochester, New York, placed a sign next to Susan B. Anthony's grave in Mount Hope Cemetery there.

The red-white-and-blue sign said: "Dear Susan B., We thought you might like to know that for the first time in history, a woman is running for President representing a major party. 144 years ago, your illegal vote got you arrested. It took another 48 years for women finally to gain the right to vote. Thank you for paving the way."

It was signed "Lovely Warren, The first female mayor of Rochester." Warren, the second African-American to hold the post, became the city's sixty-seventh mayor on January 2, 2014. A Rochester native, she is an attorney and was president of the City Council before her election. She earned a bachelor's degree from John Jay College of Criminal Justice, and a juris doctor degree from Albany Law School of Union University.

The city of Rochester posted pictures of the sign on Twitter and invited people to visit the cemetery to sign it. Women in the Rochester area have a tradition of leaving "I voted" stickers and flowers at the grave.

On November 8, the day of the presidential election, the Associated Press reported, "A steady stream of people lined up at Rochester's Mount Hope cemetery starting before dawn to pay respects to the women's suffrage leader. Women left hundreds of voting stickers as tributes."

Mayor Warren was there to pass out new stickers with Anthony's image, and the cemetery had announced extended hours to allow the tradition to continue. The crowd grew into the thousands by afternoon.

Nora Rubel, director of the Susan B. Anthony Institute at the University of Rochester, took her two daughters to the polls and the grave to share the experience.

The AP article cheerfully noted that this was "an Election Day that could put America's first female president in the White House."

It did not. Hillary Rodham Clinton lost the election to Donald Trump and conceded after a hard-fought and rough battle. She won the popular vote with 48.2 percent to Trump's 46.1, but lost the all-important Electoral College tally 232 to her opponent's 306, making it an even more heartrending loss.

She addressed an audience, mostly of staff, the following day, while her husband, former president Bill Clinton; her running mate, Tim Kaine; and many campaign aides wiped back tears or sobbed audibly.

"I know we have still not shattered that highest and hardest glass ceiling, but someday, someone will, and hopefully sooner than we might think right now," she said. "And to all the little girls who are watching this, never doubt that you are valuable and powerful and deserving of every chance and opportunity in the world to pursue and to achieve your own dreams."

It was a campaign in which talk of "assaulting women," "nasty woman," and "misogyny" became common parlance, so the loss was a bitter pill to take for many women especially, and many men.

Still, it was but one more brick in the wall of disappointments women have suffered for centuries in the long struggle to participate in the public square and to be heard. Susan B. Anthony and her fellow suffragists probably would not be all that surprised, but they would understand the pain women voters were feeling.

Susan B. Anthony died in 1906 at the age of eighty-six, fourteen years before the woman suffrage amendment was adopted. Many women have her to thank for the opportunity to vote and to hold public office.

Anthony lived in Rochester with her sister, Mary, in a modest house at 17 Madison Street near downtown for the last forty years of her life. I worked as a newspaper editor in Rochester at the end of the 1970s. Though I lived only a few blocks away from where this house stands, I don't recall if I knew then that it existed, though I was very aware that she was from the area. The house opened as a museum in the mid- to late 1990s, according to museum staff. I went back to tour it as I completed the manuscript for this book. I had been to Seneca Falls the day before to see the church where the first women's rights convention was held in 1848 and to visit the homes of Elizabeth Cady Stanton, Mary Ann M'Clintock, and Jane Hunt, who had helped organize that gathering. I wanted to feel the spirit of the women and of the suffrage movement, as much as to glean any further facts I could from their surroundings and infuse them into this story.

As a woman who went to school from the mid-1950s to the late 1970s, grade school to grad school, I knew little of the suffrage movement and the women behind it. Women received almost no mention in our history books, and women's studies courses were not in our college catalogs. Even as a feminist, voracious reader, and often reviewer of books in general and history in particular, I had rarely stumbled upon books about women's roles and contributions. When I embarked on the project to write this book, I was inspired by the upcoming centennial anniversary of the Nineteenth Amendment—known as the Susan B. Anthony Amendment—which gave all women the right to vote. I had no idea how little I knew about Anthony and the other women of the movement, and I suspect that I am not alone.

I assumed younger women, educated after women's names began to creep into history books and women's history became a recognized part of school curricula, knew more. My daughter-in-law, age thirty, born after my formal education ended, assisted me in assembling the time line for the book. When she finished her part, she remarked, "Mom, I had no idea how bad we had it." In Rochester and Seneca Falls, I bought books about Susan B. Anthony and suffrage history for her daughter, my granddaughter, age eleven then and already a history buff, so that she might know and take her right to vote very seriously when she grows up.

Seventy Years of Struggle

One hundred years from now, young women will find it difficult to believe that for nearly 150 years of the nation's history, members of their sex could not legally cast votes to elect a president or even a school board member. The drafters of the United States Constitution did not think to include women at all. The nation's Founders did not explicitly exclude women or disenfranchise them, as they did specifically for enslaved Africans. Rather, from what we know of constitutional history, the subject of women voting does not seem to have come up. If it did, it was a fleeting thought. Women were the wombs of society. Through thousands of years of biblical interpretation, law, and custom, women, especially married women, simply were not considered entities with rights separate from men's. It was as if women were part of the furniture in men's lives. They were expected to remain silent on public matters, and the vast majority of women stayed in their place.

The architects of a new democracy could have thrown off the dictates of the past and extended liberty to women, but they did not. The U.S. Constitution makes no reference to women and uses male pronouns thirty times.

The Constitution and the Bill of Rights added in 1791 make several mentions of "persons" and "citizens." The first mention of sex in regard to voting rights would come with the introduction of the Fourteenth Amendment after the Civil War, which granted the vote to formerly enslaved men. It specifically reads "male inhabitants" and "male citizens." (Suffragists would seize on its references to "citizens" having a right to vote, arguing unsuccessfully that it applied to women as well.)

The matter of who should vote was left to the states to deal with in their constitutions. Only one state, New Jersey, drew up a document that allowed women to vote, and it later reversed itself.

No doubt, young women of the next century will also find it difficult to fathom that no major party had ever selected a woman as the frontrunner on its presidential ticket until 2016, much less that no woman had ever been president.

A century ago, states had begun granting suffrage to women, some limiting it to local elections and some extending full suffrage, like New York in 1917, followed by Oklahoma and South Dakota, both in 1918, setting the stage for the final push for a constitutional amendment that would extend that right to all women. The ratification of that amendment in 1920 marked the end of more than seventy years of organized struggle that saw the formation of strong bonds, followed by divisions, reconciliations, and new disagreements over tactics.

Strong women came to the front to fight the battle. What kind of women would take up the banner at a time when women virtually were forbidden to speak in public? Early on, they were mostly white, middle-class, and most often members of the Society of Friends, known as Quakers. Their religion allowed women more agency, accepted them as equals to men, imparted a duty to see others as equal to themselves, and compelled them to seek justice for all. The early reformers tended to be more educated than women of similar social standing. At the time, few girls had any schooling beyond scant basics, no matter how well off their parents were, because few schools were open to them.

Quaker girls generally received educations equal to the boys'. Many leaders in the women's rights movement also began their careers as teachers, and many had been or became journalists and publishers to further the work.

None of these women acted alone, however. Nearly all of the early women's rights leaders had long labored for the abolition of slavery. When they stepped forward to demand rights for themselves, they quickly found allies among other abolitionists, men and women, white and black, who attended their meetings, spoke for their cause, and printed notices in newspapers. The abolitionist women were on a first-name basis with men like William Lloyd Garrison, editor of the *Liberator*, and Frederick Douglass, editor of the *North Star* and a self-emancipated black man. The women reformers shared platforms with black women like Sojourner Truth and Frances E. W. Harper.

The early leaders had mastered the skills necessary to mount a revolution through their work in the antislavery movement, some through their clandestine involvement with the Underground Railroad, as well as in the temperance movement. They were well-practiced in giving lectures, organizing conventions, putting up handbills, and petitioning lawmakers. Without the aid of smartphones, personal computers with color printers, social media, air travel, or even faxes, these women and the men who supported them organized multiple conventions, petition drives, and lecture tours. Before telegraph, radio, and television were available, the suffragists publicized their cause through letters, tracts, and newspapers. Lecturers took long rides by stagecoach, buggy, train, ferryboat, and ocean liner, often risking their own health and comfort. The stalwarts stayed in run-down hotels, boarding houses, or inns, if no friendly suffragist's home was available. Orators nailed placards to posts and trees to announce their lectures and meetings held in rented halls, barns, or the few churches that welcomed them.

For thanks, the suffrage workers were often heckled, ridiculed, pilloried in sermons, targeted in editorials, mobbed, threatened, and even hung in effigy. Even worse, as time went on, some were jailed for picketing peacefully, robbed of their civil liberties, tortured, assaulted, and force-fed. Yet for more than seventy years, a small but determined parade of women kept the cause alive.

When women won full voting rights under the U.S. Constitution in 1920, only one woman who had attended the historic gathering of the founding members of the movement in Seneca Falls, New York, in 1848 was alive to see it.

She was Charlotte Woodward Pierce, then a nineteen-year-old farm girl and glove maker. After reading a notice of the meeting in a newspaper, she rallied about a half-dozen friends and traveled in a horse-drawn wagon to attend the meeting in Seneca Falls on July 19 and 20, 1848. She was among the sixty-eight women and thirty-two men who signed the Declaration of Sentiments adopted that day. In 1920, when women could vote at last in the presidential election, she was unable to cast her ballot because of illness.

At the Ballot Box

This is a button from Walter Mondale's 1984 bid for president, with vice presidential candidate Geraldine Ferraro.

One of the arguments often raised against the Susan B. Anthony Amendment, which eventually gave all women the right to vote, was that women did not want the vote. Certainly, many of them did not, and some actively fought against it.

Having won the vote, women began to influence the political process and to serve in offices where they could make a difference. Many became active in the major movements of the century, including the civil rights movement, antiwar protests, and the feminist movement to expand women's rights, including the unsuccessful battle for the Equal Rights Amendment in the 1970s.

High points included Shirley Chisholm's run for the presidency in 1972 as the first woman to seek the Democratic Party's presidential nomination, the Democrats' selection of Geraldine Ferraro as Walter Mondale's vice presidential candidate in

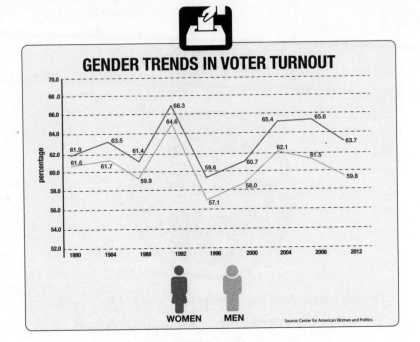

GENDER TRENDS IN VOTER TURNOUT

WOMEN   MEN

Source: Center for American Women and Politics

Men constituted the majority of voters until about 1980.
A greater proportion of women than men has voted
in every presidential election since then.

Michele Washington

1984, and, of course, Hillary Clinton's two campaigns for the presidency: in 2008, when she was defeated for the nomination by the first black man to win the office, Barack Obama; and in 2016, when she secured the nomination but lost the Electoral College vote.

Despite dire predictions, the enfranchisement of women did not bring wholesale social upheaval or the destruction of the American family or the demise of true womanhood. It did not result in women voting as a bloc and preventing men from holding office. None of the leading suffragists ran for office. Neither did giving women the vote cure all the social ills of the nation and end all wars, as many suffragists seemed to have believed it would. Southern lawmakers' fears that suffrage for black women would swell the number of votes for the race and end whites' domination dissipated, as the white power structure was able to use the same methods to block them from registering and voting as they used against black men. That began to change with the civil rights movement and the Voting Rights Act of 1965.

Women elsewhere did go to the polls, voting in steadily increasing numbers. According to an analysis of voting patterns from the Center for American Women and Politics (CAWP) at Rutgers University, a greater proportion of women than men has voted in every presidential election since 1980. CAWP said the number of women voting has exceeded the number of men voting since 1964. The center found that 65.4 percent of women and 62.1 percent of men voted in 2004. Women have cast four to seven million more votes than

men have in recent elections, CAWP said.

"It is women who decide elections," Kate Black, the vice president of research at Emily's List, told *Salon* in an interview. "It's women who show up." Emily's List is a political action committee devoted to electing pro-choice Democratic women to public office.

According to CAWP, in 2012, 63.7 percent of women and 59.8 percent of men reported voting.

Moreover, women have emerged as a force in politics because they are voting differently from men in a trend known as the gender gap. Increasingly, women are voting for Democratic tickets. In 2012, for instance, the incumbent president Barack Obama got 55 percent of the women's vote and 45 percent of the men's vote. Mitt Romney, the Republican, got 52 percent of the men's vote and 44 percent of the women's, according to a *Salon* analysis.

"Democrats are really talking about the issues that women care about," Black told *Salon*. She defined those issues as "economic security issues," including equal pay, paid family leave, job security, and access to health care, that are increasingly dominating the dialogue between women and the candidates seeking office.

"You used to see these issues siloed on candidate websites under the 'women's issues' section," she said. "Now, they're front and center."

Indeed, Kelly Dittmar, a political scientist at Rutgers and researcher for the Center for American Women and Politics, told *Salon* that women's preferences were reshaping the Democratic Party of 2016 as the campaigns worked to be more responsive to women and dropped more conservative positions.

Economic security issues were appealing to women because they "tend to be more vulnerable, still today, in terms of needing access to the social safety net, for their children and families, and for themselves," Dittmar said.

Despite their greater numbers and growing tendency to vote Democratic, the women's vote did not boost Hillary Clinton to the nomination of her party in 2008 and did not win the White House for her in 2016. In her 2008 run, she had largely played down the historical fact that she would be the first woman president if elected, until she conceded to Barack Obama in a speech to supporters that June.

"Although we weren't able to shatter that highest, hardest glass ceiling this time, thanks to you, it's got about eighteen million cracks in it," Clinton said, making reference to the number of votes she collected in the primaries. "And the light is shining through like never before, filling us all with the hope and the sure knowledge that the path will be a little easier next time."

After the campaign, she gave her staff members gifts, necklaces for women and cuff links for men with a symbolic crackled-glass emblem that read "18 million cracks HRC 2008" on the back—reminiscent of the suffrage leader Alice Paul's jail door emblems for her supporters incarcerated for protests. (See Section 6, "Jail and Hunger Strikes.") Some aides wore the crackled-glass pieces at the Democratic National Convention in 2016 in the days leading up to her formal nomination.

After the 2008 election, Hillary Clinton graciously accepted her opponent's invitation to serve in his Cabinet as secretary of state. She weathered some storms and controversies in that position, then came back to soldier on again for the nomination. After a campaign against the former Independent from Vermont, Senator Bernie Sanders, which was fought right up to the last day, she emerged as the victor for the top of the ticket.

Just before she stepped out to give her acceptance speech at the DNC in Philadelphia on July 28, 2016, the delegates and a television audience of nearly 34 million viewers, according to Nielsen ratings, saw a video depicting her as a wife, mother, grandmother, and dedicated public servant that ended with the sights and sounds of shat-tering glass. She glided onto the stage resplendent in white, like Inez Milholland, who rode her horse in the 1913 suffrage parade in Washington (see Section 6, "Welcoming Wilson"), and the New York suffragists on parade. Only on this night, Clinton was in her trademark pantsuit, not the flowing white gown Milholland chose or the long skirts of the parading suffragists.

In this campaign, Clinton readily embraced her feminine identity. She addressed it immediately in her remarks, and many people in the audience, mostly women, shed tears as she did. Women on social media confessed to crying as they watched her on television in their homes or at watch parties.

"Tonight, we've reached a milestone in our nation's march toward a more perfect union: the first time that a major party has nominated a woman for president," Clinton said. "Standing here as my mother's daughter, and my daughter's mother, I'm so happy this day has come. Happy for grandmothers and little girls and everyone in between. Happy for boys and men, too—because when any barrier falls in America, for anyone, it clears the way for everyone. When there are no ceilings, the sky's the limit."

While no woman had ever stood on that platform as the nominee of a major party, women have secured a place in elective politics throughout the country, in offices from school boards to mayoral offices, like Lovely Warren of Rochester. They have served as heads of their state governments, like Nikki Haley of South Carolina; in the U.S. House of Representatives, like Patsy Mink of Hawaii or Millicent Fenwick and Helen Meyner, both of New Jersey; and in the U.S. Senate, like Margaret Chase Smith of Maine, Shelley Moore Capito of West Virginia, and Carol Moseley Braun of Illinois.

Jeannette Rankin's election to Congress in 1916 put her in place to begin the legislative debate that eventually led to approval of the Nineteenth Amendment and the ratification process. Since 1917, when Rankin came to Congress, 325

women have served as U.S. representatives, delegates, or senators as of 2017, according to the House of Representatives' History, Art, and Archives website.

Women have also served in appointed positions: only four to date as Supreme Court justices—Sandra Day O'Connor, Ruth Bader Ginsburg, Sonia Sotomayor, and Elena Kagan; and about thirty presidential Cabinet members as of 2016, beginning with Frances Perkins, secretary of labor from 1933 to 1945, appointed by President Franklin D. Roosevelt. Cabinet women have also included such notable women as Condoleezza Rice, who was a childhood friend of the little girls killed in a Birmingham church during the civil rights movement.

Could the founding suffragists have imagined women in these political roles when they met inside the hot, stuffy, little brick church in Seneca Falls in July 1848? Would those who attended the early national women's rights conventions throughout the rest of that century have foreseen a time when women would achieve such political gains? Would the women who paraded, picketed, and went to jail in the early twentieth century believe that a woman could even stand a chance of occupying the Oval Office in 2016? A woman will be president someday, but now it will probably be someone other than Clinton.

Hillary Rodham Clinton, as former First Lady, came to Seneca Falls on July 16, 1998—150 years after the group of five organizers gathered three hundred kindred souls there for the radical purpose of discussing the rights to which women might be entitled.

In a speech there, Clinton reminded women of the power they have and of the price paid to secure it:

We must tell and retell, learn and relearn, these women's stories, and we must make it our personal mission, in our everyday lives, to pass these stories on to our daughters and sons. Because we cannot—we must not—ever forget that the rights and opportunities that we enjoy as women today were not just bestowed upon us by some benevolent ruler. They were fought for, agonized over, marched for, jailed for and even died for by brave and persistent women and men who came before us...And if we are to finish the work begun here—we must, above all else, take seriously the power of the vote and use it to make our voices heard. What the champions of suffrage understood was that the vote is not just a symbol of our equality, but that it can be, if used, a guarantee of results.

Disenfranchised

"We Are Determined to Foment a Rebellion."

Abigail Adams wrote her husband, John Adams of Braintree, Massachusetts, on March 31, 1776, as he was then attending the Second Continental Congress. She urged him to make sure his colleagues did not forget about the rights of women in their struggle for the colonies' independence from Great Britain.

I long to hear that you have declared an independency—and by the way in the new Code of Laws which I suppose it will be necessary for you to make I desire you would Remember the Ladies, and be more generous and favourable to them than your ancestors. Do not put such unlimited power into the hands of the Husbands. Remember all Men would be tyrants if they could. If perticuliar care and attention is not paid to the Ladies we are determined to foment a Rebelion, and will not hold ourselves bound by any Laws in which we have no voice, or Representation.

That your Sex are Naturally Tyrannical is a Truth so thoroughly established as to admit of no dispute, but such of you as wish to be happy willingly give up the harsh title of Master for the more tender and endearing one of Friend. Why then, not put it out of the power of the vicious and the Lawless to use us with cruelty and indignity with impunity. Men of Sense in all Ages abhor those customs which treat us

Abigail Adams, wife of President John Adams,
urged him to "Remember the Ladies."
Library of Congress

only as the vassals of your
Sex. Regard us then as Beings
placed by providence under
your protection and in immi-
tation of the Supreem Being

make use of that power only
for our happiness.

In the context of the time,
her remarks would have seemed

quite brazen if anyone had seen them besides her tolerant husband. Women of her time were not permitted a voice in public affairs of any kind. It is doubtful that more than a few of them spoke of such matters even at home, almost certainly not in the presence of husbands or fathers.

Women had little, if any, access to education that would prepare them for such discourse anyway. Mrs. Adams herself had no formal schooling or tutoring. The daughter of a Harvard-trained Congregationalist minister, she made use of his small library and learned from various family members through informal tutoring. Abigail was a voracious reader, and by the time she met the young lawyer who would become one of our nation's Founding Fathers, she was considered well educated for a woman. She was twenty years old when they married on October 25, 1764, in the family parsonage at Weymouth, Massachusetts.

John Adams, by all accounts, appreciated her mind, and theirs was as much a partnership of equals as could be imagined at the time. As his political career took him away from home for long periods, she raised their five children and ran the family farm. Their letters (more than one thousand in their lifetimes) bridged the distance. They bore news of home to him and reports on the nation-building efforts to her with commentary and gossip by both of them on the affairs of the day during the revolutionary period and at the dawn of a new nation.

In the early years of their marriage, the stage was set for the thirteen colonies established in North America to break from British rule, as the colonists chafed under the increasingly onerous attempts to tax and control them. Adams won a seat in the Massachusetts Assembly and attended the first Continental Congress as a delegate from Massachusetts in 1774. A few days after the first shots of the American Revolution were fired at Lexington and Concord on April 19, 1775, Mr. Adams was on his way to Philadelphia for the Second Continental Congress. It became the de facto government of the colonies, managing the war effort, and it was still in session when Abigail Adams's letter reached her husband.

Her bold suggestion that the Congress be mindful of women's rights stopped short of demanding a vote or asserting a role for women in governing. Her words suggest she hoped for more equitable laws regarding women as wives and mothers. In any event, her husband made light of her demands, joking that men would be foolish to give up their perquisites and were, in the end, at the mercy of women, writing in return on April 14, 1776:

> *As to your extraordinary Code of Laws, I cannot but laugh. We have been told that our Struggle has loosened the bands of Government every where. That Children and Apprentices were disobedient— that schools and Colledges were grown turbulent—that Indians slighted their Guardians and Negroes grew insolent to their Masters. But your Letter was the first Intimation that another Tribe more numerous and powerfull than all the rest were grown discontented.—This is rather too coarse a Compliment but you are so saucy, I wont blot it out.*

> *Depend upon it, We know better than to repeal our Masculine systems. Altho they are in full Force, you know they are little more than Theory. We dare not exert our Power in its full Latitude. We are obliged to go fair, and softly, and in Practice you know We are the subjects [of the women]. We have only the Name of Masters, and rather than give up this, which would compleatly subject Us to the Despotism of the Peticoat, I hope General Washington, and all our Brave Heroes would fight.*

For a man who was thought to be enlightened and was willing to consider his wife an intellectual equal, his response seems a bit flip for such a serious matter. However, it gives us a hint that women's rights was something the patriots did not even consider. The issue was not on the table, and Adams, a key player, was not going to be the one to put it there.

"All Men Are Created Equal"

John Adams was one of the most vocal advocates for the independence of the colonies when the Second Continental Congress met, and he was instrumental in writing the declaration it adopted on July 4, 1776. Thomas Jefferson was the main author, but Adams was its leading instigator. Both were on the committee appointed to write the declaration, but Adams deferred to Jefferson for his superior writing skills.

In what has been hailed as one of the most stirring statements of all time, that document declared:

> We hold these truths to be self-evident, that all men are created equal, that they are endowed by their Creator with certain unalienable Rights, that among these are Life, Liberty and the pursuit of Happiness.

The irony of this statement at a time when slavery remained legal throughout the land did not escape observers then or historians since. That Jefferson, whose livelihood derived from slavery, could write that "all men are created equal" seems disingenuous, but he was a complex man capable of entertaining conflicting beliefs.

The historian Joseph J. Ellis concluded that the revolutionary leaders had been prepared to postpone consideration of "inherently divisive issues like slavery, voting qualifications, and women's rights" for the expediency of creating a union. Jefferson's statement was a placeholder for later consideration.

"With these words, Jefferson had smuggled the revolutionary agenda into the founding document, casually and almost inadvertently planting the seeds that would grow into the expanding mandate for individual rights that eventually ended slavery, made women's suffrage inevitable, and sanctioned the civil rights of all minorities."

However, Ellis says that Jefferson would not have recognized that he was doing anything that profound.

"No one noticed it at the time," Ellis wrote. "And there is no evidence that Jefferson himself had any inkling that he had written the seminal statement of the American promise."

Consent of the Governed

The declaration makes no mention of women, presumably using "men" to mean all, and clearly the document did nothing to advance the cause of women. In fact, the women who organized the Seneca Falls Convention in 1848 turned this statement on its head by inserting "and women" in their Declaration of Sentiments.

However, Adams had written a letter to a friend on May 26, 1776, indicating that Abigail's plea pricked his conscience. His friend, James Sullivan, a politician and jurist in Massachusetts, had written a statement of principles related to the qualification of voters for their colony and governance with the "consent of the people." The Declaration of Independence used similar phrasing: "Governments are instituted among Men, deriving their just powers from the consent of the governed..."

In his letter to Sullivan, Adams asked:

> *To what an Extent Shall We carry this Principle? Shall We Say, that every Individual of the Community, old and young, male and female, as well as rich and poor, must consent, expressly to every Act of Legislation? No, you will Say. This is impossible. How then does the Right arise in the Majority to govern the Minority, against their Will? Whence arises the Right of the Men to govern Women, without their Consent?*

Whence the Right of the old to bind the Young, without theirs.

But let us first Suppose, that the whole Community of every Age, Rank, Sex, and Condition, has a Right to vote. This Community, is assembled—a Motion is made and carried by a Majority of one Voice. The Minority will not agree to this. Whence arises the Right of the Majority to govern, and the Obligation of the Minority to obey? from Necessity, you will Say, because there can be no other Rule. But why exclude Women? You will Say, because their Delicacy renders them unfit for Practice and Experience, in the great Business of Life, and the hardy Enterprizes of War, as well as the arduous Cares of State. Besides, their attention is So much engaged with the necessary Nurture of their Children, that Nature has made them fittest for domestic Cares. And Children have not Judgment or Will of their own.

True. But will not these Reasons apply to others? Is it not equally true, that Men in general in every Society, who are wholly destitute of Property, are also too little acquainted with public Affairs to form a Right Judgment, and too dependent upon other Men to have a Will of their own?...

Our people have never been very rigid in Scrutinizing into the Qualifications of Voters, and I presume they will not now begin to be so. But I would not advise them to make any alteration in the Laws, at present, respecting the Qualifications of Voters...

Depend upon it, sir, it is dangerous to open So fruitfull a Source of Controversy and Altercation, as would be opened by attempting to alter the Qualifications of Voters. There will be no End of it. New Claims will arise. Women will demand a Vote. Lads from 12 to 21 will think their Rights not enough attended to, and every Man,

who has not a Farthing,
will demand an equal Voice
with any other in all Acts of
State. It tends to confound
and destroy all Distinctions,
and prostrate all Ranks, to
one common Levell.

In fact, a few American women had exercised a right to vote. Women, for instance, voted in town halls in some cases. One, Lydia Taft, a wealthy widow, voted in town meetings in Uxbridge, Massachusetts, in 1756, as noted in *Address Delivered at the Unitarian Church, in Uxbridge, Mass., in 1864: With Further Statements, Not Made a Part of the Address, But Included in the Notes*:

Among the "honorable
women not a few," Who
Have joined Their names
and fortunes to the Taft
family, mention Should be
made of the wife of Josiah,
the son of Daniel. The days
of her widowhood Were
times of serious trouble for
the colonies. Her husband
died in 1756. The French and
Indian war was at hand; the
Revolution not far distant.
A requisition was made
upon the town of Uxbridge
for a Certain sum of money
for colonial purposes. A
meeting of the legal voters
was held to see if the money
Should be Granted. The es-
tate of Josiah Taft paid the
largest tax in Uxbridge, and
his son Bezaleel Was a mi-
nor; but with a sturdy sense
of justice That there Should
be "no taxation without rep-
resentation," The Citizens
Declared That the widow
Josiah Taft Should vote upon
the question. She did so,
and her vote was The One
That decided in the affirma-
tive That the money Should
be paid. Who wonders That
her son was a man Who Had
the unbounded confidence of
His townsmen, and served
them in various offices of
honor and trust for forty
years! Uxbridge May yet be
famous as the pioneer in the
cause of woman's suffrage.

In any case, the Declaration of Independence was just that—a declaration of intent, grievances, and war. It merely laid out the case for breaking away from British rule.

It was not a governing document, and it would not set law for the colonies in revolt.

The Founding Fathers left it to the states to decide who voted in their jurisdictions.

The Continental Congress busied itself with running the war but directed the states to reject the royal authority of the British, write state constitutions, and set up their own governments on democratic principles.

On November 15, 1777, the Congress adopted some rules, the Articles of Confederation, that served as the first national constitution, but the states retained most of the power. The document was ratified March 1, 1781. The articles named the country as the United States of America, gave sovereignty to each state, gave the states a vote in the Congress, and allowed the Congress powers to run the war and conduct foreign policy. Article IV does say, "The free inhabitants of each of these States, paupers, vagabonds, and fugitives from justice excepted, shall be entitled to all privileges and immunities of free citizens in the several States."

Even before ratification, the Congress continued managing the war, which dragged on until 1783.

"Inhabitants" and "Persons"

New Jersey became the only former colony to grant women the right to vote. As a Heritage Foundation article, "New Jersey Recognizes the Right of Women to Vote," outlined the history:

> On February 22, 1797, the New Jersey Assembly passed "An Act to regulate the Election of Members of the Legislative-Council and the General Assembly, Sheriffs and Coroners, in this State," which specifically included women in the franchise. The status of women voters had been unclear for decades. The 1776 New Jersey Constitution had vaguely stated that "all inhabitants" of the state could vote. To remedy

this, a voting law in 1790, which applied only to seven counties, had clarified the Constitution by using the phrase "he or she" in referring to voters. Finally, in an effort to create uniformity, the Assembly passed the 1797 voting law, recognizing the right of women to vote across the state.

In the constitution adopted by New Jersey in 1776, after the Congress asked the states to formalize their constitutions, all adult residents who owned a specified amount of property could vote:

> IV. That all inhabitants of this Colony, of full age, who are worth fifty pounds

proclamation money, clear estate in the same, and have resided within the county in which they claim a vote for twelve months immediately preceding the election, shall be entitled to vote for Representatives in Council and Assembly; and also for all other public officers, that shall be elected by the people of the county at large.

At least seven other state constitutions were drafted the same year, and all referred to men as eligible voters. They "defined voters as 'freeman' (Pennsylvania, Maryland, Delaware, North Carolina), 'man' (Vermont), 'white male inhabitants' (Georgia), or 'free white man' (South Carolina)," according to an article, "'The Petticoat Electors': Women's Suffrage in New Jersey, 1776–1807," by Judith Apter Klinghoffer and Lois Elkis.

A voting law in 1790 clarified the New Jersey Constitution. The Assembly approved that law with only three dissenting votes. In 1797, the Assembly passed another law recognizing women's

right to vote across the state. "And be it enacted, That every voter shall openly, and in full view deliver his or her ballot."

"New Jersey made history by recognizing the right of women to vote. The enormity of this event cannot be overstated. Never before in all of recorded history had women been given voting rights," the Heritage Foundation article said.

Because of laws restricting women's property rights, in actuality, the New Jersey law meant only widowed and single women owning property could vote. Those women who could readily took advantage of the law, voting until 1807, when the legislature suddenly discovered a need to reinterpret the constitution and passed a law stripping women of the vote and limiting it to white, male, taxpaying adult citizens.

Historians had long considered New Jersey's enfranchisement somewhat of a fluke, unique among the new states of the fledgling republic, according to Klinghoffer and Elkis. The 1776 constitution, issued July 2, was written in haste with the war drawing nearer to New Jersey after George Washington's forces suffered several defeats in New York. Perhaps the drafters merely forgot to exclude women when choosing the word "inhabitants."

Klinghoffer and Elkis argued that the decision to give women the vote was deliberate, as was the disenfranchisement of women (and black men). The authors say John Cooper, a Quaker from Gloucester County, was credited with getting the provision for women into the constitution. "Certainly, the Quaker belief in the equality of women was a major influence on the members from the southern part of the state, where they were a large percentage of the population," they wrote.

Another factor was the role women were playing in the Revolution "taking care of the farms and businesses, acting as couriers and spies, as well as providing continuous supplies of food and clothing."

The women of New Jersey embraced the vote and actively participated in the political discourse of the day. Competing political parties—the Federalists, who pushed for a stronger central government, and the Republicans, who espoused more democratic and egalitarian principles— courted the women's allegiance as they fought for dominance, though they did nothing to ease the burdens of women through the laws of the state. When a third party emerged in New Jersey, it was in the interest of the other parties to reduce their risks by narrowing the electorate, eliminating women, blacks, aliens, and the poor in the 1807 law. Some lawmakers feared that the reference to "inhabitants" would allow slaves or noncitizen aliens to vote.

"Interestingly, the women of New Jersey did not object to their exclusion with any rigor; they did not lobby or protest against the law," the Heritage Foundation noted.

The disenfranchisement of women went unchallenged for decades, as it reduced New Jersey women to the same status as their sisters throughout the nation and throughout the world.

Legal Status of Women

In general, the law of the colonies derived from English common law, which made women a lesser extension of their husbands and gave them little recourse over husbands who were cruel, drunken, or just poor providers. Upon marriage, a woman ceased to exist as a separate legal entity. In this regard, she was not really a separate "person" in her own right. Women could not hold title to their earnings, control their own property—even if they inherited it or brought it into marriage— or enter contracts. They did not have a right to custody of their own children if divorced or separated. Divorce could be granted only in extreme circumstances. They did not automatically inherit their husband's estate.

According to William Blackstone's *Commentaries on the Laws of England*, the model for the American legal system, "By marriage, the husband and wife are one person in law: that is, the very being or legal existence of the woman is suspended during the marriage, or at least is incorporated and consolidated into that of the husband."

The woman was "covered" by her husband under this legal concept of coverture.

Single women or widowed women had some rights to property, but in reality, most were still dependent on some male relative. Most women did not work outside the home or their family's farm. By custom, they generally were restricted to the "domestic sphere," while men dominated the "public sphere."

Few women received a formal education, and the vast majority of men considered them incapable of higher learning or complex reasoning. This was upheld by thousands of years of tradition, though a handful of women—such as Hatshepsut, fifteenth-century BC pharaoh of Egypt, to Elizabeth I of Britain in the sixteenth century AD—had ruled whole nations. American women really had few rights to speak of, and men were in no hurry to change that. Neither were many women.

When the war ended, life settled back into a welcomed normalcy, with little talk of women's rights until nearly the middle of the next century, in spite of Abigail Adams's declaration, and women would remain disenfranchised for another 150 years.

Reinventing the Nation

After the war, however, the Founding Fathers still had work to do to solidify the nation, which consisted of a loose affiliation of sovereign states. The Congress lacked the power to tax and to resolve conflicts among the states. It could not pay the government's debts. A unanimous vote of the states was required to amend the articles, so any state could veto a change. The articles did not set up courts or provide for a strong executive. Each state had its own currency, and trade was difficult.

Alexander Hamilton, then a military aide to George Washington, had begun calling for change before the war ended, and he was the first to suggest that representatives convene to revise the articles. The idea gained momentum and supporters with each passing year, including leaders like James Madison, then a Virginia plantation owner who had served in the Continental Congress. Representatives of several states met in September 1786 in Annapolis, Maryland, and called for a convention to reexamine the articles. In May 1787, a Constitutional Convention began in Philadelphia. Hamilton, Madison, and some other leaders already had more drastic changes in mind to produce a stronger central government by scrapping the articles and writing a new constitution. After months of deliberation, the delegates signed the new constitution on September 17 of that year, and it was ratified May 29, 1790.

As the Founding Fathers hammered out a national constitution, they debated the legality of slavery and the apportionment compromise at length, but again women's rights were not on the agenda. The Constitution neither granted women voting rights nor denied them. Voting remained a state matter.

In fact, to this day, nothing in the Constitution explicitly guarantees that the rights it protects are held equally by all citizens, male or female, in spite of efforts in the twentieth century to pass an Equal Rights Amendment.

The new Constitution of 1787 left women in legal shackles, as it left the enslaved people in full bondage but enumerated them as three-fifths of a person for purposes of allocating representation in Congress, the result of a compromise with Southern delegates.

Article I, Section 2, clause 3 states that:

Representatives and direct Taxes shall be apportioned among the several States which may be included within this Union, according to their respective Numbers, which shall be determined by adding to the whole Number of free Persons, including those bound to Service for a Term of Years, and excluding Indians not taxed, three fifths of all other Persons.

Free women were counted in the population as full persons in that regard but remained voteless and voiceless. They were not alone. Women in other parts of the world were not enfranchised, either.

While the delegates debated the three-fifths clause and the legality of slavery at length, it does not appear that they gave much thought to women. They simply ignored them. Women's place in society was enshrined by law, custom, and religious dictates, as it had been for thousands of years. It appears that it simply did not occur to the all-male assembly to address women's place in the new democracy they were creating for themselves. In the years leading up to the Revolution and during the conflict, American women had demonstrated their loyalty to the cause, vowing not to drink tea, concocting herbal substitutes, boycotting British clothing, spinning and weaving their own cloth, and staging protests of their own. They supported the patriot soldiers and often had to keep their homes, shops, and farms running in the absence of men.

Abigail Adams and other women must have hoped that the Revolution would afford them some relief from the antiquated, harsh laws of England, but none was forthcoming.

This seemed to become a pattern for American women. At the close of wars, they expected somehow that men would see the enormous contribution they had made, standing up for them in military service and standing in for them in domestic life, and would reward them, graciously granting them at least some of the rights males enjoyed. Women suffragists would have the same expectations after they put in long hours in support of the Civil War and World War I, and they would be bitterly disappointed when the rewards were denied or delayed. Having secured their own freedom from tyranny, the Founding Fathers had a myopic view of who should enjoy the rights secured from the hard-fought war, and it did not include women, not even to the patriots' own mothers, sisters, and daughters. Women who helped build this fledgling nation and sacrificed to give it birth would have little share in its liberties.

Abigail Adams did not go on to "foment a Rebelion," nor did any other woman of the time. Still, American women would not be silent forever. They were a hardy lot who individually and collectively had earned a place alongside men in determining how the nation would evolve.

The Founding Mothers

European men had mostly come to the continent without women, expecting to take what they could of the natural resources, get rich quickly, and go home. The London merchants who invested in colonies and encouraged settlement soon realized men alone could not sustain a colony and began sending women. Among the brave women who accepted the challenge was Eleanor White Dare, who gave birth to a daughter, Virginia, in 1587, not long after arriving on Roanoke Island in what is now North Carolina. Eleanor came with her husband and about 115 other settlers, only to find that a handful of men left there earlier had all died or disappeared. Virginia was the first white, Christian girl born among the British colonists. Eleanor's father, John White, returned to England to get more provisions. When he could finally find passage back three years later, the Roanoke Island settlers had all disappeared, and to date no one has learned their fate.

Jamestown was founded in 1607 with 104 men. About a year later, the first women, Mistress Anne Forrest and her maid, Anne Buras, reached Jamestown. More women came in 1609. When the settlers ran out of provisions and began starving, at least one woman may have become a victim of cannibalism.

In 1619, ninety English women came to Jamestown on one ship, sold reportedly by their own consent to settlers as wives for the price of their transportation. Eleanor Flexner, the author of *Century of Struggle: The Woman's Rights Movement in the United States,* reflected on the prospective brides' circumstances:

> *Perhaps the knowledge that each would find a husband among the several hundred bachelors eagerly awaiting them made up for the subsequent hardships, but they cannot have found life easy. Virginia was only a toehold in the wilderness, fighting an unceasing war against plague, encroaching vegetation, and the Indians, who bitterly resented the white influx.*

Native women had borne the brunt of European exploration of the "new" world, exploited, stripped of land, and exposed to deadly diseases. Pocahontas, the adolescent daughter of a powerful chief, Powhatan, was even kidnapped by the English after befriending and feeding the newcomers at Jamestown. She was soon married off to an Englishman, John Rolfe, probably in an effort to cement peace between her people and the newcomers.

When the *Mayflower* landed in Massachusetts after going off course as it headed for Virginia in 1620, eighteen married women, three of them pregnant, and eleven girls were among its approximately one hundred passengers. One woman drowned, perhaps having flung herself overboard while the ship was still at anchor. Only four of the adult women survived the first winter.

The first European women to arrive faced horrendous conditions in a strange and wild land where they had to help do some of the physical labor of clearing land, planting, and raising livestock. Conditions in the new colonies created new domestic work. Women produced goods that were not available in their new homeland—cloth, garments, soap, shoes, candles, and other necessities they might have purchased at home in England. This role was in addition to cooking, washing, and caring for children.

For men, the hardships of exploring, hunting, and fishing often proved fatal, leaving many women widowed with children to feed. Disease, famine, and childbirth in primitive conditions, not to mention invasions from native people opposed to the encroachment, also took their toll. Widowed women sometimes carried on their husband's business or took up trades of their own. These changes in women's roles began to give women in the New World a value that was more on par with the men, especially as the frontiers pushed west.

Soon it became apparent, however, that even with the women's help, the British colonists simply were too few in number to meet the labor demands of creating a new economy and building the infrastructure of a nation. They required indentured servants and eventually enslaved labor to fill the void. Some of the indentured came willingly, perhaps to escape some worse fate at home or for an adventure and a fresh start. Others were coerced, some kidnapped, and still others arrested. Those arrested faced a choice of servitude in the colonies versus jail or the gallows. Jailers could sell them or deport them for a crime.

The indentured laborers were bound to service, customarily for five to seven years, to pay for their passage. The servants faced harsh sentences for any crime they committed and often an increase in the term of indenture. They could not marry or engage in any other work without their master's permission. Many women, whites, and later blacks, arrived as indentured servants. It has become common on Internet social networks for white participants to claim that their indentured ancestors too were "slaves," but the terms of indenture were very different from what was to come, and their forced servitude would not last another 250-odd years, as that of the Africans would.

Inventing Chattel Slavery

Twenty Africans were brought to Jamestown in 1620. They served terms similar to those of the white indentured servants, and some of the Africans received land at the end of their service. Some intermarried with the white indentured people. Soon, blacks who initially came as indentured servants found themselves permanently enslaved with no indenture contract offering an out as the colonies needed more and more laborers. Indentured servants required replacement too often as their terms ended. They were in short supply, and they could more easily run away and disappear into the white population.

The supply of Africans was more abundant. Laws kept them and their children bound for life with the invention of chattel slavery, and slave ships brought thousands more men, women, and children to labor in the colonies. Any children born to them increased the masters' stock.

The white indentured women's futures often depended on the marriages they made and the successes of their husbands. Many women found themselves in dire circumstances, often with cruel or lascivious owners and few career opportunities after their service. Some hit the matrimonial lottery, marrying men who quickly prospered as planters and eventually owners of large plantations in Virginia and other colonies or of thriving businesses in the towns and cities along the Eastern Seaboard.

From this stew of native

people, explorers, outcasts, criminals, and enslaved laborers, the American population grew, spreading out first along the coast and then inward to nearby territories.

The introduction of women made it possible for the population to multiply. The introduction of a system of permanent slavery made it possible to cultivate the land with controllable costs and for white property owners to prosper in the new land.

Breaking the Silence

For nearly 250 years after nonnative women began showing up in North America, the question of women's rights seems to have taken a backseat to mere survival. Women, all women, occupied the lowest rung in society. The idea that women were inferior is perhaps as old as civilization itself, stemming in Western culture from the religious belief that women were cursed because of the sin of the biblical Eve.

It would have been difficult for even the most elite women to protest, because custom forced them into silence. The widespread notion that women should be seen and not heard in the public sphere also has been attributed to the Bible, specifically to Saint Paul's admonition:

"Let your women keep silence in the churches: for it is not permitted unto them to speak; but they are commanded to be under obedience as also saith the law" (1 Corinthians 14:34).

A few women challenged this. Among them was Anne Hutchinson, who migrated to Massachusetts in 1634. She began preaching, mostly to women, then to men as well, speaking against some Puritan teachings. Hutchinson was the wife of a merchant, a mother of fifteen, and a practicing midwife. She was the daughter of a clergyman and teacher in England who allowed her a decent education. For her preaching, she was subject to civil and religious proceedings and eventually banned from the colony

Mary Wollstonecraft published her
A Vindication of the Rights of Woman *in 1792.*

Library of Congress

of Massachusetts, settling for a time in Rhode Island. Later, she moved to disputed lands in what became the Bronx, where Native Americans massacred her and some of her children. One of her supporters had been Mary Dyer, who was herself hanged in 1660 in Boston for repeatedly defying the banishment of Quakers from the colony.

Other notable women of the colonial period who contested the status quo included Margaret

Brent, an unmarried landowner in the Maryland Colony, who became executrix for the estate of Leonard Calvert, the brother and representative of Lord Baltimore, the colony's proprietor. In 1648, she appeared before the Maryland Assembly to demand two votes—one on behalf of herself as a freeholder and one on behalf of Lord Baltimore in her capacity as his lawyer. The assembly rejected her demand, and she eventually left the colony for Virginia.

Another woman, Judith Sargent Murray, wrote an essay during the Revolution about disparities in the opportunities offered women versus men, particularly in the education and socialization of women to lean toward domesticity. She was the daughter of a prosperous merchant and sea captain in Gloucester, Massachusetts, who was a supporter of the Revolution and delegate to the convention that ratified the Constitution. Though her essay was not published until 1790, her writings on this subject came about a decade before a woman in England, Mary Wollstonecraft, published *A Vindication of the Rights of Woman* in 1792, which became a kind of manifesto for women's rights among the few well-situated, literate women who could read it.

A Suitable Education

To have a voice in society, women first had to overcome the obstacles to getting an education. Few schools existed that would accept girls, even if their parents would allow it, but attitudes toward the education of women were gradually changing. Abigail Adams was an outspoken advocate for improving the education of women.

"If we mean to have Heroes, Statesmen and Philosophers, we should have learned women," she said.

A few colleges began to accept women, and pioneering educators began opening academies specifically for women.

Dr. Benjamin Rush, a physician, professor at the University of Pennsylvania, and member of the all-male board of visitors of the Young Ladies' Academy in Philadelphia, famously penned his "Thoughts upon Female Education" in 1787. He opined that women "must be the stewards, and guardians of their husbands' property," which required an education that "teaches them to discharge the duties of those offices with the most success and reputation."

In the new republic, he said, "the equal share that every citizen has in the liberty and the possible share he may have in the government of our country, make it necessary that our ladies should be qualified to a certain degree by a peculiar and suitable education, to concur in *instructing their sons* in the principles of liberty and government" (emphasis added).

Dr. Rush elaborated on his design for a woman's education, suggesting the curriculum include English grammar, penmanship, bookkeeping, history, and geography:

> ...and thereby qualify her not only for a general intercourse with the world, but to be an agreeable companion for a sensible man. To these branches of knowledge may be added, in some instances, a general acquaintance with the first principles of astronomy natural philosophy and chemistry, particularly, with such parts of them as are calculated to prevent superstition, by explaining the causes, or obviating the effects of natural evil, and such, as are capable of being applied to domestic, and culinary purposes.
>
> Vocal musick should never be neglected, in the education of a young lady, in this country. Besides preparing her to join in that part of publick worship which consists in psalmody, it will enable her to soothe the cares of domestick life. The distress and vexation of a husband—the noise of a nursery, and, even, the sorrows that will sometimes intrude into her own bosom, may all be relieved by a song, where sound and sentiment unite to act upon the mind.

Dancing, too, was suitable as "a branch of education for an American lady," Dr. Rush said, because "it promotes health, and renders the figure and motions of the body easy and agreeable."

Instrumental music might be desirable "where a musical ear irresistibly disposes to it, and affluence at the same time affords a prospect of such an exemption from the usual cares and duties of the mistress of a family as will enable her to practice it." Ditto for art instruction.

In short, women should get only the kind of education that would serve their husbands and sons well, without disturbing domestic harmony or interfering with their womanly chores. This was still progress. Barriers to the education of girls and women were crumbling slowly.

Oberlin College opened its doors in 1833 and admitted women to the "Ladies' Course." In 1837, four women, Caroline Mary Rudd, Elizabeth Prall, Mary Hosford, and Mary Fletcher Kellogg, entered the bachelor's degree program. (In 1835, Oberlin admitted African-Americans. Soon after its founding, the college became a busy stop on the Underground Railroad and a nexus of abolitionist activity.)

Rudd, Prall, and Hosford graduated in 1841, followed in 1847 by Lucy Stone, who would become a celebrated orator for abolition and later women's rights, and Antoinette Louisa Brown, who would become the first American female to be an ordained minister.

Brown would also become a suffragist and Stone's sister-in-law. Stone married Henry B. Blackwell, and Brown married his brother Samuel Charles Blackwell and became known as Antoinette Brown Blackwell. After the Civil War, Stone would emerge as the leader of one of two major factions of the woman suffrage movement.

Educators like Emma Willard, Catharine Beecher, Sarah Pierce, and Zilpah Grant also began academies for young women in the Northeast. In 1833, Prudence Crandall, a Quaker teacher, opened a school for black girls, Miss Crandall's School for Young Ladies and Little Misses of Color, in Canterbury, Connecticut, but a mob attack forced her to shut it down. In the South, it was illegal to teach the enslaved, male or female, to read or write. Few schools were available to blacks in the North, either.

In another major educational advance for women, Mary Lyon founded Mount Holyoke Female Seminary for young women of modest means in South Hadley, Massachusetts, in 1837. It achieved collegiate status in

1893 after other colleges for women sprang up, but it is still considered the first U.S. college for women. Lyon had some education in district schools near her struggling family's farm in western Massachusetts and became a teacher. Earlier, she established Wheaton Female Seminary in Norton, Massachusetts.

Abolitionists
Take the Lead

Women were becoming empowered, and they began to use their voices in the abolitionist movement throughout the 1830s. When critics challenged their right to speak publicly, women lecturers vehemently defended their right to do so and increasingly spoke directly to the question of women's right to speak and be heard.

The famed abolitionist William Lloyd Garrison cofounded his newspaper the *Liberator* with Isaac Knapp in 1831. It was also in this period that the Underground Railroad became known by that name and gained momentum. It was a system of "agents" and "conductors" escorting those fleeing slavery through safe houses, or "sta-tions," and arranging transportation at key junctions. A rebellion in 1831 against slavery, led by Nat Turner, a plantation preacher in Virginia, stirred up Northern abolitionists, as it terrified Southerners. In the South, it led to conditions and laws that were ever more repressive. In the North, the revolt led to the founding of numerous anti-slavery societies in which blacks and whites worked together to end the evil institution, and abolitionist lecturers fanned out across the country.

A free black woman, Maria W. Stewart emerged as the first American woman on record to speak before an audience of men and women about political issues and the first to leave texts of her speeches. She

Angelina Emily Grimké (1805–1879), an abolitionist orator, was criticized for speaking in public.

Library of Congress

spoke on abolitionist ideas, educational opportunities for girls, and other issues for a brief period from 1831 to 1833. When she felt she was not well received, she gave a "Farewell Address" to friends in Boston, but defended her right to speak as a woman, asking, "What if I am a woman...?"

Born Maria Miller in 1803, in Hartford, Connecticut, she was orphaned by age five and hired out to the family of a clergyman for ten years. She moved to Boston, where she worked as a domestic and later became a teacher in New York, Baltimore, and Washington, D.C., and matron of Howard University's Freedmen's Hospital.

In Boston, Garrison published her early writings in the *Liberator*.

She was briefly married to James W. Stewart, who owned a business as a shipping outfitter, and was also active in abolitionist causes. The two of them were closely affiliated with David Walker, the writer of the famous antislavery tract "Walker's Appeal," until his death in 1830. Stewart helped him ship his pamphlet up and down the East Coast. When Stewart died a year after Walker, a probate court denied Maria any inheritance from her husband. They had no children. In later years, she was able to secure his pension from the War of 1812. She died in 1879.

A British woman, Francis Wright, also had a meteoric lecturing career in the United States, from 1828 to 1829, speaking in favor of equal education for women and against slavery.

But it was the Grimké sisters, Angelina and Sarah, who became the most well known among American women on the antislavery lecture circuit. Many people roundly criticized them for having the audacity to speak to mixed groups, and they defended their right to do so.

As women born into a Charleston, South Carolina, slaveholding family, they had learned to abhor the institution of slavery, and they spoke of its horrors with firsthand knowledge. First Sarah and then Angelina joined the Quakers and moved to Philadelphia. In 1836, Angelina wrote "An Appeal to the Christian Women of the South," urging them to rise up in opposition to slavery. ("Above all, try to persuade your husband, father, brothers and sons, that slavery is a crime against God and man, and that it is a great sin to keep human beings in such abject ignorance; to deny them the privilege of learning to read and write," she implored.)

The American Anti-Slavery Society invited the sisters to

speak to small groups of New York women gathering in homes. Three hundred women showed up at the first meeting, and they had to move to a church. Men began to attend their meetings, and some people were particularly horrified that the Grimkés spoke before mixed audiences of women and men, commonly referred to as "promiscuous audiences."

A group of ministers condemned them, issuing a "Pastoral Letter of the General Association of Massachusetts" in 1837:

We invite your attention to the dangers which at present seem to threaten the female character with wide spread and permanent injury.

The appropriate duties and influence of women, are clearly stated in the New Testament...But when she assumes the place and tone of a man as a public reformer, our care and protection of her seem unnecessary, we put ourselves in self defence against her, she

yields the power which God has given her for protection, and her character becomes unnatural...

We cannot, therefore, but regret the mistaken conduct of those who encourage females to bear an obtrusive and ostentatious part in measures of reform, and countenance any of that sex who so far forget themselves as to itinerate in the character of public lecturers and teachers.

Far from being chastened, Angelina and Sarah began to speak out against the oppression of women as much as they did against slavery—Angelina mostly in speeches and Sarah in articles in the *New England Spectator*.

Some male abolitionists, including John Greenleaf Whittier, the editor and poet, and Theodore Weld, an activist and author, who would soon marry Angelina, began to urge them to drop the women's rights talk for fear of hurting the antislavery movement. (Angelina became

Sarah Moore Grimké (1792–1873), sister of Angelina,
also spoke and wrote for the abolitionist cause.
Library of Congress

known as Angelina Grimké Weld after their marriage in 1838.)

Abolitionist women cheered them on, including Maria Weston Chapman, who wrote a scathingly satirical poem in criticism of the pastoral letter, and Lydia Maria Child, a prominent author who penned an equally witty account of an appearance of Angelina Grimké at hearings of a committee of the Massachusetts State Legislature.

Sarah wrote a defense of women's rights, "Letters on the Equality of the Sexes," in 1837. This was in response to a request from the president of the Boston Female Anti-Slavery Society, Mary S. Parker, to comment on the "Province of Woman."

Frances E. W. Harper, 1898, attended and spoke at women's rights conventions before and after the Civil War.
Library of Congress

In a letter addressing the pastoral letter, Sarah said:

No one can desire more earnestly than I do, that woman may move exactly in the sphere which her Creator has assigned her; and I believe her having been displaced from that sphere has introduced confusion into the world...Men and women were CREATED EQUAL; they are both moral and accountable beings, and whatever is right for man to do, is right for woman.

The Grimkés' insistence on their right to speak publicly paved the way for many other women to do so, notably Lucy

Stone and Lucretia Mott, both of whom who would later assume major leadership roles in the suffrage movement. Stone began traveling as an anti-slavery lecturer after graduation from Oberlin and became one of the highest-paid speakers in the country. Lucretia Mott of Philadelphia was a Quaker teacher and later preacher who was extremely sought after for her talks on abolition, women's rights, and religion. Quakers had no prohibition against women speaking, and they recognized women as preachers. To the Society of Friends, all souls carried the "inner light" of God, and all were equal. This belief in human equality also fueled their fervor for abolition.

In 1827, Mott also began reading more radical literature like Wollstonecraft's *A Vindication of the Rights of Woman*. Describing it as one of her favorites, a "centre table book," she circulated it to anyone she could get to read it. The book, asserting women's right to an education and other fundamentals, was highly influential.

In Boston, Margaret Fuller, a teacher and Transcendentalist, emerged as an important writer with her book *Woman in the Nineteenth Century* in 1845 advocating for women's independence. She initiated a series of "conversations" for women, encouraging them to read, to think about the issues of the day, and to educate each other. Women like Lydia Maria Child, Elizabeth Cady Stanton, and the wives or fiancées of intellectuals like Ralph Waldo Emerson, Nathaniel Hawthorne, and Horace Mann attended them. In 1845, Fuller became the first woman on the staff of Horace Greeley's *New York Tribune*.

Other female abolitionists who emerged as lecturers included Abby Kelley Foster, a teacher and former Quaker; Frances E. W. Harper, a free African-American poet and author; Ernestine Rose, a petitioner for women's property rights; and Sojourner Truth, the freed black orator. Later, Susan B. Anthony became a teacher and an agent, or traveling lecturer, for the American Anti-Slavery Society.

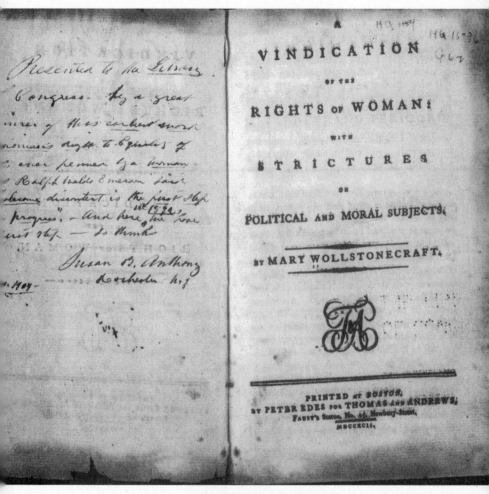

This dedication page of
A Vindication of the Rights of Woman
by Mary Wollstonecraft (Boston, 1792) has a handwritten
inscription: "Presented to the Library of Congress by a great
admirer of this earliest work for woman's right to equality...
ever penned by a woman...Susan B. Anthony,
Rochester, N.Y., Jan 1, 1904."

They would all go on to make substantial contributions to the cause of woman suffrage.

"A significant feature of the radical abolitionist movement inaugurated by William Lloyd Garrison...was the attraction it held for women. The political experience women gained through participation in this crusade and the hostility they faced in connection with it served as important roots of American feminism," Ira V. Brown wrote in an article for the journal *Pennsylvania History*.

The Anti-Slavery Society allowed women to speak at its founding meeting in 1831, encouraged them to lecture, and even paid some as agents—but it did not permit them to join. Thus, women formed their own groups, notably the interracial Philadelphia Female Anti-Slavery Society, where white, upper-echelon, abolitionist women like Lucretia Mott worked side by side with the women of the black elite for decades on behalf of people in need. The black women included Charlotte Forten and her daughters, Margaretta Forten, Sarah Forten, and Harriet Forten Purvis; Grace Bustill Douglass; and Sarah McCrummell. White members included the author Lydia Maria Child and Abigail "Abba" Alcott, mother of the famed author Louisa May Alcott. This group and two thousand other women of Philadelphia petitioned Congress to end slavery in the capital city and other jurisdictions it controlled. Even after the Civil War, the society continued its work on behalf of the freed people.

★ Lucy Stone ★
A Woman of Courage

Lucy Stone, who was born in obscurity on a farm near West Brookfield, Massachusetts, on August 13, 1818, first earned fame for flouting marital customs of her day. After resisting Henry Blackwell's initial attempts to woo her, she relented, but the couple insisted on reading a declaration of protest against the unequal nature of marriage law at the wedding. She also declined to take her husband's name. It was a scandalous act at the time, and people later called women who kept their names "Lucy Stoners."

When people scoffed at or tried to block her, she became even more determined to follow her own path. Her daughter, Alice Stone Blackwell, recalled that Lucy was "one of the very few people who seem to have been born incapable of fear."

She was among the earliest and most influential leaders of the women's rights movement for many decades. Already a popular and respected lecturer for the antislavery cause, she was often an organizer, a speaker, and a presiding officer at the earliest national and local conventions for women's rights. After the Civil War, she founded the American Woman Suffrage Association when suffragists split over the issue of whether to support the Fifteenth Amendment, which prohibited states from denying black men the right to vote. Her organization worked for its passage and initiated efforts to pass woman suffrage laws in the states.

Her fellow suffrage leaders Elizabeth Cady Stanton and Susan B. Anthony already had refused to support the amendment, and they formed the National Woman Suffrage Association to push for a federal amendment to gain the vote for women. When the two groups were reconciled twenty years later, Stone continued to fight for voting rights for women until her death in 1893. The world may never know some of her achievements, because she declined to cooperate with Stanton and Anthony on the six-volume *History of Woman Suffrage* by sending them information on her organization and her work.

Stone's views about women developed out of her experiences as a child growing up in a home where her father ruled with an iron fist and favored her brothers. The eighth child and third girl among nine children (seven surviving childhood), she grew up hearing her mother's lament that she and her sisters were not boys, because "a woman's lot is so hard." Their lot certainly was. Lucy watched her mother endure abuse from a husband who was stingy and often drunk. Living on an isolated farm in the 1800s made daily routines and chores a struggle in

any case, but Lucy's burden grew heavier as her mother's health began to fail by the time she was twelve. Lucy assumed the usual household duties of cooking, cleaning, weaving, and ironing, along with such farm tasks as milking cows and churning butter. She walked a mile to school, returned home to do chores at lunch, and went back to school for the afternoon.

Her family was not poor, though. The farm was 145 acres and provided a bounty of food. Her father was willing and able to pay for his sons' schoolbooks and college education at Amherst.

Lucy sometimes had to buy her own books, because her father thought girls did not need much education. She studied late at night and felt she was a better student than her brothers were. She already had shown signs of resisting male dominance when she insisted on voting at a meeting at the Congregational church over whether women should speak in public. When the pastor chastised her, she kept raising her hand to vote anyway. As a young woman, Lucy had heard Abby Kelley Foster, the abolitionist lecturer, speak at a nearby church, and she had also attended the meeting in which the Congregational ministers condemned the Grimké sisters for lecturing to mixed audiences of men and women.

Lucy Stone began teaching at age sixteen after begging her father to let her stay in school long enough to qualify. When she learned that Oberlin College was accepting women, she asked permission to attend. Her father refused to help, and she began trying to raise the tuition—teaching, selling produce, and making shoes for sale. It took her nine years to save enough for one year at Oberlin, but traveling by train, steamboat, and coach,

she arrived there in 1843 at the age of twenty-five and determined to stay. She excelled, and the next year, her father relented and lent her the money for tuition. Only three women had graduated from Oberlin when she arrived, and the work was rigorous. To pay her father back, she began teaching a class of African-American men to read and write.

With her fellow student Antoinette Brown, she formed a female debating club. Her classmates chose her to present an essay at graduation in 1847. The administration told her she could not read it before an audience of men and women. She could have a man read it, or she could read it to a female audience. Lucy refused to write it at all. She graduated at the age of thirty and became the first woman from Massachusetts, and one of the first in the nation, to earn a college degree.

The reformist spirit at Oberlin fed her inclinations to work in the antislavery and women's rights fields, and she declared her intentions to become a lecturer after graduation, rather than return home and continue teaching as her family expected.

"I expect to plead not for the slave only, but for suffering humanity everywhere," she said. "Especially do I mean to labor for the elevation of my sex."

She gave her first women's rights speech at her brother Bowman's church in Gardner, Massachusetts, the year she graduated. Stone soon became an agent for the Massachusetts Anti-Slavery Society. She would travel from city to city, renting halls to speak in, putting up her own handbills, and passing a hat for collection to pay expenses at the end of her speeches. She rode in buggies and stagecoaches, staying in boarding houses.

Abolitionists complained that her mixing in the message of women's rights might hurt their cause. They reached a compromise: She would speak against slavery on the weekends and women's issues on weekdays. She lectured on the social, legal, and religious impediments to women's fulfillment of their capabilities.

Lecturing provided her a good income, and she was determined not to marry anyone and have her rights subsumed by a man's. When she met Henry Blackwell at his hardware store during her travels, he began a prolonged pursuit in 1853, even attending women's rights conventions to hear her. He was sincere in his support of women's rights, however, and already active in antislavery work. Blackwell also had five educated and independent sisters, including Dr. Elizabeth Blackwell, the first formally trained female doctor in the United States, and a younger sister, Dr. Emily Blackwell, who was also one of the first women to be a physician.

Finally, Stone became smitten after learning that Henry Blackwell had risked prosecution under the Fugitive Slave Act of 1850, his business standing, and possibly his life by daring to rescue an escaped girl who was being returned to slavery. He boarded a train passing through Ohio, snatched her from her captors, and escorted her off. Lucy could admire that kind of heroism. It also helped that the couple had a long correspondence about the terms of a marriage of equals and worked out an agreement that would pre-serve her independence and autonomy. At their marriage at the Stone family farm on May 1, 1855, the couple read their "protest" of laws and customs that gave husbands dominance over women, and Henry Blackwell pledged not to invoke them during their marriage. The minister who officiated the ceremony, the Rev. Thomas Wentworth Higginson, an abolitionist friend and advocate for women's rights, sent a copy of the protest to a newspaper, and it went as "viral" as possible in their day.

The notice appeared in the *Worcester Spy* and is reprinted in *History of Woman Suffrage*, Volume 1.

MARRIAGE OF LUCY STONE UNDER PROTEST.

It was my privilege to celebrate May day by officiating at a wedding in a farm-house among the hills of West Brookfield. The bridegroom was a man of tried worth, a leader in the Western Anti-Slavery Movement; and the bride was one whose fair name is known throughout the nation; one whose rare intellectual qualities are excelled by the private beauty of her heart and life.

I never perform the marriage ceremony without a renewed sense of the iniquity of our present system of laws in respect to marriage; a system by which "man and wife are one, and that one is the husband." It was with my hearty concurrence, therefore, that the following protest was read and signed, as a part of the nuptial ceremony; and I send it to you, that others may be induced to do likewise.

Rev. Thomas Wentworth Higginson.

PROTEST

While acknowledging our mutual affection by publicly assuming the relationship of husband and wife, yet in justice to ourselves and a great principle, we deem it a duty to declare that this act on our part implies no sanction of, nor promise of voluntary obedience to such of the present laws of marriage, as refuse to recognize the wife as an independent, rational being, while they confer upon the husband an injurious and unnatural superiority, investing him with legal powers which no honorable man would exercise, and which no man should possess. We protest especially against the laws which give to the husband:

1. The custody of the wife's person.
2. The exclusive control and guardianship of their children.

3. The sole ownership of her personal, and use of her real estate, unless previously settled upon her, or placed in the hands of trustees, as in the case of minors, lunatics, and idiots.

4. The absolute right to the product of her industry.

5. Also against laws which give to the widower so much larger and more permanent an interest in the property of his deceased wife, than they give to the widow in that of the deceased husband.

6. Finally, against the whole system by which "the legal existence of the wife is suspended during marriage," so that in most States, she neither has a legal part in the choice of her residence, nor can she make a will, nor sue or be sued in her own name, nor inherit property.

We believe that personal independence and equal human rights can never be forfeited, except for crime; that marriage should be an equal and permanent partnership, and so recognized by law; that until it is so recognized, married partners should provide against the radical injustice of present laws, by every means in their power.

We believe that where domestic difficulties arise, no appeal should be made to legal tribunals under existing laws, but that all difficulties should be submitted to the equitable adjustment of arbitrators mutually chosen.

Thus reverencing law, we enter our protest against rules and customs which are unworthy of the name, since they violate justice, the essence of law.

(Signed),
Henry. B. Blackwell,
Lucy Stone.
Worcester Spy, 1855.

At the National Woman's Rights Convention in Cincinnati, Ohio, a few months after her wedding, Lucy Stone responded to a man who had suggested that the movement consisted of "a few disappointed women."

"From the first years to which my memory stretches, I have been a disappointed woman," she said. "I was disappointed when I came to seek a profession worthy [of] an immortal being—every employment was closed to me, except those of the teacher, the seamstress, and the housekeeper. In education, in marriage, in religion, in everything, disappointment is the lot of woman."

Henry Blackwell worked closely with Stone in the woman suffrage movement, and national convention proceedings often mentioned him as an officer and debater. They edited a suffrage newspaper, the *Woman's Journal*, and he continued to publish it for years after her death. Alice, born in 1857, was their only child, and she grew up to be a suffragist as well. Alice Stone Blackwell was a force behind the reunification of the suffrage factions in 1890. She wrote the first biography of her mother, *Lucy Stone: Pioneer of Women's Rights*, in 1930.

In it, she declared that her mother had "much personal magnetism, and a singularly sweet voice," qualities that made her a persuasive and influential speaker.

"She had also a mind as bright and swift as quicksilver, and that indescribable something which radiates from a character strong, simple and sincere," Alice Blackwell wrote.

The London Encounter

In 1838, after Britain ended slavery, American abolitionists received invitations to a World Anti-Slavery Convention called in London. Lucretia Mott was to attend as a delegate of Garrison's American Anti-Slavery Society, the Philadelphia Female Anti-Slavery Society, the American Free Produce Association, and the Association of Friends for Promoting the Abolition of Slavery.

Seven other American women were among those named delegates: Mary Grew, Sarah Pugh, Elizabeth Neall, Abby Kimber, all of Philadelphia; and Ann Greene Phillips, Abby Southwick, and Emily Winslow from New England. When British organizers heard of the Americans' intent to send women, they sent out another call specifying preference for "gentlemen" as representatives. The Americans ignored it. Lucretia and her husband, James Mott, sailed from New York City on May 7, 1840, and arrived in Liverpool on May 27.

They stayed at a rooming house where Henry Stanton, an abolitionist with the American and Foreign Anti-Slavery Society, and his bride, Elizabeth Cady Stanton, who was not a delegate, were staying. This trip was part of the Stantons' honeymoon, and the two women made an immediate connection.

Upon the start of the convention, the majority voted to ban women from participating but permitted them to sit in a section separated by a rail. Some of the male delegates sat with them, including Charles Lenox Remond, an African-American from Massachusetts who, like his sister, Sarah Remond, was an antislavery lecturer; Nathaniel P. Rogers, a white abolitionist editor from New Hampshire; and Garrison.

When they were not in session, Lucretia Mott and Elizabeth Cady Stanton talked and walked about London. The young bride was in awe of Mott.

"It seemed to me like meeting a being from some larger planet...when I first heard from the lips of Lucretia Mott that I had the same right to think for myself that Luther, Calvin, and John Knox had," Stanton recalled, listing the great theologians and religious reformers.

Stanton also has been widely quoted as saying the two women discussed calling a women's convention on their return. However, Mott, who kept a diary during that trip and for the only known time in her life, did not mention such an intention at that time, nor did her husband in his writings about their travels. Lucretia Mott later acknowl-edged to Stanton that the two women might have discussed organizing a meeting on a later occasion in Boston.

Elizabeth Stanton considered the London showdown over seating women as the start of a movement for women's rights. Mott apparently did not. She dated the women's movement from the first national Anti-Slavery Convention of American Women, held May 9, 1837, in New York City. One biographer argued that for Lucretia Mott, the question of women's rights never took precedence for her over the fight against slavery. She never wavered on that, not even in later years when Stanton and her co-agitator, Susan B. Anthony, split from other suffragists over the Reconstruction amendments that gave black men the vote decades before women could get it. Stanton was not a Quaker, and she appears to have been a lukewarm abolitionist at best and then largely by association.

In any case, neither Mott nor Stanton did anything to bring about such a convention until eight years later, when another encounter would set the stage for the most famous "first" women's rights gathering where the question of voting was on the agenda.

Yet they and other American women had laid the groundwork for that discussion to take place through their significant role in carving out a new nation in a strange and unforgiving land, finding their collective voice, and refusing to accept less than equality for themselves and others. Abolitionist women, especially the Quakers, would become the backbone of the women's movement, nurturing it and propelling it forward for the remainder of the century.

★ Lucretia Mott ★
Uncompromising Reformer

While history has tended to recall Lucretia Mott as a saintly, mild-mannered woman, she embraced the term "heretic" and urged others to agitate for human rights and justice.

She belonged to the Society of Friends, known as Quakers. Her story also shows how the Friends' ideals of equality and social conscience underpinned the women's movement in its infancy, as Quaker women would lead the way. She worked for woman suffrage as a humanitarian issue, although she followed her faith's dictates against voting and involvement in politics. She was the moral compass for the movement.

On the abolition issue, she was an uncompromising purist. The life and work of Lucretia Mott demonstrate how closely aligned were the antislavery and women's rights movements, and through her, we can see how relationships among abolitionist men and women, whites, and blacks laid the foundation for the woman suffrage movement and sustained it for decades. The names of people involved in her life appear repeatedly in the annals of woman suffrage.

Lucretia Coffin was born on January 3, 1793, in the seaport town of Nantucket, Massachusetts, into a family whose forebears had been its first nonnative settlers and carried on a long tradition of Quakerism. Her ancestor Mary Coffin Starbuck had converted virtually the entire island to Quakerism. As a Quaker, Lucretia was accustomed to attending school with boys and to equal treatment. The women of Nantucket also were used to taking care of business affairs as their husbands spent weeks and sometimes years away at sea as whalers. A visit to the island in 1801 by a Quaker minister, Elizabeth Coggeshall, influenced Lucretia to focus on the "inner light" and to follow her conscience.

At the age of thirteen, she went with her sister Eliza to a Quaker school in Dutchess County, New York, the Nine Partners School. She excelled and became a teacher at a young age and met James Mott, grandson of the headmaster. While it was unusual for families to invest in girls' education, hers did so enthusiastically. Nine Partners provided her an education superior to what most men would have had at the time, and it instilled a fine-tuned sense of justice and morality. Her family later moved to Boston and then Philadelphia, where Lucretia and James settled after their marriage.

Lucretia Mott became a preacher in 1821 and traveled broadly to speak on matters of faith and abolition. By the mid-nineteenth century, she was one of the most famous women in the United States. As a Quaker, she could not receive pay for preaching, and she customarily spoke extemporaneously. As a result, the only speeches of hers that survive are from newspapers, transcriptions of proceedings, or pamphlets.

She was a devoted wife for fifty-seven years to James Mott, also a leading abolitionist, and they raised five children to adulthood. Despite her outside activities, Lucretia Mott took pride in her domestic skills and her hospitality. Whites and blacks mingled at her home often, which was not a common practice at the time. A fellow abolitionist brought Henry "Box" Brown, the man who escaped slavery by having himself shipped in a box, to meet Lucretia Mott at her home.

When she helped form the Philadelphia Female Anti-Slavery Society, she was on the committee to write the constitution, along with Margaretta Forten, daughter of James Forten, a free black abolitionist and wealthy businessman, and Sarah Mc-Crummell, wife of James McCrummell. Another of the Fortens' daughters, Harriet, was married to Robert Purvis, founder of the Colored Free Produce Society, and the Motts knew him through their work on that cause. James Mott had started the Free Produce Society of Philadelphia to disseminate information on where to get goods that slave labor had not produced.

Lucretia Mott favored immediate, absolute emancipation, in contrast to those who would accept schemes for gradual progress, and advocated the boycotting of all products produced by slave labor, including sugar, molasses, cotton, and rice, despite the inherent hardships of doing so. Abolitionists, who called it the free produce movement, reasoned that if the market for such goods dried up, the justification for slavery would evaporate. Mott even urged her own husband to give up a business in the cotton trade and switch to wool.

Lucretia Mott also spoke against colonization, or deportation of freed blacks to resettle them in new territories, an idea often advocated among abolitionists and others. Many whites feared immediate emancipation would lead to social chaos and violent retribution if blacks remained in the country. The American Colonization Society had advocated sending African-Americans to Africa as colonizers and missionaries, but free blacks in Philadelphia opposed it.

William Lloyd Garrison had favored gradualism, but an encounter with Mott radicalized him to share her absolutist stance against slavery, according to one of her biographers, Carol Faulkner. Mott also may have inspired him to start his newspaper. They formed a lifelong friendship, and Garrison mobilized a movement.

She also opposed payments to slaveholders to purchase the freedom of individuals, as some abolitionists had done for Frederick Douglass after his escape from a Maryland plantation. Some white Southern Quakers were bequeathing slaves to the Philadelphia society as a means of freeing them, but the Motts questioned the morality of taking ownership even if it was to free them.

The abolitionists argued that such purchases acknowledged the right of one person to own another. Mott also thought Douglass was a more authentic force as someone who still lived under the threat of re-enslavement. Nevertheless, they shared mutual admiration, and Lucretia and James traveled the lecture circuit in the West for a week with Douglass and Garrison in 1847.

Douglass greatly admired Lucretia Mott, as reflected in his autobiography:

I shall never forget the first time I ever saw and heard Lucretia Mott. It was in the town of Lynn, Massachusetts. It was not in a magnificent hall, where such as she seemed to belong, but in a little hall over Jonathan Buffum's store, the only place then open, even in that so-called radical anti-slavery town, for an anti-slavery meeting on Sunday...

The speaker was attired in the usual Quaker dress, free from startling colors, plain, rich, elegant, and without superfluity—the very sight of her a sermon. In a few moments after she began to speak, I saw before me no more a woman, but a glorified presence, bearing a message of light and love from the Infinite to a benighted and strangely wandering world, straying away from the paths of truth and justice into the wilderness of pride and selfishness, where peace is lost and true happiness is sought in vain. I heard Mrs. Mott thus, when she was comparatively young. I have often heard her since, sometimes in the solemn temple, and sometimes under the open sky, but whenever and wherever I have listened to her, my heart was always made better, and my spirit raised by her words; and in speaking thus for myself I am sure I am expressing the experience of thousands.

Mott readily joined the women's movement, beginning with her involvement at Seneca Falls, and remained active through most of her life, often chairing conventions before the Civil War. Even when the movement later split over the issue of enfranchising black men, she kept peace with both sides.

In her eulogy to Lucretia Mott in 1881, Elizabeth Cady Stanton said, "Lucretia Mott was a philanthropist; her life was dedicated to the rights of humanity. When the poet, the novelist, the philosopher, and the metaphysician have been forgotten, the memory of the true reformer will remain engraven on the hearts of the multitude."

The Radical Quakers

The Motts became supporters of Elias Hicks, a preacher who criticized the hierarchy among the Quakers, alleging abuse of disciplinary authority and equivocation on slavery. (Some owned slaves or ran businesses that profited from slavery.) After the split from the orthodox Quakers in 1827, James and Lucretia followed the Hicksite branch, which emphasized following individual conscience over strict scriptural guidance. Lucretia Mott's outspokenness sometimes rattled even the Hicksites. Some chafed at her attacks on the hierarchy but thought it best to keep her in the fold because of her gifts as a speaker.

James joined the Pennsylvania Abolition Society and served as secretary from 1822 to 1823. Ben Franklin, a cousin to Lucretia Mott, had founded the colony of Pennsylvania as a haven of religious freedom for Quakers and other sects that did not accept the Church of England. Philadelphia was not only a hub for Quakers. It was home to the largest community of free blacks in the North. The combined forces of the African-American leaders and sympathizing Quakers made the city a hotbed of abolitionist activity and ideas.

The Pennsylvania Abolition Society formed in Philadelphia in 1775, and Franklin was its president in the 1780s. Many other prominent citizens were members, and the society offered legal assistance to fugitives. The city became a major stopover for blacks fleeing slavery, as the first major point north of the border with Delaware, a slave state, and because of its proximity to other slave states. By 1810, the black population was 9,656, or 10.5 percent of the city's population of 91,877.

Pennsylvania adopted gradual abolition in 1780, the first state to do so, to free children born to enslaved parents in the future. By 1847, slavery had ended in the state. State law recognized fugitives as free as soon as they reached Pennsylvania soil.

Garrison formed the American Anti-Slavery Society, a national, interracial organization to advocate for immediate emancipation. It held its founding meeting in December 1833 in Philadelphia. He publicly abandoned support of colonization and gradual abolition, committing the organization to racial equality and "immediatism," an idea that Elizabeth Heyrick, an abolitionist and philanthropist, had promoted in Britain. Seventy delegates, all male, attended, including James Mott and black abolitionists like Robert Purvis and James McCrummell (or McCrummill), a black barber/dentist from Philadelphia.

Lucretia Mott attended with her mother, a sister, and her older daughter, and interjected suggestions for the Declaration of Sentiments, violating the norms of women not speaking up in "promiscuous" audiences.

Lydia White and Esther Moore, both Hicksite Quakers, attended, as did Sidney Ann Lewis, an Orthodox Quaker and supporter of the free produce movement.

Four days later, Mott and a group of black and white women formed the Philadelphia Female Anti-Slavery Society. The convening of this meeting was a breakthrough for female activism, and its existence challenged notions about race and gender.

The women asked McCrummell to preside, because they had little experience with parliamentary procedure and voting practices. Quakers made decisions by consensus, and Lucretia Mott had been to only two other conventions in her life, including the American Anti-Slavery Society days earlier. The Philadelphia Female Anti-Slavery Society recruited other women and urged them to take public roles. The female society disseminated information about slavery, donated to the American Anti-Slavery Society, supported abolitionist newspapers, sponsored lectures, and aided schools, including a school run by Sarah Mapps Douglass, an African-American abolitionist, educator, lecturer, and writer.

Meanwhile, the Boston Female Anti-Slavery Society suggested the formation of a national executive committee to oversee groups of this nature. The Philadelphia women had misgivings, but agreed to hold a national Anti-Slavery Convention of American Women. This time, Lucretia Mott chaired the meeting, and members elected her vice president, along with Grace Douglass of Philadelphia.

A resolution on women's duties in the abolitionist movement, offered by Angelina Grimké, was accepted. It read, "Resolved, that as certain rights and duties are common to all moral beings, the time has come for woman to move in that sphere which Providence has assigned her."

This meeting has been described as the first national convention at which women discussed women's rights, and Mott said in her time that she considered it the beginning of the great women's movement.

When the antislavery women held a second convention, in May 1838 in Pennsylvania Hall, a new building paid for by abolitionists, mobs surrounded and disturbed an evening session. After another session, as the attendees left the hall, facing an angry crowd, the white women took black women by the arm to make sure they passed through safely. The mob continued to grow and later broke in and burned the building to the ground four days after it opened.

What they could not do was break the spirit of the abolition movement. It was a much more complex force than most Americans probably realize, with men and women, blacks and whites, working together to force change. The abolitionists were more passionate, more committed, and more organized than we tend to understand and acknowledge. Their movement made it possible to apply those strengths and their principles to a new movement, and the coalition that emerged in the antislavery cause could be marshaled to foster a women's movement.

We hold these truths to be self-evident:

that all men and women are created equal;

that they are endowed by their Creator with certain

inalienable rights; that among these are life, liberty, and

the pursuit of happiness; that to secure these rights

governments are instituted, deriving their just powers

from the consent of the governed.

Declaration of Sentiments,

Seneca Falls Convention, July 19–20, 1848

These are portraits of seven prominent figures
of the women's rights movement, including Lucretia Mott, Elizabeth
Cady Stanton, and Susan B. Anthony.
Library of Congress

Section 2

The Awakening

A Declaration of Sentiments

I have no idea of submitting tamely to injustice inflicted either on me or on the slave. I will oppose it with all the moral powers with which I am endowed. I am no advocate of passivity.

Lucretia Mott

The First Convention

In July 1848, Lucretia Mott, Elizabeth Cady Stanton, Martha Wright, and nearly three hundred other women and men, including the abolitionist editor Frederick Douglass, gathered for a convention at Seneca Falls, New York. It became a high-water mark in the struggle for women's rights, including the right to vote. A group primarily made up of Quaker women organized the conference, advertising it as "a Convention to discuss the social, civil, and religious condition and rights of Woman."

The group presented "A Declaration of Sentiments" and resolutions. The assembly seemed inclined to omit the voting rights plank until Douglass spoke fervently in its favor. Mythologies have crept into the Seneca Falls story, and historians still debate what the meeting was the "first" of. Different histories and biographies vary greatly in detail, but one thing seems clear from the myriad accounts: The meeting took place when and where it did because Lucretia Mott, the famed Quaker preacher and reformer, happened to be there visiting the hub of an area known for its reformist spirit.

The area in the Finger Lakes region was a breeding ground of religious reform and social experimentation. People called it the "burned over" region because so many reformist ideas had swept over the area like a forest fire, and many had taken root there. One example was in the nearby utopian community at Oneida, whose leaders advocated spiritual perfection and "free love," the idea that one can freely choose sexual partners, as many as, as often as, and for however long one might choose, without government regulation of marriage.

The Hicksite Friends had congregated in the area, relocating from Philadelphia, New Jersey, and elsewhere. At the Genesee Yearly Meeting, an organizational division for Quakers, one faction had split off from the Hicksites to form the Progressive Friends, emphasizing more equal standing for women and promoting greater activism in the antislavery cause.

That spring, Lucretia and James Mott had embarked on an extended trip to attend several meetings and make several visits in line with their many reform interests. In March 1848, Lucretia and James traveled to Boston for the Anti-Sabbath Convention, called to counter "the attempt to compel the observance of any day as 'THE SABBATH,' especially by penal enactments." As Quakers, the Motts reserved

the right to worship according to their own conscience. They attended an anniversary convention of the American Anti-Slavery Society in New York City and the Genesee Yearly Meeting in upstate New York. They visited the Cattaraugus Seneca Indian Reservation near Buffalo, where Quakers had helped establish a school, and checked on settlements of African-Americans escaped from slavery who were living across the border in Canada.

Finally, the Motts traveled to Auburn, New York, to visit Lucretia's sister Martha Wright, six months pregnant, a writer and abolitionist in her own right. The Society of Friends "disowned" her for marrying an outsider in 1824—Captain Peter Pelham of Kentucky, a hero in the War of 1812. (He died two years later, and she married David Wright, a lawyer.) The Motts also planned to visit the Wrights' neighbor, William Seward, the former governor and antislavery senator (later Abraham Lincoln's secretary of state) about a treaty issue involving the Cattaraugus Senecas. During her visit, Lucretia Mott also spoke at a prison and at the Universalist Church in Auburn.

The region was an abolitionist stronghold where the Wrights and their neighbors thought nothing of hiding runaways in their barns, basements, or even kitchens as part of the Underground Railroad. The heroic "conductor" Harriet Tubman by then lived near the Wrights there in Auburn and continued to do her part for the escapees. The well-known abolitionist politician Gerrit Smith, a cousin to Elizabeth Cady Stanton, lived in the area, and his house served as a depot of the Underground Railroad. The area's proximity to the Canadian border made it a strategic junction.

When the National Liberty Convention met in Buffalo on June 14 and 15, 1848, Smith expressed support of "universal suffrage in its broadest sense, females as well as males being entitled to vote." (Though she was not present, Lucretia Mott received one vote in the nomination for president.)

In another harbinger of reform that year, on March 15, 1848, forty-four women of Genesee and Wyoming Counties petitioned the New York State Assembly, declaring that they owed no allegiance to the government in which they were deprived of political rights. "When women are allowed the privileges of rational and accountable beings, it will be soon enough to expect from them the duties of such," it said.

An Invitation to Tea

Elizabeth Stanton had moved from Boston to nearby Seneca Falls in 1847 with her husband, Henry Stanton, lured by fresh air, the prospect of living in a vibrant community of like-minded people, and the gift of a house from Elizabeth's father. Henry was a lawyer and a leading abolitionist whom she had met at Gerrit Smith's home. At this point, they had three sons, and Elizabeth had spent much of the year making the neglected lakeside house habitable. She was often alone, as her husband traveled and the children stayed with relatives during the renovations.

In early July 1848, she was one of the guests at a tea party at the home of Jane Hunt, wife of Richard Hunt, a merchant and mill owner, in Waterloo, only a mile or two from Seneca Falls. Mrs. Hunt had just given birth two weeks earlier.

Lucretia Mott was the guest of honor, accompanied by her sister Martha. Mary Ann M'Clintock, wife of Thomas M'Clintock, a pharmacist and officer in the American Anti-Slavery Society, also attended. All the women present were Quakers or disowned Quakers, except Stanton, who grew up in a stalwart Presbyterian family. She had become a skeptic about organized religion by adulthood.

Stanton and Mott had been in touch over the years since their meeting in London, and Mott might have suggested that Jane Hunt invite her friend. The women probably knew of each other because of their anti-slavery activities. Stanton had become interested in abolitionist causes after meeting William Lloyd Garrison in London, and her husband was one of the leading orators and writers of the movement in the country.

The Hunts and the M'Clintocks were among the most radical abolitionists, and their homes were stations on the Underground Railroad. (They are part of the National Park Service Underground Railroad Network to Freedom.) They would have known of Elizabeth Stanton's cousin Gerrit Smith, whose home was also a station. The M'Clintocks also boycotted slave-made goods at home and in their store.

The women who gathered that day discussed the Boston Anti-Sabbath Convention and the Genesee Yearly Meeting that the Motts had attended (and in which all of them sided with the progressives), the National Liberty Convention, and the passage that April of the New York Married Women's Property Act, which let wives retain property they brought into marriage. This was the law for which Ernestine Rose had long petitioned. It would also permit Stanton to own the home her father had given her in her own right.

As the afternoon progressed, the tea party talk elicited an outpouring of frustration from Stanton regarding the plight of women. The daughter of a judge from Johnstown, New York, she was well educated and well versed in the laws that restricted women's lives. Living in a small town, raising three children while her husband traveled frequently on behalf of abolitionist causes, legal work, and politics, she was now well acquainted with the daily drudgery of running a household in the nineteenth century. This included cooking, baking, washing, and tending babies. She could afford hired help but could not always find it. Stanton recalled that her reflections on the oppression of women moved the other women to act. (She had a tendency to portray herself as the heroine in the stories she told of her life.)

Hunt family lore suggests Divine Intervention also might have played a role. According to one story, Richard Hunt was within earshot, and hearing the women's discussion, urged them to act on their convictions. He issued a charge to them from the scriptures: "Faith without works is dead." (James 2:17: "Even so faith, if it hath not works, is dead, being alone.")

However they came to the decision, by the afternoon's end the women had called a convention. They insisted on having it while Lucretia Mott was still in the vicinity, because her reputation could draw a crowd. They secured a site at Wesleyan Chapel. Built by Methodist antislavery activists, it welcomed reformist speakers. The organizers placed a notice in the local paper, the *Seneca County Courier*.

"A Convention to discuss the social, civil and religious condition and rights of Woman will be held in the Wesleyan Chapel, at Seneca Falls, N.Y., on Wednesday and Thursday the 19th and 20th of July current; commencing at 10 o'clock A.M. During the first day, the meeting will be exclusively for Women, which all are earnestly invited to attend. The public generally are invited to be present on the second day, when Lucretia Mott, of Philadelphia, and others both ladies and gentlemen, will address the Convention."

Lucretia Mott also sent the notice to Douglass, who published it in the *North Star* a few days later, and other regional papers published it as well. She and Martha returned to the Wright home in Auburn, about twenty miles away from Waterloo and Seneca Falls, to tend to a sick James.

A few days after the tea party, Stanton, Mary Ann M'Clintock, and M'Clintock's two grown daughters, Elizabeth and (also) Mary Ann, gathered at the M'Clintock home to write a declaration of sentiments and resolutions for the convention, similar to those they were familiar with from antislavery conventions. Stanton had done some work on a draft, and they perused several other documents. They found them unsatisfactory until one of them offered the Declaration of Independence as an example. They decided to model their proclamation on that and modified it to read, "that all men and women are created equal." They pored over various law books and documents to define the list of grievances.

Later, Stanton's husband reviewed the document, making suggestions, but when he read the demand for the vote, he said he would have nothing to do with it and would leave town if she insisted on presenting it— and he did so, taking off for one of his many speaking engagements.

The Mott biographer Carol Faulkner speculated that the document might have been far different if Mott had been at the M'Clintocks' to participate in the drafting. She, in keeping with Quaker teaching and her uncompromising views, rejected any political participation, and thus did not see the vote as a goal or a remedy for women's oppression.

When Mott learned of the demand, she exclaimed, "Lizzie, thee will make us ridiculous!"— or subject to ridicule, so far-fetched was the idea of women having the vote and so deep was the opposition to their obtaining it.

"And Women Are Created Equal"

The organizers feared that hardly anyone would show up for the meeting. When the day arrived, they were pleasantly surprised to find nearly three hundred people, including men. The women let the men stay even though the organizers had reserved the first day for women, but they asked the men not to speak until the next day.

The people had come from a fifty-mile radius. The crowd was waiting outside, because the church doors were locked, and no one had secured a key. Someone's son climbed through the window and unlocked the doors. Finally, the meeting could begin. Young Mary Ann M'Clintock, the daughter of the elder Mary Ann and Thomas, took notes. The organizers sat up front.

Stanton read the sentiments, and attendees asked her to read them again, paragraph by paragraph, for discussion.

★ *Declaration of Sentiments* ★

When, in the course of human events, it becomes necessary for one portion of the family of man to assume
among the people of the earth a position different
from that which they have hitherto occupied, but one
to which the laws of nature and of nature's God enti-
tle them, a decent respect to the opinions of mankind
requires that they should declare the causes that impel
them to such a course.

We hold these truths to be self-evident: that all men
and women are created equal; that they are endowed
by their Creator with certain inalienable rights; that
among these are life, liberty, and the pursuit of happiness; that to secure these rights governments are instituted, deriving their just powers from the consent of
the governed. Whenever any form of Government becomes destructive of these ends, it is the right of those
who suffer from it to refuse allegiance to it, and to insist upon the institution of a new government, laying
its foundation on such principles, and organizing its
powers in such form as to them shall seem most likely
to effect their safety and happiness. Prudence, indeed,
will dictate that governments long established should
not be changed for light and transient causes; and
accordingly, all experience hath shown that mankind are
more disposed to suffer, while evils are sufferable, than
to right themselves by abolishing the forms to which
they are accustomed. But when a long train of abuses and
usurpations, pursuing invariably the same object, evinces
a design to reduce them under absolute despotism, it is

their duty to throw off such government, and to provide new guards for their future security. Such has been the patient sufferance of the women under this government, and such is now the necessity which constrains them to demand the equal station to which they are entitled.

The history of mankind is a history of repeated injuries and usurpations on the part of man toward woman, having in direct object the establishment of an absolute tyranny over her. To prove this, let facts be submitted to a candid world.

He has never permitted her to exercise her inalienable right to the elective franchise.

He has compelled her to submit to laws, in the formation of which she had no voice.

He has withheld from her rights which are given to the most ignorant and degraded men—both natives and foreigners.

Having deprived her of this first right of a citizen, the elective franchise, thereby leaving her without representation in the halls of legislation, he has oppressed her on all sides.

He has made her, if married, in the eye of the law, civilly dead.

He has taken from her all right in property, even to the wages she earns.

He has made her, morally, an irresponsible being, as she can commit many crimes with impunity, provided they be done in the presence of her husband. In the covenant of marriage, she is compelled to promise obedience to her husband, he becoming, to all intents and purposes, her master—the law giving him power to deprive her of her liberty, and to administer chastisement.

He has so framed the laws of divorce, as to what shall be the proper causes of divorce; in case of separation, to whom the guardianship of the children shall be given, as to be wholly regardless of the happiness of women— the law, in all cases, going upon the false supposition of the supremacy of man, and giving all power into his hands.

After depriving her of all rights as a married woman, if single and the owner of property, he has taxed her to support a government which recognizes her only when her property can be made profitable to it.

He has monopolized nearly all the profitable employments, and from those she is permitted to follow, she receives but a scanty remuneration.

He closes against her all the avenues to wealth and distinction, which he considers most honorable to himself. As a teacher of theology, medicine, or law, she is not known.

He has denied her the facilities for obtaining a thorough education—all colleges being closed against her.

He allows her in Church as well as State, but a subordinate position, claiming Apostolic authority for her exclusion from the ministry, and, with some exceptions, from any public participation in the affairs of the Church.

He has created a false public sentiment, by giving to the world a different code of morals for men and women, by which moral delinquencies which exclude women from society, are not only tolerated but deemed of little account in man.

He has usurped the prerogative of Jehovah himself, claiming it as his right to assign for her a sphere of action, when that belongs to her conscience and her God.

He has endeavored, in every way that he could to destroy her confidence in her own powers, to lessen her self-respect, and to make her willing to lead a dependent and abject life.

Now, in view of this entire disfranchisement of one-half the people of this country, their social and religious degradation,—in view of the unjust laws above mentioned, and because women do feel themselves aggrieved, oppressed, and fraudulently deprived of their most sacred rights, we insist that they have immediate admission to all the rights and privileges which belong to them as citizens of these United States.

In entering upon the great work before us, we anticipate no small amount of misconception, misrepresentation, and ridicule; but we shall use every instrumentality within our power to effect our object. We shall employ agents, circulate tracts, petition the State and national Legislatures, and endeavor to enlist the pulpit and the press in our behalf. We hope this Convention will be followed by a series of Conventions, embracing every part of the country.

Firmly relying upon the final triumph of the Right and the True, we do this day affix our signatures to this declaration.

The debate on the sentiments continued into the afternoon, but the organizers put off a vote on the resolutions until the second day. That day, the crowd grew larger. The hard wooden pews on the main floor and the side balconies of the simple brick church were packed. James Mott, who had recovered from his illness, chaired. The women asked for a man to preside, because they did not feel any of them had the experience and knowledge of parliamentary procedure to do so. Richard Hunt, Thomas M'Clintock, and Frederick Douglass were among the men present. Elizabeth M'Clintock, who knew Douglass through a local abolitionist group, had invited him.

The drafters had composed resolutions based on the eighteen grievances the colonists had presented to King George III, substituting the injustices to which women were subjected.

The Resolutions ★

Whereas, the great precept of nature is conceded to be, "that man shall pursue his own true and substantial happiness," Blackstone, in his Commentaries, remarks, that this law of Nature being coeval with mankind, and dictated by God himself, is of course superior in obligation to any other. It is binding over all the globe, in all countries, and at all times; no human laws are of any validity if contrary to this, and such of them as are valid, derive all their force, and all their validity, and all their authority, mediately and immediately, from this original; Therefore,

Resolved, That such laws as conflict, in any way, with the true and substantial happiness of woman, are contrary to the great precept of nature, and of no validity; for this is "superior in obligation to any other."

Resolved, That all laws which prevent woman from occupying such a station in society as her conscience shall dictate, or which place her in a position inferior to that of man, are contrary to the great precept of nature, and therefore of no force or authority.

Resolved, That woman is man's equal—was intended to be so by the Creator—and the highest good of the race demands that she should be recognized as such.

Resolved, That the women of this country ought to be enlightened in regard to the laws under which they live, that they may no longer publish their degradation by declaring themselves satisfied with their present position, nor their ignorance by asserting that they have all the rights they want.

Resolved, That inasmuch as man, while claiming for himself intellectual superiority, does accord to woman moral superiority, it is pre-eminently his duty to encourage her to speak and teach, as she has an opportunity, in all religious assemblies.

Resolved, That the same amount of virtue, delicacy, and refinement of behavior that is required of woman in the social state should also be required of man, and the same transgressions should be visited with equal severity on both man and woman.

Resolved, That the objection of indelicacy and impropriety, which is so often brought against woman when she addresses a public audience, comes with a very ill grace from those who encourage, by their attendance, her appearance on the stage, in the concert, or in the feats of the circus.

Resolved, That woman has too long rested satisfied in the circumscribed limits which corrupt customs and a perverted application of the Scriptures have marked out for her, and that it is time she should move in the enlarged sphere which her great Creator has assigned her.

Resolved, That it is the duty of the women of this country to secure to themselves their sacred right to the elective franchise.

Resolved, That the equality of human rights results necessarily from the fact of the identity of the race in capabilities and responsibilities.

Resolved, therefore, That being invested by the Creator with the same capabilities and the same consciousness of responsibility for their exercise, it is demonstrably the right and duty of woman, equally with man, to promote every righteous cause by every righteous means; and especially in regard to the great subjects of morals and religion, it is self-evidently her right to participate with her brother in teaching them, both in private and in public, by writing and by speaking, by any instrumentalities proper to be used, and in any assemblies proper to be held; and this being a self-evident truth, growing out of the divinely implanted principles of human nature, any custom or authority adverse to it, whether modern or wearing the hoary sanction of antiquity, is to be regarded as self-evident falsehood and at war with the interests of mankind.

The resolution calling for women "to secure to themselves their sacred right to the elective franchise" met with great opposition from those who argued that such a controversial platform could diminish support for other resolutions. Different attendees felt that other barriers—social, civil, and religious—were more pressing. Stanton defended the resolution, arguing that political rights were necessary for women to make other gains through laws.

Douglass Speaks

Anticipating controversy, given her husband's reaction, Elizabeth Stanton had asked Frederick Douglass, whom she knew from abolitionist activities, to speak on the elective franchise resolution's behalf. He did so eloquently. Douglass, the only African-American known to have attended the meeting, was familiar to the audience, as probably the most famous black man in the country at age thirty-two. He had escaped slavery ten years earlier, moved to New Bedford, Massachusetts, and started attending antislavery meetings. He soon met William Lloyd Garrison and became an agent for the American Anti-Slavery Society, and one of its most popular lecturers. His autobiography, *The Life and Times of Frederick Douglass*, published in 1845, was already an international best seller. The *North Star* carried the motto "Right is of no Sex—Truth is of no Color—God is the Father of us all, and we are all brethren."

Rising to speak for woman suffrage at Seneca Falls, he said he could not accept the right to vote for himself as a black man if women could not also claim that right. Douglass argued that women's involvement in politics would have a positive effect. "In this denial of the right to participate in government, not merely the degradation of woman and the perpetuation of a great injustice happens, but the maiming and repudiation of one-half of the moral and intellectual power of the government of the world," he said.

The resolution regarding suffrage passed by a small margin, and it was the only resolution the body did not adopt unanimously.

The declaration was passed unanimously. That day, sixty-eight women and thirty-two men signed the "Declaration of Rights and Sentiments."

A newspaper report carried in the *Seneca County Courier* on July 21, 1848, and reprinted in William Lloyd Garrison's *Liberator* on August 25, 1848, said it was "well drawn and contain[ed] a succinct statement of alleged grievances."

Although Mott's visit was the impetus for the meeting, Stanton carried the day with her insistence on demanding women's political equality, and Mott credited her for her contribution.

The report of proceedings, printed at Douglass's newspaper office, described Mott as "the moving spirit of the occasion," and the *Seneca County Courier* commented on Mott's contribution:

The lady is so well known as a pleasing and eloquent orator...Her discourse on that evening, whatever may be thought of its doctrines, was eminently beautiful and instructive. Her theme was the Progress of Reforms. In illustrating her subject, she described the gradual advancement of the causes of Temperance, Anti-Slavery, Peace, &c., briefly, but in a neat and impressive style. She then alluded to the occasion which had brought the audience together...and expressed the hope and belief that the movement in which she was then participating, would soon assume a grandeur and dignity worthy of its importance.

Others who spoke during the meetings included both of the M'Clintock daughters who helped draft the declaration, and their father, who read aloud from laws restricting women's rights.

Christopher Densmore, in an article on the role of radical Quaker women in the women's rights movement, noted, "The First Woman's Rights Convention...was conceived, organized and carried to a successful conclusion within eleven days...The rapid and successful organization of the Convention was possible because of the availability of a preexisting network of radical reformers."

After the sessions at Seneca Falls, Douglass wrote in the *North Star* on July 28, 1848:

One of the most interesting events of the past week, was the holding of what is technically styled a Woman's Rights Convention at Seneca Falls. The speaking, addresses, and resolutions of this extraordinary meeting were almost wholly conducted by women; and although they evidently felt themselves in a novel position, it is but simple justice to say that their whole proceedings were characterized by marked ability and dignity. No one present, we think, however much he might be disposed to differ from the views advanced by the leading speakers on that occasion, will fail to give them credit for brilliant talents and excellent dispositions. In this meeting, as in other deliberative assemblies, there were frequent differences of opinion and animated discussion; but in no case was there the slightest absence of good feeling and decorum. Several interesting documents setting forth the rights as well as the grievances of women were read. Among these was a Declaration of Sentiments, to be regarded as the basis of a grand movement for attaining the civil, social, political, and religious rights of women...Many who have at last made the discovery that the negroes have some rights as well as other members of the human family, have yet to be convinced that women are entitled to any...In respect to political rights, we hold woman to be justly entitled to all we claim for man. We go farther, and express [our] conviction that all political rights that it is expedient for man

Frederick Douglass defended Elizabeth Cady Stanton's resolution for woman suffrage.

Library of Congress

to exercise, it is equally so for woman. All that distinguishes man as an intelligent and accountable being, is equally true of woman; and if that government only is just which governs by the free consent of the governed, there can be no reason in the world for denying to woman the exercise of the elective franchise, or a hand in making and administering the laws of the land. Our doctrine is that "right is of no sex." We therefore bid the women engaged in this movement our humble Godspeed.

Whether the Seneca Falls Convention alone had set in motion anything that could yet be called "a movement" for suffrage, much less a "grand movement," was open to debate. The assembly at Seneca Falls did not make any effort to form a national organization. Among the organizers, only Mott, Stanton, and Wright would remain in the struggle for woman suffrage for the rest of their lives. It was clear, however, that the Seneca Falls meeting was the start of something.

"This convention was novel in its character, and the doctrines broached in it are startling to those who are wedded to the present usages and laws of society," the *Seneca County Courier* concluded. "The resolutions are of the kind called radical. Some of the speeches were very able—all the exercises were marked by great order and decorum."

★ Signers of the Declaration ★ of Sentiments at Seneca Falls

On Thursday, July 20, 1848, sixty-eight women signed the Declaration of Sentiments under the heading, "Firmly relying upon the final triumph of the Right and the True, we do this day affix our signatures to this declaration":

Lucretia Mott

Harriet Cady Eaton

Margaret Pryor

Elizabeth Cady Stanton

Eunice Newton Foote

Mary Ann M'Clintock

Margaret Schooley

Martha C. Wright

Jane C. Hunt

Amy Post

Catherine F. Stebbins

Mary Ann Frink

Lydia Mount

Delia Matthews

Catharine C. Paine

Elizabeth W. M'Clintock

Malvina Seymour

Phebe Mosher

Catherine Shaw

Deborah Scott

Sarah Hallowell

Mary M'Clintock

Mary Gilbert

Sophrone Taylor

Cynthia Davis

Hannah Plant

Lucy Jones

Sarah Whitney

Mary H. Hallowell

Elizabeth Conklin

Sally Pitcher

Mary Conklin

Susan Quinn

Mary S. Mirror

Phebe King

Julia Ann Drake

Charlotte Woodward

Martha Underhill

Dorothy Matthews

Eunice Barker

Sarah R. Woods

Lydia Gild

Sarah Hoffman

Elizabeth Leslie

Martha Ridley

Rachel D. Bonnel

Betsey Tewksbury

Rhoda Palmer

Margaret Jenkins

Cynthia Fuller

Mary Martin

P. A. Culvert

Susan R. Doty

Rebecca Race

Sarah A. Mosher

Mary E. Vail

Lucy Spalding

Lavinia Latham

Sarah Smith

Eliza Martin

Maria E. Wilbur

Elizabeth D. Smith

Caroline Barker

Ann Porter

Experience Gibbs

Antoinette E. Segur

Hannah J. Latham

Sarah Sisson

Thirty-two men signed the Declaration of Sentiments under the heading "...the gentlemen present in favor of this new movement":

Richard P. Hunt

Samuel D. Tillman

Justin Williams

Elisha Foote

Frederick Douglass

Henry W. Seymour

Henry Seymour

David Salding

William G. Barker

Elias J. Doty

John Jones

William S. Dell

James Mott

William Burroughs

Robert Smalldridge

Jacob Matthews

Charles L. Hoskins

Thomas M'Clintock

Saron Phillips

Jacob Chamberlain

Jonathan Metcalf

Nathan J. Milliken

S. E. Woodworth

Edward F. Underhill

George W. Pryor

Joel Bunker

Isaac Van Tassel

Thomas Dell

E. W. Capron

Stephen Shear

Henry Hatley

Azaliah Schooley

The Rochester Convention

Some participants, mostly Quakers again, called a follow-up meeting for August 2, 1848, in Rochester to consider the "rights of women, Politically, Socially, Religiously and Industrially." They wanted another opportunity to discuss the implications of the first meeting before the Motts left the area. Amy Kirby Post, another Hicksite Quaker abolitionist who had been at the Seneca Falls meeting, pressed Lucretia Mott to be the keynote speaker. They would meet at the Unitarian Church.

The following notice appeared in Douglass's newspaper on July 28, 1848:

A meeting to discuss the Rights of Women will be held in this city on Wednesday, 2d August. The place of meeting will be announced in the city papers. A meeting preliminary to this will be held on the evening of the 1st, in Protection Hall, Stone's Buildings. We are happy to announce that James and Lucretia Mott, with other persons from abroad, will be present.

When they convened, according to a report of the convention, "Amy Post called the meeting to order and reported on behalf of the [organizing] committee the following persons to serve as officers: Abigail Bush, president, Laura Murray, vice prest., Catharine A. F. Stebbins, Sarah L. Hallowell, and Mary H. Hallowell, secretaries."

Objections raised by Mott, Stanton, and the elder Mary Ann M'Clintock over the advisability of having a woman preside were quickly quashed by a vote of the attendees, and Bush, who was not a Quaker but was an abolitionist and activist, assumed the chair.

At this meeting, all who wished to speak from the floor were encouraged to do so. Mott challenged and sparred with various speakers, including some men objecting to women's rights. In one exchange, according to the report, a man asked what would happen if a man and his wife had a disagreement about politics or a child's education: "When the two heads disagree who must decide? There is no Lord Chancellor to whom to apply, but does not St. Paul strictly enjoin obedience to husbands, and that man shall be head of woman?"

Mott replied that within "the Society of Friends she had never known any difficulty to arise on account of the wife's not having promised obedience in the marriage contract. She had never known any other mode of decision except a resort to argument, an appeal to reason; and, altho in some of the meetings of this society women are placed on an equality, none of the results so much dreaded have occurred. The opposers of Woman's Rights who 'tho they bid us obey the bachelor St. Paul, themselves reject his counsel. He advised them not to marry.'"

The Rochester organizers read the Declaration of Sentiments from Seneca Falls, and 107 people signed it. The second meeting was smaller but important to keep the momentum going. At neither meeting did the attendees appear to have made any attempt to formalize an organization or adopt any strategies for achieving the aims set out in the declaration.

7

ensued in which Mrs Mott Mrs Stanton
and Mr Pickard participated. Mr Pickard asked, who
after marriage should hold property and whose name
should be retained? he thought an umpire necessary
— all business must cease, untill the consent of both parties
be obtained; he saw an impossibility of introducing
such a rule into society, the gospel has established
the unity of the married pair — they two are one —

Mrs Stanton thought property might be held join
-tly and the choice of names discretionary with
the parties. concerned. the custom of taking
the husbands name is not universal —

The following resolutions were now passed adopted with
but two or three dissenting voices —   A

                                        B.

                B.

Resolved That we tender a vote of thanks to the trustees
of the Unitarian Church for kindly granting the use of it for
this convention —

Resolved that The funds intended in this movement gratefully accept
the kind offer of the trustees of Protection hall for to hold our
meetings whenever we choose —

            Abigail Bush   President
            Laura Murray   Vice do
            Catherine A. F. Stebbins
            Sarah L. Hallowell   } Secretaries
            Mary H. Hallowell

These minutes of the Woman's Rights Convention
held in Rochester, New York, on August 2, 1848, are from
the papers of Phebe Post Willis and Henry Willis. They were given
to the University of Rochester Library by their grandson, the late
Henry Willis. This convention followed the one at Seneca Falls on
July 19 and 20, 1848. Those attending that convention were urged
to hold similar meetings in other cities. Representatives from
Rochester returned home and organized a convention held in the
Unitarian Church less than two weeks later. This page lists the
officers as Abigail Bush, president; Laura Murray, vice president;
and secretaries Catherine A. F. Stebbins,
Sarah L. Hallowell, and Mary H. Hallowell.

Courtesy of the Department of Rare Books & Special Collections and Preservation,
University of Rochester River Campus Libraries

A Call to Action

For Elizabeth Stanton, the meetings had been the catalyst she needed to commit herself to a lifelong quest to see that women got the ballot and all the rights due them. However, she had four more children over the following eleven years, for a total of seven. Thus encumbered by family obligations, she would limit her travel. She continued to contribute through her writing and intellectual gifts, often signing the call for conventions she could not attend, sending letters of support to be read, and offering resolutions.

Lucretia Mott wrote Stanton of her hopes to call another meeting in Philadelphia but acknowledged the difficulties of finding a venue and speakers. Mott also wrote about her 1848 travels that year, including the Seneca Falls and Rochester conventions, in the *Liberator*, declaring that she was encouraged by attention to "this long-neglected subject" of women's rights.

The Seneca Falls Convention seemed to help Lucretia Mott crystallize her own thoughts about women's rights and commit to advocating for them. It also established her as the primary leader of the movement. In 1849, Mott published a "Discourse on Woman," from a lecture she gave in Philadelphia to a full house at the Assembly Building in answer to one by Richard H. Dana, a poet and critic, ridiculing the idea of political equality for women. Mott spoke in defense of women's right to participate in the public sphere and even to gain the right to vote, in spite of her views as a Quaker about avoiding political participation. "Far be it from me to encourage women to vote, or to take an active part in politics in the present state of our government," she said, but women's "right to the elective franchise, however, is the same and should be yielded to her, whether she exercise that right or not." She urged women to demand their rights.

Her "Discourse" had been widely circulated, read, and discussed by the time of the next significant gathering to discuss women's rights. That would be in Salem, Ohio, about a year and a half after the New York meetings. The Second Baptist Church was the site of a convention on April 19–20, 1850, according to the *History of Woman Suffrage*, Volume 1, first published by Stanton, Susan B. Anthony, and Matilda Joslyn Gage in 1881. Emily Robinson called that meeting to order. Mariana W. Johnson served as president pro tem and Sarah Coates as secretary pro tem.

Johnson read the call, which urged the women of Ohio to meet "to concert measures to secure to all persons the recognition of equal rights, and the extension of the privileges of government without distinction of sex, or color."

Men were present but forbidden to speak at all during the meeting. Nevertheless, they took it graciously, according to the *History*. It said,

This Convention had one peculiar characteristic. It was officered entirely by women; not a man was allowed to sit on the platform, to speak, or vote. Never did men so suffer. *They implored just to say a word; but no; the President was inflexible—no man should be heard. If one meekly arose to make a suggestion he was at once ruled out of order. For the first time in the world's history, men learned how it felt to sit in silence when questions in which they were interested were under discussion. It would have been an admirable way of closing the Convention, had a rich banquet been provided, to which the men should have had the privilege of purchasing tickets to the gallery, there to enjoy the savory odors, and listen to the after-dinner speeches. However, the gentlemen in the Convention passed through this severe trial with calm resignation; at the close, organized an association of their own, and generously endorsed all the ladies had said and done. [Emphasis in the original.]*

The convention adopted twenty-two resolutions covering women's social, political, civil, and religious rights.

Johnson read a memorial outlining the myriad ways in which women were denied rights and urging that in the constitution the state was about to draft, "women shall be secured, not only the right of suffrage, but all the political and legal rights that are guaranteed men."

An "Address to the Women of Ohio," reprinted in the *History*

("said to have been written by J. Elizabeth Jones"), implored them to: "Let it not be our fault if the rights of humanity, and not alone those of 'free white male citizens,' are recognized and protected."

The account of the convention, submitted by Frances Gage, also makes note of the presence of Josephine Sophia White Griffing, another abolitionist whose home was an Underground Railroad station.

"It was here Josephine S. Griffing uttered her first brave words for woman's emancipation, though her voice had long been heard in pathetic pleading for the black man's rights," the report stated.

Griffing had moved to Litchfield, Ohio, in 1842 from Hebron, Connecticut, with her husband, Charles. She helped found the Ohio Women's Rights Association and became its president in 1853. Josephine Griffing gained national prominence as a speaker and writer and later lobbied for creation of the Freedman's Bureau after the Civil War.

In conclusion, the report pronounced the convention "largely attended and entirely successful."

With the meetings in New York State and the Ohio meeting, American women had given notice that a new era in their relationship to their government had begun and they would no longer be silent about "taxation without representation." They had laid claim to their rights and would not rest until they were secured.

★ Elizabeth Cady Stanton ★ The Mother of the Movement

Elizabeth Cady Stanton emerged as the face and the voice of the women's movement after the Civil War, working side by side with Susan B. Anthony. Stanton's writing, oratory, and intellect were her gifts to the movement, and she used them skillfully to bombard opponents with facts and arguments. Words were her weapon of choice.

Her first experience as a reformer was in the temperance movement, and during the Civil War, she led women's efforts to support passage of the Thirteenth Amendment formalizing emancipation. She precipitated a split in the women's movement that lasted decades, rather than support passage of the Fifteenth Amendment, which gave black men the vote without enfranchising women.

Born November 12, 1815, in Johnstown, New York, Elizabeth Cady was the eighth child of Daniel Cady, a lawyer, and Margaret Livingston Cady, daughter of a Revolutionary War hero. Elizabeth's father was in Congress when she was born, serving one term as a Federalist member of the

House of Representatives. Afterward, he returned to his law practice, then became a judge and later a New York State Supreme Court justice.

Elizabeth was one of eleven children, but five of her siblings died in childhood, including four brothers. The only brother who had lived almost to adulthood, Eleazar, died at the age of twenty, leaving five sisters. Her parents grieved for years over the loss of the six children.

Among her earliest memories was hearing her father express regret that she was not a boy, a sentiment he repeated in later years. He loved her and appreciated her brilliance, but a girl in those times realistically could never fulfill his dreams of having a son to carry on his legacy. Elizabeth spent a lot of her life trying to prove she could do as much as a boy could and fighting the injus-

tices of law that subjugated women.

Their house was a place where law clerks convened to study with the judge, and Elizabeth loved reading the law books and engaging in argument with the aspiring lawyers. She also heard the legal complaints of the neighbors aired, often those of women impoverished because of a drunken husband or deserted by a scoundrel.

The family did not want for material wealth and had servants, including free blacks and three enslaved men, until New York abolished slavery in 1827. Elizabeth's parents were not reformers and abolitionists like those of Lucretia Mott and Susan B. Anthony. The Cadys were stalwart Presbyterians, but Elizabeth developed a distaste for organized religion early in life.

Elizabeth attended the Johnstown Academy and studied Greek and Latin with a local Presbyterian minister. She later boarded at the Troy Female Seminary, the school founded in Troy, New York, by the forward-thinking Emma Willard and later named for her. The best school for girls available at the time, it provided girls education comparable to that offered to boys. Elizabeth Cady, however, was not particularly thrilled that she could not go to Union College in Schenectady, where her male classmates and brother Eleazar had gone. Nor was she enamored of most of the subjects because she had already studied them, but she took to French, dancing, and music. She described leaving school after being extremely unnerved by the fire-and-brimstone messages of a revivalist visiting the seminary, and she apparently did not graduate.

She returned home at age seventeen to a leisurely life. Unlike Lucretia Mott, Susan B. Anthony, or Lucy Stone, Elizabeth Cady did not seek a calling or a cause at that age. She did not need to work, and her parents did not expect her to do more than light chores at home.

With so much free time, she did spend long periods in the home of her cousin Gerrit Smith. (Their mothers were sisters.) He was the son of Peter Smith, who had made a fortune in real estate. Gerrit Smith was a radical reformer and abolitionist who gifted vast acreages of land to freed blacks for farms in upstate New York. He became a staunch friend of the women's rights movement. (Smith also became a presidential candidate for the Liberty Party and a financial backer of John Brown's raid on the federal arsenal at Harpers Ferry, in what was then Virginia and later West Virginia.)

The Smith home was a kind of crossroads for the abolitionists, all kinds of other reformers, revolutionaries,

Dutch immigrants, Native Americans, free blacks, fugitives, and relatives. Elizabeth liked to spend time there with Smith's daughter Elizabeth, or "Libby," who would be credited with importing the "Bloomer" fashion that proved an albatross to the movement a few years later.

Elizabeth Cady Stanton recalled in History of Woman Suffrage:

Here one would meet the first families in the State, with Indians, Africans, slaveholders, religionists of all sects, and representatives of all shades of humanity, each class alike welcomed and honored, feasting, fêting, dancing—joining in all kinds of amusements and religious worship together (the Indians excepted, as they generally came for provisions, which, having secured, they departed). His house was one of the depots of the underground railroad. One day Mr. Smith summoned all the young girls then visiting there, saying he had a great secret to tell them if they would sacredly pledge themselves not to divulge it. Having done so, he led the way to the third story, ushered us into a large room, and there stood a beautiful quadroon girl to receive us. "Harriet," said Mr. Smith, "I want you to make good Abolitionists of these girls by describing to them all you have suffered in slavery." He then left the room, locking us in. Her narrative held us spell-bound until the lengthening shadows of the twilight hour made her departure safe for Canada…We had the satisfaction to see Harriet dressed in Quaker costume, closely veiled, drive off in the moonlight that evening, to find the liberty she could not enjoy in this Republic, under the shadow of a monarch's throne.

The encounter does not seem to have inspired her to take up the cause of abolition instantly, but in their house she found mental stimulation, exposure to new ideas, and soon enough a husband. Elizabeth recalled the home as "a charming resort for lovers of liberty as well as lovers of Eve's daughters. In his leisure hours my cousin had a turn for match-making, and his chief delight in this direction was to promote unions between good Abolitionists and the sons and daughters of conservative families."

One frequent visitor there was Henry Brewster Stanton, a lecturer for the antislavery cause, who at thirty-four was ten years her senior. He was tall, good-looking, and facile at conversation, and Elizabeth was soon under his spell, as he was hers. Within a month, they were engaged. He came from a good family, descended from Puritans who had arrived on the *Mayflower*. His father was a merchant and manufacturer. However, Elizabeth soon broke off the engagement because her father disapproved. In his view, other than lecturing as one of the first full-time agents of the American Anti-Slavery Society, Stanton had no real occupation or future prospects. By all accounts, however, he was a talented organizer and speaker who was passionate about abolition. (His family had owned a man, and as a youth, Henry hated the idea of slavery. As an adult, he vowed to take up the cause of freedom.) Frederick Douglass credited one of Stanton's speeches with bringing him into the abolitionist movement soon after his escape.

The engagement was back on after Henry announced plans to attend the World Anti-Slavery Convention in London in 1840. Not wanting to endure a long separation, they married in a rush on May 11 of that year with a few relatives and friends present. Elizabeth declined to include "obey" in her vows and insisted on retaining "Cady" in the usage of her name. They traveled to New York and embarked on a three-week voyage to London.

At the time, Elizabeth was uninitiated in antislavery politics, but she would soon realize her husband was at the center of a splintering of antislavery organizations over strategies to achieve emancipation, religious influences, and views of women's rights that were at odds with William Lloyd Garrison's wing and with the women in the abolitionist movement. Henry Stanton spent much of the voyage tutoring his bride on the antislavery cause with help from James G. Birney, the Liberty Party nominee for president.

At that conference, the American women were denied their place as delegates and relegated to sit behind a partitioning rail. Some of the men from the United States, including Garrison, refused their own places on the convention floor and sat with the women in solidarity.

At their boarding house, Elizabeth met one of the spurned delegates, Lucretia Mott, and her husband, James. The Motts and the other U.S. women came prepared to fight for women's right to be active participants in the convention.

Elizabeth found herself on the wrong side of the question, "though I really knew nothing of the merits of the division, having been outside the world of reforms," she recalled later.

"I supposed they would all have a feeling of hostility toward me," she said. "However, Mrs. Mott, in her sweet, gentle way, received me with great cordiality and courtesy, and I was seated by her side at dinner." During a lively debate over dinner, Elizabeth Stanton recalled, she spoke up for women's rights.

Lucretia and Elizabeth

Elizabeth Cady Stanton, handwritten inscription:
Elizabeth Cady Stanton and her daughter, Harriot. from a daguerreotype 1855

Elizabeth Cady Stanton, shown with her daughter
Harriot in 1856, had seven children.
Library of Congress

struck up a friendship, and Elizabeth Cady Stanton often told the story that they walked the streets of London "arm in arm" and, angered by the rejection of the women, made a vow to hold a women's rights conference back home. Various historians have cast doubt on that story, arguing that Mott apparently did not share Stanton's fury over the slighting of women and did not concur that they talked in London about convening a meeting on their return home. Mott did later recall that Stanton may have proposed the idea a year or so later in Boston.

After London, the Stantons traveled in Europe, where Henry gave lectures. After returning home, they lived with Elizabeth's parents in Johnstown for a time while Henry studied law with her father. There, the Stantons had their first child, Daniel, before moving to Boston. Henry had become more deeply entrenched in antislavery work and became further estranged from the Garrisonians, especially over the questions of political participation.

(The Garrisonians believed that the U.S. Constitution was a proslavery document, because of the compromise embedded in it that allowed slavery to continue. They wished to do nothing to advance the government—by voting or taking part in partisan politics. The American Anti-Slavery Society, formed in 1833, split in 1839 over this difference and others, including women's rights. One faction left to form the more moderate American and Foreign Anti-Slavery Society. Stanton was part of a third division who wished to take a more proactive role in government. He and others had withdrawn from the American Anti-Slavery Society to form the Liberty Party, and he was busy campaigning to elect candidates who would fight for abolition.)

Boston had not been that fruitful for Henry's law practice and political ambitions, and Elizabeth's father offered them an abandoned farmhouse in Seneca Falls, then a busy center for manufacturing and commerce. Elizabeth looked forward to being part of that "magnetic circle of reformers" of upstate New York, as she called it in her memoir. They moved there in the spring of 1847. Now, with two more children born in Boston—Henry Jr. in 1844 and Gerrit Smith Stanton in 1845—she busied herself taking care of her household and enjoying her children. (In succession came four more: Theodore, Margaret, Harriot, and Robert Livingston, the last in 1859, when she was forty-four.)

Her husband increasingly traveled to organize the Liberty Party (1840s) and later the Free Soil Party (1848), both founded to oppose slavery. He served in the New York legislature in 1850–1851 and later helped organize the Republican Party.

At first, she spent much of her time supervising the renovation of the house and making it livable after it had sat vacant for years. She lamented:

> I now fully understood the practical difficulties most women had to contend with in the isolated household, and the impossibility of woman's best development if in contact, the chief part of her life, with servants and children…The general discontent I felt with woman's portion as wife, mother, housekeeper, physician, and spiritual guide, the chaotic conditions into which everything fell without her constant supervision, and the wearied, anxious look of the majority of women impressed me with a strong feeling that some active measures should be taken to remedy the wrongs of society in general, and of women in particular.

A little over a year after her move, Elizabeth Cady Stanton must have let out a great sigh of relief when she heard that the woman who had opened her mind to the infinite possibilities of women's elevation was coming to town, and she was invited to a tea in her honor.

"In this tempest-tossed condition of mind I received an invitation to spend the day with Lucretia Mott, at

This drawing of Elizabeth Cady Stanton was found at the Frederick Douglass home in Washington, D.C.
Library of Congress

Richard Hunt's, in Waterloo," she said. "There I met several members of different families of Friends, earnest, thoughtful women. I poured out, that day, the torrent of my long-accumulating discontent, with such vehemence and indignation that I stirred myself, as well as the rest of the party, to do and dare anything."

Elizabeth Cady Stanton probably took the train a short distance from Seneca Falls to Waterloo and walked to the elegant, white-columned home of Jane and

Richard Hunt on the main street with great anticipation. There, her hosts probably greeted her warmly, but the fact could not have escaped her that she was different from the others. They were all Quakers, part of the radical Friends who had split off from another reform group. They were probably wearing their customary plain dress and white caps, and most of them were related in some way to someone else there. All were ardent abolitionists. Among them, in addition to Jane Hunt, possibly with her two-week-old infant nearby, were Lucretia Mott and her expectant sister, Martha C. Wright, who had come by train from Auburn; and Mary Ann M'Clintock and her grown daughters, Elizabeth and Mary Ann. They had many things to talk about, notably the fractious Genesee Yearly Meeting of area Friends that the Motts had come to attend, each family's most recent antislavery activities, and the recent passage of the New York Married Women's Property Act.

With the opportunity to talk about women's issues in a room full of sympathetic women—Quakers, kind, generous, accepting of the stranger, willing to hear her out—the words of pent-up frustration over women's lot must have come gushing out. In Stanton's telling, she is the one who stirs up the others. However, the other women, long accustomed to organizing, speaking, acting on their convictions of being treated as equals to men, probably had much to say. They decided on the spot to call a convention, and some of them met a few days later to draw up a declaration. It was Elizabeth Cady Stanton who had insisted on including a demand for the vote and defended it with the help of Frederick Douglass. To the Garrisonian Quakers, the voting issue was a conflict. Henry Stanton, who believed in partisan politics for men, refused to attend the convention if the resolution was included, and he left town to lecture. All the other organizers' husbands attended and signed the declaration—James Mott, Richard Hunt, and Thomas M'Clintock.

If the convention at Seneca Falls had not included a demand for the vote, that event might have been long forgotten. No one might ever have heard of Elizabeth Cady Stanton. For her singular courage to voice that demand, and for the many years of her exceptional leadership and dogged determination throughout her long life to keep the issue alive, she will be long remembered.

She had lit the flame.

Section 3

The Early Conventions

I doubt whether a more important movement
ever launched touching the destiny of the race, than this
in regard to the equality of the sexes.

William Lloyd Garrison

Cartoon: Which? A timely question—a man labeled "popular vote" looks at Republican, Democratic, woman suffrage, and temperance advocates.

Library of Congress

"Let Us Convene"

The conventions at Seneca Falls, Rochester, and Salem were significant because they set the stage for a movement to begin and helped the organizers determine that others shared their quest. They identified the central issues and put the world on notice that women were demanding change.

However, those meetings had been largely local or regional. Women eagerly answered a call for the first national convention on women's rights. Over the next decade, supporters would convene annually, airing grievances, building consensus, and, most important, establishing alliances and friendships that would drive the movement. In addition to the national conventions, three more held in Ohio also had historic significance. The movement would remain dominated by abolitionists and would remain a Northern and Midwestern phenomenon until late in the century. The proceedings of these meetings help track who joined the movement and when. No central organization or political agenda congealed during this period. The leadership seems to have shifted with each convention, and the discussions ranged over a wide array of issues related to women's rights—marriage, property ownership, custody, education, and their roles in the churches.

The meetings themselves served as a form of agitation, and this was a necessary stage in the revolution, akin to the "consciousness raising" phase of the feminist movement of the 1960s and '70s or to the civil rights movement before a leader arose in the form of Martin Luther King Jr. The reformers first had to air their concerns among themselves and build up their own fortitude. Meeting face-to-face was also necessary, because people had few ways to communicate in those days except by letter or by reading the newspapers. Regular use of telegrams would come later. So people were not in frequent contact of any kind. The conventions presented opportunities to hear what others thought and to share ideas.

The meetings followed a standard format. Organizers issued a call, which went out to the press. A nominating committee selected officers to serve in various posts for the duration of the convention. Organizers solicited and read letters from well-wishers not in attendance. Participants read resolutions, debated, and voted them up or down. Some designated speakers offered remarks, others commented from the floor, and nonsupporters had their say. The organizing committee had the proceedings written up and sometimes printed for circulation.

Many men, supporters and opponents, some of them very prominent, attended these meetings, helping to frame the issues and narrow the agenda. They were mostly motivated to stand up for women out of devotion to human rights and justice concerns, as well as devotion to their own mothers, wives, and daughters.

Men often served as officers of the conventions, and among them were some of the leading ministers, philosophers, and reformers of the day. Their presence lent legitimacy to the proceedings and underscored their importance. They brought parliamentary, political, and business expertise that few women could have had in that era. They also occasionally provided security. Other men sometimes came as curiosity seekers, hecklers, and agitators.

The conventions served to publicize the cause and crystallize the issues but neither a concrete agenda nor specific strategies would emerge from this era. Nevertheless, this was an important stage in the making of a movement.

Worcester, Massachusetts, 1850

Paulina Kellogg Wright Davis, of Rhode Island, organized and presided over the first National Woman's Rights Convention, which was held October 23 and 24, 1850, in Worcester, Massachusetts. Davis had studied medicine and had spent several years traveling to lecture women on anatomy. An active abolitionist, she also had worked with Ernestine Rose on petitioning the New York legislature for the law giving property rights to married women. She later started a women's rights periodical, the *Una*.

Recalling details of the planning twenty years later, she said:

In May, 1850, a few women in Boston attending an Anti-Slavery meeting, proposed that all who felt interested in a plan for a National Woman's Rights Convention, should consult in the anteroom. Of the nine who went out into that dark, dingy room, a committee of seven were chosen to do the work...However, the work soon devolved upon one person [herself]. Illness hindered one, duty to a brother another, duty to the slave a third, professional engagements a fourth, the fear of bringing the gray hairs of a father to the grave prevented another from serving; but the pledge was made, and could not be withdrawn.

**The Reverend Antoinette Brown Blackwell,
an Oberlin College graduate, was the first American woman
to be ordained as a minister.**

The Granger Collection, New York

Eighty-nine people signed the call. It said the convention would convene "to consider the question of Woman's Rights, Duties, and Relations. The men and women who feel sufficient interest in the subject to give an earnest thought and effective effort to its rightful adjustment, are invited to meet each other in free conference at the time and place appointed."

Lucretia Mott, Elizabeth Cady Stanton, and Lucy Stone were among the signers. Stone was one of the women who had helped organize the convention but nearly missed it because of a brother's illness and then her own.

A number of men signed the call, including the white abolitionist vanguard: Garrison; Gerrit Smith; Wendell Phillips (also signing for his wife, Ann Greene Phillips); Amos Bronson Alcott, an educator and Transcendentalist, and father of the author Louisa May Alcott; and William H. Channing, a Unitarian clergyman and Transcendentalist philosopher. The philosopher-poet Ralph Waldo Emerson sent a letter of support. Many men attended, among them Douglass, who would become a constant at women's rights conventions throughout his life.

An estimated one thousand people poured into Brinley Hall for the meeting. The attendees came from nine of the thirty-one states in the Union. The U.S. population was just a little over 23 million people. New York was the largest with 3 million residents, followed by Pennsylvania with 2.3 million. The country was still growing, and the population was pushing westward.

Sarah H. Earle of Worcester (identified as the wife of John Milton Earle, editor of the *Worcester Daily Spy*) called the meeting to order, and Paulina Davis was elected president of the convention. Addressing those assembled, she said,

The reformation we propose in its utmost scope is radical and universal. It is not the mere perfecting of a reform already in motion, a detail of some established plan, but it is an epochal movement—the emancipation of a class, the redemption of half the world, and a conforming reorganization of all social, political, and industrial interests and institutions…We claim for woman a full and generous investiture of all the blessings which the other sex has solely, or by her aid, achieved for itself. We appeal from man's injustice and selfishness to his principles and affections.

Speakers included Lucy Stone, Antoinette L. Brown, and Dr. Harriot K. Hunt.

Among the attendees

was Sojourner Truth, the formerly enslaved preacher and anti-slavery lecturer from Ulster County, New York, who participated in the debates.

Among the resolutions passed was this:

> *Resolved, That women are clearly entitled to the right of suffrage, and to be considered eligible to office; the omission to demand which, on her part, is a palpable recreancy to duty, and a denial of which is a gross usurpation on the part of man, no longer to be endured; and that every party which claims to represent the humanity, civilization, and progress of the age, is bound to inscribe on its banners, "Equality before the Law, without distinction of Sex or Color."*

This was considered "highly controversial because of its shocking support of equality for black women," according to an article by Jessie M. Rodrique, PhD, published by the Worcester Women's History Project, 2002.

Rodrique says that this convention "marked the beginning of the organized movement for women's rights and called for the total reorganization of 'all social, political, industrial interests and institutions'...The convention was applauded by a few local and national newspapers, but disparaged by most of them. The issues raised at the convention, however, were heard throughout the world. It became a touchstone for international feminism."

An unnamed writer from the *New York Herald* was not impressed. The headline read:

WOMAN'S RIGHTS CONVENTION.

AWFUL COMBINATION

OF

SOCIALISM, ABOLITIONISM, AND INFIDELITY.

THE PANTALETTES STRIKING FOR THE PANTALOONS.

BIBLE AND CONSTITUTION REPUDIATED.

The paper reported under a dateline of October 23, 1850, that a "motley mingling of abolitionists, socialists, and infidels, of all sexes and colors, called the Woman's Rights Convention, assembled in this city, to-day."

The article devoted several paragraphs to describing the leading women's appearances.

"Miss Davis, the President or Presidentess, is a tall, handsome lady, fair complexion, blue eyes, auburn ringlets and of a very amiable expression of countenance."

Lucretia Mott was "in the modest dress of a Quakeress—muslim cap and scarf, rich Quaker gown and white silk shawl. Her countenance wears the hard iron expression of [a general], all bone, gristle, and resolution. We should take her to be an elderly lady, indomitable as Caesar."

The writer deemed Abby Kelley Foster "a very striking personage—tall and thin, with an eye wild and resolute...dress, plain black, open collar, dark hair, dressed plain."

The article noted the presence of several abolitionist leaders and "several dark colored sisters...visible in the corners."

The article outlined some of the debate and concluded:

The objects of the Convention, as disclosed to-day, are:

1. To abolish the Bible.

2. To abolish the constitution and the laws of the land.

3. To re-organize society upon a social platform of perfect equality, in all things, of sexes and colors.

4. To establish the most free and miscellaneous amalgamation of sexes and colors.

5. To elect Abby Kelly Foster President of the United States, and Lucretia Mott Commander-in-Chief of the Army.

6. To cut throats ad libitum.

7. To abolish the gallows.

Such appear to us the actual designs of that piebald assemblage called the Woman's Rights Convention.

The convention named a National Central Committee to guide future proceedings, with Davis as chair, Sarah H. Earle as secretary, and Wendell Phillips as treasurer, along with state representatives. Stone and Channing were among its members.

Worcester, Massachusetts, 1851

The committee called a second convention in Worcester for October 15 and 16, 1851, also at Brinley Hall.

A notice had appeared in Frederick Douglass's paper on September 4, announcing a convention "to consider the Rights, Duties, and Relations of Woman" and inviting men and women to "the free and full discussion of this great question."

The announcement continued:

The cause itself, affecting as it does, the destiny of the race, takes the front rank in those reform movements which the progressive spirit of the age has called into being; and invites to its aid all who see and feel the wrongs which grow out of the false position occupied by women and who, having no dread of what is called for by the instinct of mankind, dare give to such a movement the sanction of their presence, and to embody, in word and deed, the thought and feeling which they must have, who see that woman socially, civilly, religiously and educationally, occupies an unnatural and unworthy position.

More than merely announcing a meeting, the notice proclaimed that "a movement" was in progress. The *History of Woman Suffrage* reported that on the day of the meeting, "at an early hour the house was filled, and was called to order by Paulina Wright Davis, who was again chosen permanent President. This Convention was conducted mainly by the same persons who had so successfully managed the proceedings of the previous year."

The abolitionist leader Wendell Phillips read the resolutions prepared for consideration. Prefacing that task, he said, "I rejoice to see so large an audience gathered to consider this momentous subject, the most magnificent reform that has yet been launched upon the world. It is the first organized protest against the injustice which has brooded over the character and the destiny of one-half of the human race. Nowhere else, under any circumstances, has a demand ever yet been made for the liberties of one whole half of our race. It is fitting that we should pause and consider so remarkable and significant a circumstance."

Syracuse, New York, 1852

The committee convened a third national convention in Syracuse on September 8–10, 1852, at the densely packed City Hall. Paulina Wright Davis, as chair of the Central Committee, called the meeting to order, and the Reverend Samuel J. May, pastor of the Unitarian Church in Syracuse, offered a prayer. He had written letters in support of previous conventions and had been preaching for several years advocating the social, civil, and political rights of woman. The delegates came from eight states and Canada. Among those in attendance who had been at the Seneca Falls Convention were Martha C. Wright, who served as one of the secretaries, and the elder Mary Ann M'Clintock and her husband, Thomas.

The delegates elected Lucretia Mott as president. Only her husband, James, shouted "No!" when the vote was called. Perhaps it was in jest, but her agreement to serve in that position for a "promiscuous assemblage" was significant, the *History of Woman Suffrage* noted, given her objections to having a woman preside at the Rochester meeting four years earlier.

"Mrs. Mott, who sat far back in the audience, walked forward to the platform, her sweet face and placid manners at once winning the confidence of the audience," the report said.

In opening remarks, she said that she did not know parliamentary procedures and felt unprepared to make a speech, but apparently did so quite ably, according to the account in the *History*:

> *She asked the serious and respectful attention of the Convention to the business before them, referred to the success that had thus far attended the movement...and closed by inviting the cordial co-operation of all present.*
>
> *In commenting upon Mrs. Mott's opening address, the press of the city declared it to have been "better expressed and far more appropriate than those heard on similar occasions in political and legislative assemblages." The choice of Mrs. Mott as President was pre-eminently wise; of mature years, a member of the Society of Friends, in which woman was held as an equal, with undoubted right to speak in public, and the still broader experience of the Anti-Slavery platform, she was well fitted to guide the proceedings and encourage the expression of opinions from those to whom public speaking was an untried experiment. "It was a singular spectacle," said the* Syracuse Standard, *"to see this gray-haired matron presiding over a Convention with an ease, dignity, and grace that might be envied by the most experienced legislator in the country."*

At the Syracuse convention, Stone read the call, urging all to participate in the debates, even if they disagreed with the women's demands. One of the high points of the Syracuse meeting came after the reading of a letter from Elizabeth Cady Stanton, suggesting that all women who owned property refuse to pay taxes as long as they were unrepresented in government.

The letter generated fervent debate and "resolutions of the most radical character," most of them adopted by the convention. "Thus at that early day was the action of those women, who have since refused to pay taxes, prefigured and suggested," the report said.

Matilda Joslyn Gage helped edit the History of Woman Suffrage.

Library of Congress

"One of the remarkable aspects of this reform, is the fact that from the first its full significance was seen by many of the women who inaugurated it."

Attendees debated at length whether to form a women's party or permanent organization, but several women objected to doing so. They adopted a resolution instead to encourage women to convene meetings in their states and regions, and from 1850 to 1860 national women's rights gatherings were held every year, except 1857.

Among those attending a women's rights convention for the first time were Susan B. Anthony, who was appointed an officer, and Matilda Joslyn Gage of Onondaga County, New York. The youngest person there, at twenty-six, according to the report, Gage spoke publicly for the first time on women's rights, notably on equal access to education. She and Anthony would go on to make significant contributions to the movement. In the 1880s, Stanton, Anthony, and Gage produced the early books of the *History*, which eventually grew to six volumes.

Ohio Conventions, 1851–1853

Women in several states answered the call to hold meetings. Ohio in particular was ripe for this new wave of reform, because it had also called a convention to rewrite its constitution, and women and blacks were eager to see their rights written into it.

The state, divided by only a river from slave territory in Kentucky and, to the east, a sliver of what was then Virginia, had been a beacon for runaways and an epicenter of debate over the evils of slavery. Agitation grew after the passage of the Fugitive Slave Act of 1850, requiring the cooperation of officials and citizens of free states in capturing and returning runaways to their masters. Many abolitionists and Underground Railroad agents lived along the Ohio shore and brazenly resisted the law.

Ohioans were no strangers to protest and reform. Throughout the state, word of the Salem women's rights convention in 1850 spread (see Section 2, "A Call to Action"), building enthusiasm for a second state convention in Akron on May 28, 1851. Most of the speakers had honed their skills in the antislavery movement or the growing temperance movement. Frances Dana Barker Gage, a writer from McConnelsville whose family was part of the antislavery underground, presided. (Gage signed the account of the convention in the *History of Woman Suffrage*.) After demurring that she was not entirely pleased at the honor, since she had never attended a regular business meeting of any kind and was unfamiliar with "the forms and ceremonies of a deliberative body," she proceeded to give a very eloquent and long speech.

In conclusion, she said:

Let woman speak for herself, and she will be heard. Let her claim with a calm and determined, yet loving spirit, her place, and it will be given her...Oh, if all women could be impressed with the importance of their own action, and with one united voice, speak out in their own behalf, in behalf of humanity, they could create a revolution without armies, without bloodshed, that would do more to ameliorate the condition of mankind, to purify, elevate, ennoble humanity, than all that has been done by reformers in the last century.

At this convention, the emancipated orator Sojourner Truth also made her first known speech on women's rights.

"Some of our younger readers may not know that Sojourner Truth was once a slave in the State of New York and carries today as many marks of the diabolism of slavery, as ever scarred the back of a victim in Mississippi," the *History* noted.

★ Sojourner Truth: ★ Powerful Orator

Born Isabella "Bell" Baumfree around 1797, Sojourner Truth escaped slavery in 1826, about a year before slavery ended in New York, because her slaveholder had gone back on a promise to free her. Her next employer paid the owner for her year's labor, and she chose the name Sojourner Truth. Though illiterate, the History noted, she was "a woman of rare intelligence and common-sense."

The History presented Frances Gage's account of the famed "And a'n't I a woman?" speech, which includes repeated uses of that refrain, as the one delivered at the Akron Convention in 1851. This version—though read, memorized, and recited by countless numbers of people for generations—has been widely discredited by historians. For one thing, Gage quotes Truth as speaking in a Southern dialect, which several scholars have found implausible. She was raised in upstate New York and learned Dutch as a first language, as was common in her community. Gage also describes heckling and "hissing" from the audience, but others at the time said Truth was fondly received.

In the Gage version, Truth says she has seen most of her thirteen children sold into slavery. In reality, her biographers say that she had five children, perhaps one sold away in slavery, and that she never claimed more. Gage did not publish her account until twelve years after the event, and she offered a slightly different version four years later for the History of Woman Suffrage.

The earliest reports of the speech appeared in newspapers shortly after the conference, and a fuller version appeared in an Ohio paper in June 1851. Marius Robinson, editor of the *Anti-Slavery Bugle*, who had also acted as the recording secretary of the convention, wrote it in Standard English. He did not include the question "A'n't I a woman?" even once in his reporting of it, and the remarks differ on other points. He wrote:

One of the most unique and interesting speeches of the convention was made by Sojourner Truth, an emancipated slave. It is impossible to transfer it to paper, or convey any adequate idea of the effect it produced upon the audience. Those only can appreciate it who saw her powerful form, her whole-souled, earnest gesture, and listened to her strong and truthful tones. She came forward to the platform and addressing the President said with great simplicity: "May I say a few words?" Receiving an affirmative answer, she proceeded:

"I want to say a few words about this matter. I am a woman's rights. I have as much muscle as any man, and can do as much work as any man. I have plowed and reaped and husked and chopped and mowed, and can any man do more than that? I have heard much about the sexes being equal. I can carry as much as any man, and can eat as much too, if I can get it. I am as strong as any man that is now. As for intellect, all I can say is, if a woman have a pint, and a man a quart—why can't she have her little pint full? You need not be afraid to give us our rights for fear we will take too much,—for we can't take more than our pint'll hold. The poor men seems to be all in confusion, and don't know what to do. Why children, if you have woman's rights, give it to her and you will feel better. You will have your own rights, and they won't be so much trouble. I can't read, but I can hear. I have heard the bible and have learned that Eve caused man to sin. Well, if woman upset the world, do give her a chance to set it right side up again. The Lady has spoken about Jesus, how he never spurned woman from him,

***Sojourner Truth, seen here in 1864, often spoke up
at the national women's rights conventions.***
Library of Congress

and she was right. When Lazarus died, Mary and Martha came to
him with faith and love and besought him to raise their brother.
And Jesus wept and Lazarus came forth. And how came Jesus into
the world? Through God who created him and the woman who bore
him. Man, where was your part? But the women are coming up
blessed be God and a few of the men are coming up with them. But
man is in a tight place, the poor slave is on him, woman is coming
on him, he is surely between a hawk and a buzzard."

Robinson might have edited his version, and Gage might have embellished hers for whatever reason, and blended various speeches by Truth. No one will ever know. Truth spoke extemporaneously, and it was long before the era of voice recording, but it is clear from both accounts that her delivery had a powerful impact on her audience, and she continued to be a presence at women's rights conventions.

Addressing the American Equal Rights Association in 1867, Truth said, "I suppose I am about the only colored woman that goes about to speak for the rights of the colored woman. I want to keep the thing stirring, now that the ice is cracked." She was not the only one. Harriet Tubman also made some speeches on women's rights. *Century of Struggle* mentions among early leaders "the Negro women who, while their first interest inevitably lay in the anti-slavery struggle, consistently pointed out the relationship between freedom for the slave and equality for women of any color— Sojourner Truth, Frances E. W. Harper, Sarah Remond." Of these, Eleanor Flexner wrote, "none did more valiant service than the almost legendary Sojourner Truth."

Massillon, Ohio, 1852

A third Ohio convention took place at Massillon, about twenty miles south of Akron, on May 27, 1852, where attendees formed the Ohio Women's Rights Association. They named Hannah Maria Conant Tracy Cutler, then an abolitionist writer and educator, president. (Cutler, who later became a physician, remained active in the national suffrage movement until her death in 1896.)

In 1853, a national convention for women's rights met in Cleveland on October 5–7. Frances Gage opened the meeting with a brief history of the women's rights meetings since Seneca Falls and concluded by asserting that she hoped the discussions at this convention "will be a little more extensive than the call would seem to warrant, which indicates simply our right to the political franchise."

Lucretia Mott readily agreed that the previous convention had left it to the Central Committee to issue the call but had not anticipated being restricted to discussing voting rights.

"It was not supposed that they would specify any particular part of the labor of the Convention, but that the broad ground of the presentation of the wrongs of woman, the assertion of her rights, and the encouragement to perseverance in individual and combined action, and the restoration of those rights, should be taken," Mott said.

The meeting proceeded with a lively discussion on a broad

range of issues, including property rights, custodial rights, taxation without representation, and access to education.

Gage had urged everyone to participate, even those who disagreed with the positions being taken.

I extremely regret that while we have held convention after convention, where the same liberty has been given, no one has had a word to say against us at the time, but that some have reserved their hard words of opposition to our movement, only to go away and vent them through the newspapers, amounting, frequently, to gross misrepresentation.

By the time of that convention in Cleveland, suffragists were holding national conventions regularly, as well as state and regional meetings, and many were wearing a new fashion—a dress over pantaloons that became known as the Bloomer.

★ The Bloomer: ★ "Dress Reform"

Official proceedings and news accounts of the various women's conventions in the early 1850s frequently took note of a new fashion statement, generally lampooning it and insulting the wearers.

Many of the attendees were donning an innovative kind of dress that freed them from many pounds of fabric in layers—long skirts, multiple petticoats, stockings, and corsets with whalebone stays—that restricted breathing and constrained movement. The dresses of the day also often had high, stiff collars and long, full sleeves. The new attire consisted of a loosely fitted tunic with a belt, and a skirt that reached just below the knees with Turkish-inspired pantaloons underneath that buttoned at the ankle.

The "Bloomer" style was popularized by Amelia Bloomer.

Though nicknamed for Amelia Jenks Bloomer of Seneca Falls, New York, the origins of this look remain somewhat murky. Bloomer's name is associated with them (even in dictionaries today) because she publicized the fashion in her periodical, the Lily, the first newspaper for women. Susan B. Anthony recalled that Bloomer and Elizabeth Cady Stanton were wearing the outfits when she met Stanton after an antislavery meeting in Seneca Falls in 1851.

One theory is that the modified dress originated in Europe, popularized there by a leading British actress of the day, Fanny Kemble, who wore the style. Then, an American woman, Elizabeth

Amelia Bloomer (1818–1894),
publisher of the Lily, *popularized the Bloomer.*

Smith Miller, reportedly saw them while abroad and brought the style home to upstate New York. She was the daughter of the well-known abolitionist and suffrage advocate Gerrit Smith and a cousin of Elizabeth Cady Stanton.

When Bloomer saw them, she started wearing them, as did many of the leading suffragists—Stanton, Susan B. Anthony, and Lucy Stone among them. The History of Woman Suffrage simply said Miller introduced them in 1850, and she wore them in Washington while her father served in the House of Representatives (1853–1854) and for some years after.

"The facts of history may as well be stated here in regard to the 'Bloomer' costume," the History said in its account of the 1853 National Woman's Rights Convention in Cleveland. A newspaper had noted that some of the most prominent women of the movement were there, and some were in Bloomer garb.

Alice Stone Blackwell recalled that her mother wore the Bloomer for three or four years, beginning around 1850. After wearing it mostly at home for a year, she began wearing the style all the time, including at the conventions, and she wore it well. Blackwell said the Bloomer "was not half so ugly" as many of the styles of that era.

"It was not beautiful, but was very comfortable and convenient, and entirely modest," Blackwell wrote. Blackwell, who also called it the "freedom dress," attributed the style to Miller, who wanted something she could wear for long walks around her father's vast property in upstate New York.

Even as it became a popular sensation and solved the problems of excruciatingly uncomfortable attire for women, the style drew unwanted attention and harsh commentary. At the 1853 convention, Henry B. Blackwell, not yet married to Lucy Stone, "complimented those women who were just inaugurating a movement for a new costume, promising greater freedom and health. He thought the sneers and ridicule so unsparingly showered on the 'Bloomers,' might with more common sense be turned on the 'tight waists, paper shoes, and trailing skirts of the fashionable classes,'" according to the proceedings.

The Bloomer outfits became associated with the women's rights movement and vice versa. Soon, they became a distraction. Since the fad took root as the women's rights meetings spread, many people probably saw them for the first time when these fashion-forward women gathered en masse, adding to the shock value. They also became associated with other unpopular ideas of the day, including "free love," "easy divorce," and "amalgamation" (race mixing) that the suffragists were accused of promoting—and that a few were promoting. The visual, or the "optics," was clearly taking them "off message," as pundits would say in modern times.

"It invoked so much ridicule, that they feared the odium attached to the dress might injure the suffrage movement, of which they were prominent representatives," the History continued. "Hence a stronger love for woman's political freedom, than for their own personal comfort, compelled them to lay it aside."

Among those who clung to it the longest was Susan B. Anthony, because it was a more practical option for her frequent travels than the other fashions of the day. The pantaloons did not drag in the mud, weigh her down, or hamper her in getting in and out of coaches. The outfit did attract stares and heckling. Lucy Stone told a story in which a mob of men encircled Anthony and her on a New York City corner, jeering and laughing at their Bloomers until an acquaintance asked police to rescue them.

Anthony, Stone, and Stanton exchanged numerous letters about their fashion dilemma as Anthony expressed angst over the thought of giving them up. She had abandoned her plain Quaker clothing years before and now paid close attention to her wardrobe. Stanton and Stone had reverted to traditional dress.

"If Lucy Stone with all her reputation, her powers of eloquence, her loveliness of character, that wins all who once hear her voice, cannot bear the martyrdom of the dress, I ask, who can?" Anthony wrote to Stone.

Both Stone and Stanton

urged Anthony to give up the attire, arguing that it was unwise to expend so much energy and emotion defending it. Stanton urged Anthony, in vain, to "let the hem out of your dress to-day" before a meeting scheduled the next day. Eventually, Anthony relented.

In remarks later, Anthony said that while she had hoped to "establish the principle of rational dress," the attire was "a physical comfort but a mental crucifixion" because people fixated on her appearance. Comparing the old cumbersome dress to "intellectual slavery," she said she learned that audiences could accept only one reform at a time. "I have felt ever since that experience that if I wished my hearers to consider the suffrage question I must not present temperance, the religious, the dress or any other besides, but must confine myself to suffrage."

The History cheerily reported, "The experiment, however, was not without its good results. The dress was adopted for skating and gymnastic exercises, in seminaries and sanitariums...Many farmers' wives, too, are enjoying its freedom in their rural homes" (presumably out of the public eye).

It was unfortunate in many ways, because "dress reform" was a subject of serious discussion at the time, as the History noted:

In demanding a place in the world of work, the unfitness of her dress seemed to some, an insurmountable obstacle. How can you, it was said, ever compete with man for equal place and pay, with garments of such frail fabrics and so cumbrously fashioned, and how can you ever hope to enjoy the same health and vigor with man, so long as the waist is pressed into the smallest compass, pounds of clothing hung on the hips, the limbs cramped with skirts, and with high heels the whole woman thrown out of her true equilibrium. Wise men, physicians, and sensible women, made their appeals, year after year; physiologists lectured on the subject; the press commented, until it seemed as if there were a serious demand for some decided steps, in the direction of a rational costume for women. The most casual observer could see how many pleasures young girls were continually sacrificing to their dress: In walking, running, rowing, skating, dancing, going up and down stairs, climbing trees and fences, the airy fabrics and flowing skirts were a continual impediment and vexation. We can not estimate how large a share of the ill-health and temper among women is the result of the crippling, cribbing influence of her costume.

The Lily ran dozens of letters, comments from other papers, and editorials about dress reform, which helped to boost its circulation tenfold, from a few hundred readers up to as many as four thousand.

In an unsigned editorial on October 16, 1854, it said, "Let [woman] rise to eminence in any profession or trade, for which she has talent or inclination...Let her dress suitable to her work, and to her taste, if she has sense enough to do so, and don't hoot at her because her dress don't suit you. I would like to do man's work, if I could wear a man's working dress, or be respected as a working man is."

Comfort would have to wait, however, while more pressing matters were at issue, because the Bloomer had caused "quite an agitation," Elizabeth Cady Stanton wrote in the History of Woman Suffrage.

"I wore the dress two years and found it a great blessing," recalled Stanton. "What a sense of liberty I felt...What emancipation from little petty vexatious trammels and annoyances every hour of the day. Yet such is the tyranny of custom, that to escape constant observation, criticism, ridicule, persecution, mobs, one after another gladly went back to the old slavery and sacrificed freedom to repose."

It would be decades before women's form of dress changed significantly. Certainly, these women could not have imagined that the time would come when fashions like bikinis, miniskirts, Daisy Dukes, hot pants, leggings, or see-through ball gowns would become commonplace.

Stanton wrote that Gerrit Smith was deeply troubled when women like her and his own daughter gave them up, so disappointed that "women had so little courage and persistence, that for a time he almost despaired of the success of the suffrage movement; of such vital consequence in woman's mental and physical development did he feel the dress to be."

New York City, 1853

A month before the Cleveland convention, a New York State women's rights convention convened in New York City at the Broadway Tabernacle on September 6–8, 1853, after a confluence of reformist conventions had stirred up the city, including antislavery and temperance conventions.

As the *History of Woman Suffrage* explained:

> The opening days of the autumn of this year were days of intense excitement in the city of New York. Added to the numbers attracted by the World's Fair [the Exhibition of the Industry of All Nations] was the announcement of the Anti-Slavery, Woman's Rights, and two Temperance Conventions. The reformers from every part of the country assembled in force, each to hold their separate meetings, though the leaders were to take a conspicuous part in all...and every day two or three of these conventions were in session, all drawing crowds to listen or to disturb. William Henry Channing, William Lloyd Garrison, Wendell Phillips and Thomas Wentworth Higginson eloquently pleading for the black man's freedom on the anti-slavery platform, and for the equality of their mothers, wives, and daughters on the woman's rights platform, and for both the woman and the

black man on the temperance platform.

When the women's convention met, one of the temperance conventions, the World's Temperance Convention, had already disintegrated after delegates rejected the Reverend Antoinette L. Brown's credentials from two affiliate organizations, as well as those of an African-American delegate, James McCune Smith. Protestors held their own convention, the Whole World's Temperance Convention. Lucretia Mott addressed it, linking the reform movements of peace, temperance, abolition, and women's rights. Rowdy thugs disrupted all the meetings, however, and they continued their mob agitation under the direction of the city's Democratic political machine, Tammany Hall.

When the Whole World's Temperance Convention adjourned, up to three thousand people crowded into the hall for the women's convention, including the mob elements. "At every session every man of them was promptly in his place," the *History* noted. Vigorous debate ensued, and one eloquent speaker after another rose to speak, but the ruffians interrupted every one of them for two days, most especially Sojourner Truth.

When she appeared on the platform, the *History of Woman Suffrage* related, it "was the signal for a fresh outburst from the mob...Sojourner combined in herself, as an individual, the two most hated elements of humanity. She was black, and she was a woman, and all the insults that could be cast upon color and sex were together hurled at her; but there she stood, calm and dignified, a grand, wise woman, who could neither read nor write, and yet with deep insight could penetrate the very soul of the universe about her."

Men hissed at her, and she gave as good as she got, telling them, "We'll have our rights; see if we don't; and you can't stop us from them; see if you can. You may hiss as much as you like, but it is comin'."

The cacophony continued, as the crowds shouted down women

and men, regardless of color. Lucretia Mott presided, but the chaos grew to the point that she feared they would need to seek police intervention. As a Quaker, she could not ask for or condone a use of force. Rather than do that, she vacated the chair, giving it to Ernestine Rose. Twice, Rose asked from the platform that the police quiet the disruptions, but the situation got worse.

The second day, amid what the *History* called a "terrific uproar, shouting, yelling, screaming, bellowing, laughing, stamping," Mott praised the women for their courage in the face of such ill treatment and adjourned the meeting. As they exited, the mob jostled and shoved. Mott told a man escorting her to take care of some other women while she took one of the roughest combatants by the arm and asked him to get her out safely, and so he did.

The one "redeeming feature" of the mob, organizers reported, was that the hecklers had paid twenty-five cents to attend each session, just as the women and their supporters had, helping organizers to pay the overhead. However, their presence was also a personification of the opposition that the movement would face, an omen of the decades of struggle ahead. Because of the noise and dissonance, the recording secretaries and the press could give only sketchy reports of what might otherwise have been a highly successful convention with stellar speakers and insightful debate.

"A Surfeit of Conventions," 1854–1861

The poor reception in New York City did not slow the pace of the conventions. They continued as the leadership continued to shift. National conventions were held in Philadelphia in 1854, with Ernestine Rose presiding; Cincinnati in 1855, with Martha C. Wright; New York City in 1856, with Lucy Stone (there was no convention in 1857); and New York City every year from 1858 to 1860, with Susan B. Anthony presiding in 1858, Lucretia Mott in 1859, and Martha C. Wright in 1860. In the prewar years, local, state, or regional meetings were also convened.

Supporters and opponents alike began to complain that the movement was all talk and no action. In 1855, even the ever-patient Lucretia Mott complained of a "surfeit of conventions."

Mott, who had chaired and spoken at more than her share of meetings, thought that the gatherings were draining the supporters' energies and merely repeating the now-familiar complaints without producing any results. For her, women's rights work was also taking time away from the antislavery activities to which she was more committed. This was at a crucial time in the decade between the passage of the Fugitive Slave Act of 1850 and the outbreak of the Civil War. The radical abolitionist Quakers were busy enough aiding fugitives and resisting the law.

The Fugitive Slave Act of

Martha C. Wright,
one of the conveners of the Seneca Falls Convention,
took a leading role in the women's rights movement of the 1850s.
Library of Congress

1850 increased the urgency of ending the institution. Under the law, even those who escaped and made it to Cincinnati, Philadelphia, or New York were not safe. Aiding and abetting an escapee was a crime. An alleged fugitive had to prove he or she was free, and bounty hunters could claim any African-American was a fugitive. Abolitionist activity intensified, and Mott's Philadelphia Female Anti-Slavery Society and the Pennsylvania Anti-Slavery Society were engaged in fund-raising and other activities. For the next several years, Mott was far more absorbed in the anti-slavery movement than in the women's movement.

She urged Lucy Stone to let a year go by without a convention, but the gatherings continued. The following year, Mott addressed the convention but complained that everyone had heard everything possible about women's rights, while most women in society remained complacent and oblivious to their compromised status. In 1857, Stone, newly wed and a new mother, was finally prepared to let a year go by without one. In 1858, a convention was held, but Lucretia Mott skipped it.

Susan B. Anthony ascended to the presidency of the 1858 convention. She had become more involved with women's rights and less in temperance activities after being silenced at some meetings herself. Mott attended in 1859, but her short speech on progress was not well received, and she vowed never to return. In May 1860, her sister Martha Wright chaired the convention at Cooper Institute in New York City and defended the worth of the conventions:

I shall leave it to others to speak of the purposes of this great movement and of the successes which have already been achieved.

There are those in our movement who ask, "What is the use of these Conven-

tions? What is the use of this constant iteration of the same things?" When we see what has been already achieved, we learn the use of this "foolishness of preaching:" and after all that we demand has been granted, as it will be soon, The New York Observer *will piously fold its hands and roll up its eyes, and say, "This beneficent movement we have always advocated," and the pulpits will say "Amen!" (Laughter and applause). Then will come forward women who have gained courage from the efforts and sacrifices of others, and the great world will say, "Here come the women who are going to do something, and not talk."*

In February 1861, the last national convention before the Civil War took place in Albany, New York, where delegates also had a hearing before the judiciary committee of the New York legislature on a bill to liberalize divorce laws. After that, the women's rights advocates set aside their concerns to focus on supportive roles as the nation prepared for war. Seven slave states had already seceded and formed the Confederacy.

After years of holding meetings, the women's rights advocates had made no real effort to form a national organization. They had no national office. No ongoing leadership was in place. No clear consensus emerged on which issues to prioritize and how to push an agenda forward, though participants were beginning to discuss petitioning governmental bodies and taking similar measures. Suffrage was an issue, but it was never the only issue on the table. The debates still covered a range of topics with talk of property rights, marriage and divorce laws, educational opportunities, religious constraints, reproductive issues, and other grievances. While important, they were unrelated to voting rights.

What the flurry of meetings had done was to help the women find their own voices and hear their own frustrations with the restrictive laws and customs articulated aloud. By convening, they had forced the outside world to pay attention to their grievances. The conventions also had helped the women discern friends from foes and attract male allies.

Perhaps most important, the movement had produced leaders. It helped them polish organizational skills and identify who among them excelled at what tasks. Mott had emerged as the moral force of the movement, Wright as a trusted sounding board for all the leaders, Stone as a silver-tongued orator, and many others as warriors and willing workers. In the next decade, Stanton would emerge as its philosopher and Anthony as its consummate organizer. What began as not-so-idle talk over tea was indeed a movement, and they were ready to carry it forward.

★ *The Temperance Movement* ★

As noted throughout this book, many of the women and men involved in the women's movement got their start in the reform arena through the temperance movement, and many were active simultaneously in both.

The temperance movement was an organized effort to encourage abstinence from or moderation in the consumption of intoxicating beverages, especially hard liquor. It took root in the United States early in the nineteenth century, not so much out of moral or religious concerns but out of practical ones. Early Americans drank alcohol as a matter of course, and alcoholism became rampant, as *Century of Struggle* noted. (By 1830, adults consumed an estimated seven gallons of alcohol a year per capita, or three times current norms.)

As Jean H. Baker observed in *Sisters: The Lives of America's Suffragists*, Americans enjoyed a bounty of apples and grains to make alcohol cheaply. Most employers gave their workers a ration of spirits as part of their pay, and getting together to drink on payday became a bonding ritual for workmen. Taverns sprang up everywhere and became havens for men. The trend began to alarm public leaders, clergy, employers, and women's rights advocates.

Drunken servants were not good workers. Drunken neighbors were a threat to society as a whole, and drunken husbands could be a disaster for women. Wives of drunkards were generally unable to provide for themselves or protect themselves and their children in their own homes. Hence, sobriety became a primary women's rights issue.

"What might be a moral injustice if the latter was a sober citizen became sheer tragedy if he were a heavy drinker who consumed not only his own earnings but his wife's, and reduced her and her children to destitution," Eleanor Flexner observed in *Century of Struggle*.

Recall that under the laws, a woman in such a state could not divorce her husband, could not retain custody of her children, and probably had no property rights. Neither in all likelihood could she get a job to support herself.

Early temperance societies solicited drinkers to sign pledges of sobriety. In the nineteenth century, they shifted from mere moral suasion against the personal consumption of liquor to putting pressure on local, state, and federal lawmakers to restrict or ban the sale of such beverages. The temperance leaders wielded tremendous influence.

Women formed their own organizations because they either could not speak up or were not welcome at all in men's organizations, the same way they had been shut out of most male abolition organizations. An evangelical-based movement swept through the Midwest in the 1870s, with bands of women singing, praying, and roaming through towns, invading saloons and forcing them to shut down, at least temporarily. The most infamous among these reformers was Carrie Nation, a Kentucky-born temperance advocate, who was arrested frequently for wielding a hatchet to bust up saloons, breaking glass and smashing kegs.

In 1874, women in Cleveland, Ohio, founded the Woman's Christian Temperance Union, with Annie Wittenmyer, an Iowa editor who had been active in Civil War relief work, as president and Frances Willard, an educator, as corresponding secretary. Willard saw woman suffrage as a natural extension of their agenda, but when Wittenmyer forbade her to speak on the issue, Willard challenged her. She rose to the presidency in 1879 and took the organization to new levels, melding the twin causes of temperance and women's rights under the argument that women needed a voice and a vote in politics to protect their interests. Willard, who had served as the first dean of women at Northwestern University, used her influence to draw in women who might have been reticent to support the woman suffrage cause. Willard urged followers to "speak for woman's ballot as a protection for her home."

She did more than talk—Willard put the mighty forces of the WCTU behind the effort, creating a suffrage department within the organization. She called for a "do everything" strategy to accomplish their goals, applying every means necessary: petitioning, lobbying, and persuading.

The WCTU was active in every state and claimed to represent up to five hundred thousand members by the 1890s. It was the most powerful women's organization in the nation, and its members campaigned actively for suffrage. Still, many women in the organization remained less than enthusiastic about joining forces with the suffragists.

Against this alliance, a liquor lobby emerged, becoming a formidable and deep-pocketed enemy of local and national suffrage campaigns that was not above sleazy and mean tactics. Liquor interests feared that if women got the vote, prohibition was certain, and at the very least laws to restrain drinking would proliferate.

This led some woman suffrage leaders to question the wisdom of having the issues of suffrage and temperance closely associated in the public mind. Some attributed the many defeats for suffrage and the protracted struggle to attain the vote to the perception that suffrage and prohibition were linked. After Willard's death in 1896, the WCTU turned back to its roots to focus on temperance, getting localities to restrict alcohol sales and educating the public on the evils of drink.

It was the rise of another organization, the Anti-Saloon League, formed in 1893 with men at the helm, that led to Prohibition, pushing for the Eighteenth Amendment to ban the manufacture, sale, and transportation of alcohol throughout the United States. By 1916, twenty-three states had passed antisaloon legislation or prohibited the manufacture of alcoholic beverages. When Congress began deliberating the Eighteenth Amendment, the liquor lobby's attentions had been diverted to state efforts. Prohibition passed Congress in December 1917. Ratification was completed in January 1919, and the amendment went into effect a year later. (It was repealed in 1933 by the Twenty-First Amendment.)

Apparently, the liquor lobby had spent its energies fighting these laws and was not so much a force when the Nineteenth Amendment went to the states for ratification in June 1919, though it was still a formidable opponent.

Section 4

A
Division

One cause at a time. This hour belongs to the Negro.

Wendell Phillips, president of

the American Anti-Slavery Society,

1865

Susan B. Anthony died in 1906,
fourteen years before ratification of the amendment
that bore her name. This portrait was taken by S. A. Taylor,
probably not long before her death.

The Abolitionist Lecture Tour

In the next decade, women began to see the vote as the answer to all the issues they had been debating since 1848. Woman suffrage would emerge as the primary goal of the movement, but factions would split over how to achieve it, causing a fissure that would take decades to heal, sundering alliances and straining relationships. The divisions would also diffuse energies, squander resources, and stall progress.

After the election of Abraham Lincoln in 1860, some of the women who had been most active in the women's cause to date—including Elizabeth Cady Stanton, Susan B. Anthony, and Lucretia Mott—joined other abolitionists in a lecture tour in New York State to advocate for emancipation, facing mobs and threats along the way from anti-abolitionists in the North.

Far from being ecstatic about the election of the president we know today as the Great Emancipator, many of the radical abolitionists regarded him with suspicion. He came to his final decision on emancipation slowly. Though he was morally opposed to slavery in principle and to its extension to the new territories, he considered the institution constitutionally protected. Lincoln was not an abolitionist in the way many of the leaders in the women's movement were; most favored immediate and absolute emancipation and bestowing full citizenship rights on the formerly enslaved. The abolitionists opposed

compensation of slaveholders, gradual emancipation, or
"colonization"—removal of the
formerly enslaved to some other
territory or land—all ideas that
Lincoln and many others had
floated. He was a moderate on
slavery, and the radical abolitionists did not trust that they
could win him over to their side.
The antislavery women and men
who had fought together for
women's rights feared Lincoln
would be willing to compromise
with the South on slavery to
keep the Union intact.

A cadre of them set aside
the work for women's rights to
barnstorm for emancipation,
with slogans vowing "No Compromise with Slaveholders" and
"Immediate and Unconditioned
Emancipation." Hateful mobs
ran them offstage in Rochester,
Syracuse, and Buffalo. Stanton
and Anthony had organized the
tours to stir up public sentiment
and to keep pressure on Lincoln.

Martha Wright presided over
some of these meetings and
organized one in her town of Auburn, New York, in January 1861.
Experienced at running women's

conventions, where heckling
was common, Wright had anticipated some trouble, and police
were present at her request.
Still, a mob of 100 to 150 broke
up the meeting, and the abolitionists had to take sanctuary in
Wright's home to complete their
business.

Undeterred, they met again
February 4 and 5 in Albany.
Though the threat of violence
followed them, a police show of
force averted disaster.

The mayor, George H.
Thacher, had refused a request
from citizens that he block the
meetings, and he insisted on
protecting the abolitionists' free
speech rights. He escorted the
attendees from their hotel to the
hall.

According to *The Life and
Work of Susan B. Anthony*, "The
mayor went on the platform and
announced that he had placed
policemen in various parts of
the hall in citizens' clothes,
and that whoever made the
least disturbance would be at
once arrested. Then he laid a
revolver across his knees, and
there he sat during the morning,

afternoon and evening sessions. Several times the mob broke forth, and each time arrests were promptly made."

Frederick Douglass also stood at the edge of the platform and faced the crowd as if daring anyone to advance toward the speakers, Wright recalled later. Hooligans sat among the attendees shouting down speakers, including Lucretia Mott, Susan B. Anthony, and Gerrit Smith, but the meeting proceeded. The mayor and Douglass escorted Mott and Wright as a rowdy bunch followed the convention-eers back to their hotel. Mayor Thacher told Anthony that if they insisted on continuing the meetings a second day he would offer protection but was not certain if he could hold back "this rabble."

The disruptions were evidence of increasing tensions. The breakup of the Union had already begun, and detractors characterized the abolitionists as traitors to the United States. Lincoln had campaigned on his determination to keep slavery out of new territories, and the Southern states feared his election was a step toward abolition. Lincoln won his election on November 6, 1860. South Carolina seceded on December 20, 1860, and by February 1, 1861, six more states had followed its lead, seceding before he could take the oath of office in March 1861. By mid-April of that year, the country was at war.

Once the Civil War opened, the cause of woman suffrage took a backseat to saving the Union. After the antislavery convention in Albany, New York, Wright had presided over one last state women's rights convention, and the New York State Women's Rights Committee had circulated a petition demanding the ballot and presented it to the legislature.

Elsewhere, conventions were suspended. Anthony had begun planning a national women's rights convention for 1861 but soon realized she had no support for one and no speakers. The women's movement was at a standstill.

★ *The Party of Lincoln* ★

The political parties active throughout the era of the women's rights and suffrage movements do not align with the parties of the same names in modern times. Parties often dissolved, changed focus, took new names, or divided. This is similar to the way the Democratic and Republican Parties metamorphosed, nearly reversing positions and ideologies, in the twentieth century, and third parties continued to emerge. The Democratic and Republican Parties of the twenty-first century have ideologies almost directly opposite to what they were a hundred years ago.

The Republican Party that eventually elected Abraham Lincoln president was formally organized in July 1854 in Jackson, Michigan. The name "Republican" was a nod to the Democratic-Republican Party that Thomas Jefferson and James Madison formed in the 1790s in opposition to Alexander Hamilton's party, the Federalists, who wanted a strong central government. The Democratic-Republican Party came to power in 1800 with the election of Jefferson as president, and it remained the dominant party until around 1824, when it splintered. Presidents Jefferson, James Madison, and James Monroe were members of the party. They opposed a strong national government, emphasized states' rights, and despised Hamilton's fiscal policies.

Meanwhile, a faction who called themselves Republicans evolved into the National Republicans and eventually the Whig Party in 1834. A Democratic Party also formed by 1828, led by Andrew Jackson, who was elected president and served from 1829 to 1837.

When the Democrats' platform in 1848 failed to support

the exclusion of slavery in the Western territories acquired from Mexico, some members helped form the Free Soil Party, along with some Whigs and members of the Liberty Party. From 1848 to 1852, the Free Soil Party was active in presidential races and a few local ones. The party's rallying cry was "free soil, free speech, free labor, and free men." Its members were not abolitionists per se, but opposed slavery as an economic threat to jobs and business, as well as on moral grounds. They believed that containing slavery to where it already existed would lead to the demise of the system. The Free Soil Party had few victories. It nominated Martin Van Buren, then a former president (1837–1841), to lead the ticket, but he did not win in 1848, and its 1852 candidate, John P. Hale, was also defeated.

By 1854, the Whigs were in disarray and divided over the issue of slavery, after the Kansas-Nebraska Act of that year dissolved the terms of the Missouri Compromise of 1820. It had prohibited slavery in the former Louisiana Territory north of the 36°30' parallel, except within the proposed state of Missouri. The new law allowed voters, "free white male inhabitants" of a territory, to decide whether to allow slavery, but many saw the act as an economic threat to free white men who wanted the opportunity the new territory represented. If slavery were allowed there, paid labor would be scarce.

It was "a monumental fiasco which inflamed the slave controversy worse than ever," the Lincoln biographer Stephen B. Oates wrote.

On May 9, 1854, the day after the Kansas-Nebraska Act passed Congress, a small group of Northern antislavery congressmen of various parties met at a boarding house near the Capitol in Washington, D.C., to discuss plans for a new party. It would be devoted to the Jeffersonian principles of "inalienable rights of life, liberty, and the pursuit of happiness." Its immediate aim was to keep slavery from spreading into the West.

The first convention was held in 1856 in Philadelphia, and delegates nominated John C. Frémont for the presidency. He ran unsuccessfully against James Buchanan, a Democrat, and Millard Fillmore, the nominee of another new party, the American, or Know-Nothing, Party. They were anti-immigrant and anti-Catholic but did not take sides on slavery. Buchanan won, but the Republican Party quickly gained ground.

Lincoln had been a Whig but shifted his loyalties and helped start the Republican Party in Illinois. The national Republicans nominated him for president in 1860, as the Northern and Southern Democrats nominated different candidates and the new Constitutional Union Party, made up of conservative Whigs, nominated another. Lincoln beat them all. The Southern slave states threatened to secede if Lincoln won, and they began to do so within six weeks of his election and formed the Confederacy. Its forces attacked Fort Sumter in April 1861, launching the bloody Civil War.

After the war, Republicans, especially the most radical faction within the party that now dominated Congress, pushed through the Reconstruction amendments, abolishing slavery, establishing citizenship for the formerly enslaved, and giving black males the right to vote. African-Americans identified with the Republicans and shunned Southern Democrats, who were anti-Reconstruction and prosegregation. The early suffragists were almost uniformly Republican, because they had been solidly abolitionists. A Republican first introduced the Susan B. Anthony Amendment in Congress.

The Republican Party dominated presidential politics until the election of Franklin D. Roosevelt in 1933. The party retained the loyalty of African-Americans until the 1930s, when many supported Roosevelt and the New Deal policies. The shift to the Democratic Party was nearly complete by the 1960s when Barry Goldwater, the Republican nominee, opposed the 1964 Civil Rights Act in the Senate on constitutional grounds. It cost him the race against the incumbent Lyndon B. Johnson, a Southern Democrat, who signed the act, and all but a few African-Americans left the Republican Party for good.

The Loyal Women

Many of those who had been the women's movement's foot soldiers now put their energies into the war effort. A few women, like Lucy Stone, continued lecturing. Her sisters-in-law Dr. Elizabeth Blackwell and Dr. Emily Blackwell set up an organization to train nurses and standardize sanitation practices. Dorothea Dix, a social reformer from Maine, became superintendent of Union Army nurses. Women like Louisa May Alcott, not yet a famous author, and Clara Barton (later founder of the American Red Cross) went off to nurse the wounded.

A brave handful of women posed as men and fought on the battlefields. Some, like Harriet Tubman, already famed for leading hundreds out of slavery, conducted relief efforts among African-Americans freed as the Union Army advanced south. Tubman and Pauline Cushman, an actress, also spied for the Union. Other women worked the jobs men left when they went to fight, becoming factory workers, teachers, or government office workers. Volunteers also rolled bandages, collected food, and held fairs to raise money for the relief efforts. In the North and South, many women took over the running of farms or plantations. Even women writers contributed. Julia Ward Howe wrote the poem that became the Union anthem, "The Battle Hymn of the Republic," and Lincoln teased Harriet Beecher Stowe

**Julia Ward Howe helped Lucy Stone
start the American Woman Suffrage Association.**
Library of Congress

that she had started "this great war" with her book *Uncle Tom's Cabin*, which rallied the North and rattled the South.

In the greatest sacrifice of all, women accepted the death and injuries of their husbands, fathers, brothers, and sons.

As the authors of the *History of Woman Suffrage* reflected:

At this eventful hour the patriotism of woman shone forth as fervently and spontaneously as did that of man...While he buckled on his knapsack and marched forth to conquer the enemy, she...gathered needed supplies for the grand army; provided nurses for the hospitals; comforted the sick; smoothed the pillows of the dying; inscribed the last messages of love to those far away; and marked the resting-places where the brave men fell. The labor women accomplished, the hardships they endured, the time and strength they sacrificed in the war that summoned three million men to arms, can never be fully appreciated.

In the midst of war, Lincoln issued the Emancipation Proclamation on September 22, 1862, ending slavery in the ten states where the people "shall then be in rebellion" effective January 1, 1863. (It did not apply to the border slave states that had remained in the Union or anywhere else.)

The proclamation did not appease some of the abolitionist women, including Anthony and Stanton, who still feared that opponents could overturn the proclamation or that the war would end in some kind of compromise with the South on slavery. Restless for something to do, they jumped at the opportunity when Henry Stanton suggested in a letter to Anthony that they work on behalf of a constitutional amendment to end slavery permanently throughout the United States.

"You have no idea how dark the cloud is which hangs over us," Henry Stanton wrote. "We must not lay the flattering unction to our souls that the proclamation will be of any use if we are beaten and have a dissolution of the Union. Here then is work for you. Susan, put on your armor and go forth!"

Elizabeth Cady Stanton and Susan B. Anthony called a meeting of the Loyal Women of the Nation in New York for May 14, 1863, where hundreds of women joined them, including their old allies Ernestine Rose and Angelina Grimké Weld. Lucy Stone presided. Weld had retired from public speaking decades before, but rose to speak:

My heart is full, my country is bleeding, my people are perishing around me.

But I feel as a South Carolin-
ian, I am bound to tell the
North, go on! go on! Never
falter, never abandon the
principles which you have
adopted.

During their meeting, the conventioneers pledged their support of the war: "Resolved, That we, loyal women of the nation...do hereby pledge our-selves one to another in a Loyal League, to give support to the Government in so far as it makes the war for freedom." Perhaps more important, they pledged to collect one million signatures on petitions to present to Congress, where the proposed Thirteenth Amendment would require pas-sage by a two-thirds majority of each house before it went to the states for ratification. Petitions would show that the people of the North favored emancipation.

The women at this historic meeting also did what they had not accomplished for the women's rights movement. They established an organization, the Women's Loyal National League, electing Elizabeth Cady Stan-ton as president and Susan B. Anthony as secretary. In another key step, the new organization also set up an office, which opened in Cooper Union within the month. Anthony headed the office, gaining valuable experi-ence. She drew a salary of $12 a week, made possible by a donor, and boarded with the Stantons, who had moved to New York City because Henry was deputy collector at the Customs House.

Thousands of women, men, and children enlisted to collect signatures, and five thousand members joined the League. The leaders rolled up the petitions into large bundles to present to Congress. When Senator Charles Sumner, Republican of Massa-chusetts, received the first bun-dle of one hundred thousand on February 9, 1864, he addressed the Senate:

Mr. President: I offer a
petition which is now lying
on the desk before me. It is
too bulky for me to take up.
I need not add that it is too
bulky for any of the pages of
this body to carry.

This petition marks a stage of public opinion in the history of slavery, and also in the suppression of the rebellion. As it is short I will read it: "To the Senate and House of Representatives of the United States:

"The undersigned, women of the United States above the age of eighteen years, earnestly pray that your honorable body will pass at the earliest practicable day an act emancipating all persons of African descent held to involuntary service or labor in the United States."

There is also a duplicate of this petition signed by "men above the age of eighteen years"...

This petition is signed by one hundred thousand men and women, who unite in this unparalleled number to support its prayer. They are from all parts of the country and from every condition of life. They are from the seaboard, fanned by the free airs of the ocean, and from the Mississippi and the prairies of the West, fanned by the free airs which fertilize that extensive region. They are from the families of the educated and uneducated, rich and poor, of every profession, business, and calling in life, representing every sentiment, thought, hope, passion, activity, intelligence which inspires, strengthens, and adorns our social system. Here they are, a mighty army, one hundred thousand strong, without arms or banners; the advance-guard of a yet larger army.

But though memorable for their numbers, these petitioners are more memorable still for the prayer in which they unite. They ask nothing less than universal emancipation; and this they ask directly at the hands of Congress.

With four hundred thousand signatures in hand, the League was short of its ambitious goal, but it disbanded in August 1864 as victory in Congress appeared within reach. The Thirteenth Amendment passed Congress on January 31, 1865, and the states ratified it by December 6, 1865. Its intent was to make sure no one could undo the proclamation after the war.

It declared, "Neither slavery nor involuntary servitude, except as a punishment for crime whereof the party shall have been duly convicted, shall exist within the United States, or any place subject to their jurisdiction."

The war ground on until April 9, 1865, with General Robert E. Lee's surrender in Virginia, but the nation was plunged into chaos when John Wilkes Booth assassinated President Lincoln within the week. Confederate forces elsewhere began their surrenders, and Andrew Johnson became president. He declared the war over on May 9, 1865.

Whose Hour?

When the last guns of war fell silent that spring, the tasks that lay ahead included how to reconstitute the nation and what to do with the four million newly freed people. Republicans in Congress sought to define freedmen's status and their rights.

The Supreme Court's *Dred Scott* decision of 1857 had effectively declared that enslaved black people were not persons and had no rights. A constitutional amendment could recognize African-Americans as persons and citizens by virtue of being born in the country or being naturalized.

Congress began to debate a Fourteenth Amendment to the Constitution that said in part, "All persons born or naturalized in the United States, and subject to the jurisdiction thereof, are citizens of the United States and of the State wherein they reside."

Further, if the rebel states rejoined the Union, the government would have to apportion their representatives based on all the people. For the original Constitution, the Founders had counted "all other persons" who were not "free persons" as "three-fifths" of one.

The new amendment also offered equality to all "male citizens." The word "male" appears three times in the amendment: "when the right to vote...is denied to any of the *male inhabitants* of such state, being twenty-one years of age, and citizens of the United States, or in any way abridged...the basis of representation therein shall be reduced in the proportion which the number of such *male citizens* shall bear to the whole number of *male citizens* twenty-one years of age in such State" (emphasis added). Up to then the Constitution had made no reference to sex.

The vanguard of women who had fought for the freedom of those in bondage long before the war and who had served the nation so loyally throughout the conflict took notice. They thought one other item should be on the agenda: suffrage for women. The proposed amendment called into question whether women were even "citizens."

They had set aside their own ambitions to have a voice in government for the sake of their country, and now they felt it was their turn for some consideration. Before the war, the women's conventions had debated the many inequities women endured in the home, in the church, and in the public square. The war had helped galvanize them and narrow the goal

to enfranchisement. With the vote, women could take their fate in their own hands.

"By their active labors all through the great conflict, women learned that they had many interests outside the home," the *History of Woman Suffrage* observed. "In the camp and hospital, and the vacant places at their firesides, they saw how intimately the interests of the State and the home were intertwined; that as war and all its concomitants were subjects of legislation, it was only through a voice in the laws that their efforts for peace could command consideration."

Optimistic that their own victory was at hand, they soon learned they had been naïve in their assumption that their government would act justly in return. Now, they could not even count on their friends, the men who had been with them since the earliest days of the women's rights movement. Men who had spoken out for their rights, shared their platforms, and protected them from mobs were not on their side.

As the last embers of the war were still smoldering, the American Anti-Slavery Society met in May 1865 to decide whether it still had a mission, now that emancipation was a reality. William Lloyd Garrison, the leading white abolitionist of his day, argued that the society had completed its work, and it should be disbanded. Wendell Phillips insisted they must stay in the fight until they had secured the black man's right to vote. Phillips, whose support for the women's cause dated at least to the 1840 antislavery conference in London, became president of the American Anti-Slavery Society.

A white man and a member of the Boston elite, Phillips believed that establishing the freedman's right to vote would be hard enough without the burden of trying to secure the vote for all women, too. He and others were alarmed by reports of violence against blacks in the South perpetrated by bitter ex-Confederates, and they feared that without the vote the freedmen would be virtually re-enslaved.

Women like Anthony and Stanton fumed when he declared, "This hour belongs to the Negro. As Abraham Lincoln said, 'One war at a time,' so I say, 'One cause at a time.' This is the Negro's hour."

Universal Suffrage Demand

Up to this point, the right to vote was still a state issue, and women had focused on battles in the individual states to win the franchise. Now they realized if Congress had the power to make voting a federal right by proposing a constitutional amendment, it was possible for Congress to use that power on behalf of women. An amendment would still need state ratification, but it would bypass the cumbersome process of amending each state's constitutions or laws.

In December 1865, Stanton, Anthony, and Lucy Stone petitioned Congress for a constitutional amendment that would prohibit states from interfering with the franchise of citizens on account of sex. They began to call for "universal" suffrage, incorporating all women and black men, and they began to refer to themselves as "suffragists."

The first Senate debate over woman suffrage took place in 1866, when the lawmakers considered a bill to extend the vote to black men in the District of Columbia. Senator Edgar Cowan of Pennsylvania offered an amendment to strike the word "male." Opponents argued that women's "elevated social position" gave them more power than mere political clout would give them, and extending the franchise to them would disrupt domestic harmony. Women had "a higher and holier mission" than engaging in the battles of public life, one senator argued. The measure lost 37–9.

The Civil Rights Act of 1866, which became law April 9, 1866, guaranteed citizenship without regard to race, color, or previous condition of slavery or involuntary servitude.

On May 10, 1866, the Eleventh National Woman's Rights Convention met in New York City, bringing the old coalition together for the first time in six years. The discussions centered on the suffrage question.

Stanton presided, opening the meeting with remarks, "We have assembled to-day to discuss the right and duty of women to claim and use the ballot. Now in the reconstruction is the opportunity, perhaps for the century, to base our government on the broad principle of equal rights to all. The representative women of the nation feel that they have an interest and duty equal with man in the struggles and triumphs of this hour."

Susan B. Anthony read a declaration: "That disfranchisement in a republic is as great an anomaly, if not cruelty, as slavery itself." One resolution denounced the attempt to insert "male" into the Constitution as a "cruel injustice to the women of the nation."

Responding, Frances E. W. Harper, an African-American, rejected the comparison between the women's status and slavery, one that suffragists frequently made.

Harper, who was born free in Baltimore, Maryland, was a poet and an eloquent antislavery lecturer well known to the abolitionists, and recently she had been working among the new freedwomen in the South. Few people had addressed the rights of the freedwomen or sought the opinions of black women in the North.

She called on the audience to remember that the rights of white women and men were all "bound up together" with those of black women and men. It was, therefore, pointless to argue over who should have the vote first. In conclusion, she said, "Talk of giving women the ballot-box? Go on...The white women of this country need it. While there exists this brutal element in society which tramples upon the feeble and treads down the weak, I tell you that if there is any class of people who need to be lifted out of their airy nothings and selfishness, it is the white women of America."

Anthony presented a resolution: "Whereas, By the act of Emancipation and the Civil Rights bill, the negro and woman now hold the same civil and political status, alike needing only the ballot; and whereas the same arguments apply equally to both classes, proving all partial legislation fatal to republican institutions, there-fore, Resolved, That the time has come for an organization that shall demand Universal Suffrage, and that hereafter we shall be known as the 'American Equal Rights Association.'" The participants adopted it unanimously.

Thus, a new organization devoted to working for voting rights for blacks and women was born. Some local or regional suffrage groups were active, but this was the suffragists' first attempt at building a national organization to press the cause for the vote.

"The Last Straw"

The American Equal Rights Association barely got started before the issue of whose voting rights should take priority caused division. Elizabeth Cady Stanton became very vocal in her opposition to black men having the vote first, while women like Lucy Stone and Abby Kelley Foster and most of the men argued that establishing the right to vote for black men was more urgent and that women could wait if necessary. Called on at one of the Equal Rights conventions, Sojourner Truth disagreed. "I am glad to see that men are getting their rights, but I want women to get theirs, and while the water is stirring I will step into the pool. Now that there is a great stir about colored men's getting their rights is the time for women to step in and have theirs," she said.

The Fourteenth Amendment achieved ratification and became effective in July 1868. With it, the federal government guaranteed the civil rights of blacks, but some Republicans in Congress became concerned that they had not specifically assured the political rights of the freedmen. They began drafting the Fifteenth Amendment, declaring that the "right of citizens of the United States to vote shall not be denied or abridged by the United States or by any state on account of race, color, or previous condition of servitude."

"Stanton and Anthony were outraged," Garrett Epps wrote in *Democracy Reborn: The Fourteenth Amendment and the Fight for Equal Rights in Post–Civil War America.* "For them, women needed the vote as much as men of any color. And the word 'male' in the Constitution would offer antisuffragists an argument that votes for women were unconstitutional as well as unimportant. Anthony presciently remarked that the new language would delay female voting for a hundred years. And besides, there were those insidious questions that, once asked, could not be unasked—who 'needed' the vote more, who 'deserved' it more, who would make 'better' use of it?"

While the Republicans in control of Congress were concerned about the welfare of the newly freed, they also were mindful that the two to three million black men in the South would gratefully reward the party that freed them with their votes. If they granted women the vote, they could not count on gaining all their votes for the party.

Nevertheless, Senator S. C. Pomeroy of Kansas became the first person in Congress to offer a woman suffrage amendment in December 1868, followed by U.S. Representative George W. Julian of Indiana, offering a joint resolution in March 1869. Nothing apparently came of either effort.

Angry and frustrated, Stanton began using language in speeches and written commentaries that denigrated both black men and poor immigrants who had begun pouring into the country. In a December 1868 newspaper editorial, she wrote: "Think of Patrick and Sambo and Hans and Yung Tung who do not know the difference between a Monarchy and a Republic, who never read the Declaration of Independence or Webster's spelling book, making laws for Lydia Maria Child, Lucretia Mott, or Fanny Kemble...Would these gentlemen who, on all sides, are telling us 'to wait until the negro is safe' be willing to stand aside and trust all *their* interests in hands like these? The educated women of this nation...are as sure that the highest good of all alike demands the elevation and enfranchisement of woman" (emphasis in the original).

The Fifteenth Amendment passed both houses of Congress in February 1869, and the ratification process was under way when the American Equal Rights Association met in New York City on May 12, 1869.

At the convention, Stephen Foster, a former abolitionist lecturer and a longtime ally of the women's movement (not the famous songwriter of the same name), objected to a slate of officers with Stanton's name as vice president, suggesting she resign from the organization because she had "repudiated the principles of the society." He questioned her commitment to universal suffrage and her apparent shift to support for "educated suffrage," requiring some proof of learning.

"What are these principles?" he said. "The equality of men—universal suffrage...I put myself on this platform as an enemy of educated suffrage, as an enemy of white suffrage, as an enemy of man suffrage, as an enemy of every kind of suffrage except universal suffrage."

Frederick Douglass, who had stood by Stanton since she looked to him for support on the suffrage question at Seneca Falls twenty-one years earlier, rose to speak. First he praised her for her long years of service—"There is no name greater than that of Elizabeth Cady Stanton in the matter of woman's rights and equal rights"—and then thoroughly rebuked her:

I must say that I do not see how any one can pretend that there is the same urgency in giving the ballot to women as to the negro. With us, the matter is a question of life and death...When women, because they are women, are hunted down through the cities of New York and New Orleans; when they are dragged from their houses and hung upon lamp-posts; when their children are torn from their arms, and their brains dashed out upon the pavement; when they are objects of insult and outrage at every turn; when they

*are in danger of having
their homes burnt down
over their heads; when their
children are not allowed to
enter schools; then they will
have an urgency to obtain
the ballot equal to our own.*

Someone from the assembly
asked, "Is that not all true about
black women?" Douglass replied,
"Yes, yes, yes;...but not because
she is a woman, but because she
is black."

Susan B. Anthony defended
Stanton's position and suggested
that as downtrodden as blacks
were, Douglass would not switch
places with a woman. Lucy Stone
spoke against the principle of
educated suffrage, adding that
she would be "thankful in my
soul if *any* body can get out of
the terrible pit." She urged that
the divisive debates over who
should have priority end, but
they continued into a second
day. Douglass introduced a resolution calling for the organization to support the Fifteenth
Amendment, while continuing
to work for woman suffrage.
Frances Harper spoke in support

of it. She said that "if the nation
could only handle one question,
she would not have the black
women put a single straw in the
way."

After an acrimonious debate,
the question was deferred over
the objection of the crowd. The
meeting ended in discord and
confusion.

"The last straw was laid on
the camel's back when Frederick
Douglass rose in our convention
in Steinway Hall with a series of
resolutions, saying that our Association rejoiced in the passage
and prospective adoption of the
Fifteenth Amendment," Stanton
wrote later. "I am happy to say
that there was too much pride,
self-respect, and womanly dignity on that platform to rejoice."

It is probably true that
Congress did women a grave
disservice at this juncture in
history by not extending them
the vote and instead actively
disenfranchising them through
these amendments, despite
their long years of agitation
and loyalty. Yet there is much
to be said for the arguments
that blacks in the South were

in grave peril, facing violent backlash from white attackers, if lawmakers did not act to protect their rights. The dreadful war was barely ended and the country, particularly the South, was in dire shape. Lincoln had just been reelected in 1864 while the war was still raging and promptly assassinated in April 1865, a little more than a month after his second inauguration. For the second election, he had run on the National Union Party ticket with Andrew Johnson, a Democrat, as his running mate, to try to attract voters from that party. Johnson was no friend to the Reconstruction cause, and after succeeding Lincoln, he repeatedly clashed with the Republican-dominated Congress, resulting in his impeachment in the House in 1869 and narrow acquittal in the Senate.

Men like Douglass and Phillips were known allies of the women and supporters of suffrage who vowed to continue working for their cause as well. They were not saying that women could not or should not have suffrage. The men who had legislative experience were saying that it probably was not politically feasible in the highly charged postwar atmosphere to accomplish two very difficult things.

For one suffragist faction to alienate their former abolitionist allies and to refuse compromise might not have been the wisest course. Furthermore, the women's frequent suggestion that their status was akin to that of the slave had a grain of truth but ignored the privileges of race, class, and relative wealth that nearly all the suffragists shared. Indeed, Stanton had grown up in a home with a few enslaved servants when slavery was legal in New York State and later, like some other suffragists, employed household help.

By this time, however, Stanton had demonstrated that she was not capable of seeing other people's views as valid. She was a woman largely driven by anger from childhood on, not by humanitarian or holy instincts as many of the suffragists and their supporters were. She seems never to have looked past her father's slights to recognize her parents' pain over losing so many children. As a young woman, she was angry she couldn't go to college with the men. She remained angry about women's exclusion from the London convention for years even though she wasn't a delegate. As a wife, she was probably angry that her husband's frequent political travels left her with a household of children to manage.

Stanton became angrier with each passing year over women's status in society. She was angry at Douglass, who had stood with her when she needed him at Seneca Falls and who remained loyal to the women's cause to the day he died, because he defended the freedmen's need for the vote. She certainly was angry over the declaration of "the Negro's hour." Later, she would become increasingly angry over religious dictates. Perhaps her anger was justified, and it certainly served as a motivator, but it also clouded her judgment. While Stanton's contributions to the movement are incalculable, her attitudes and actions often put the effort in peril and alienated potential allies. This was one of those times.

The Split

Two days after the New York convention adjourned, Stanton and Anthony held a reception and formed the National Woman Suffrage Association (NWSA). It would work specifically for the enfranchisement of women through a proposed federal amendment and against the Fifteenth Amendment. Acting quickly and secretively, Stanton and Anthony had not invited Lucy Stone or many others who had been active in the movement to the organizing meeting. The new organization, headed by Stanton, met weekly in New York City and began planning conventions for that summer at Saratoga and Newport. Its leadership was to be all female, apparently because the organiz-ers believed their former male allies had betrayed them.

A few months later, Stone organized a separate organization, the American Woman Suffrage Association (AWSA), with the help of the "Battle Hymn" poet Julia Ward Howe, who had joined the woman suffrage movement a few years earlier after hearing Stone speak.

The *History of Woman Suffrage* called the formation of Stone's new group "a secession from our ranks" and alluded to "personal hostilities among the leaders of the movement" in addition to differences of opinion on support for the Fifteenth Amendment.

Henry Ward Beecher, a regular at the women's conventions, accepted the presidency of the new organization. Beecher, a Congregationalist minister in Brooklyn, was active in all the reform movements. (He was also a brother of the educator Catharine Beecher and Harriet Beecher Stowe, whose novel *Uncle Tom's Cabin* was an international best seller.)

Unlike Anthony and Stanton, Stone had reached out to a broad coalition of people and called for a convention in Cleveland on November 24 and 25, 1869. She sent out hundreds of letters to women and men, explaining that the new organization would not oppose the Fifteenth Amendment or debate extraneous issues. The letters bore fruit. Leading reformers signed the call for the first convention. She sent the call to Stanton with a letter, explaining that she did not intend for the new group to be a rival and expressing the hope that they could work in harmony, attracting different members and using different methods. Stanton never answered but wrote a scathing commentary.

Long-standing friends like Martha Wright criticized Stone and urged reunification, but the breach was too wide. Wright's sister Lucretia Mott began to believe that they should have never started any formal organization for women's rights. Distressed by Stanton's rhetoric and her ties to a questionable financial backer, Mott tried to straddle the fence for a while, attending meetings of both organizations. She was torn between loyalty to her old friend Stanton and to Stone for her stand on universal rights. Mott had resigned from the leadership of the American Equal Rights Association in May 1868 and recommended disbanding it. The organization continued to list her as president.

Hundreds of people, representing twenty-one states, attended the convention Stone organized. Susan B. Anthony attended and addressed a packed hall, denouncing the effort as a scheme to undermine the NWSA. She did urge attendees to join one or the other organization to work for a Sixteenth Amendment for woman suffrage.

The Revolution

One of the underlying issues in the schism that surfaced at the May 1869 meeting of the American Equal Rights Association was a newspaper, the *Revolution*, that Anthony and Stanton had started with the help of a wealthy donor, George Francis Train. Stanton used it as a vehicle for her many pronouncements against the Fifteenth Amendment and in favor of educated suffrage.

They had met Train while campaigning for woman suffrage in Kansas in 1867. Kansas had scheduled a referendum on separate measures to give women and blacks the vote. This offered suffragists their first opportunity to test support at the polls for the woman's vote, and Kansas supporters asked for help from suffragist leaders. Lucy Stone and her husband, Henry Blackwell, headed to Kansas to campaign for both propositions. Upon their arrival, Colonel Sam N. Wood, a state senator supporting woman suffrage, declared, "With the help of God and Lucy Stone, we shall carry Kansas!"

Anthony, Stanton, Train, and the Reverend Olympia Brown, of Massachusetts, quickly followed them. Brown was an active suffragist whom Anthony and Stone had called upon many times for help. It was a grueling campaign under frontier conditions, and they found little support. Both proposals lost, woman suffrage by 30,000 to 9,000. The black voter proposal did only slightly better.

The first issue of the Revolution, edited by Elizabeth Cady Stanton and Parker Pillsbury, was issued in New York on January 8, 1868. Susan B. Anthony was the "Proprietor and Manager."

Library of Congress

Train, an eccentric financier and speculator, traveled and lectured with Anthony, Stanton, and Brown in Kansas, speaking only on behalf of the women's vote proposal, not the black vote. He paid for their travel and during the trip volunteered to give them the money to start a newspaper. He also paid for lecture engagements along the way back.

He filled his speeches with racial remarks and jokes, which horrified friends of Anthony and Stanton as reports of their travels drifted back home. Lucretia Mott thought he brought out the worst in Stanton. True to his word, however, with the help of another backer, he set them up in a newspaper, headquartered in New York City. They named it the *Revolution*. They printed the first issue January 8, 1868, with Anthony as publisher. The financial backing soon dried up, leaving her in debt. Anthony sold it to a joint stock company in 1870, and it continued publication until February 1872, with Laura Curtis Bullard as editor, chronicling women's news and providing a forum for debate. It served as the official publication of the National Woman Suffrage Association.

Lucy Stone started a newspaper for the American Woman Suffrage Association, the *Woman's Journal*, two years to the day after the *Revolution* first went to press, on January 8, 1870. Stone, Henry Blackwell, and Mary Livermore (who had edited a Chicago newspaper, the *Agitator*) edited it. The *Woman's Journal* headquarters was in Boston, and it was well funded, backed by a joint stock company.

A Difference
in Strategies

The two associations had adopted different strategies. The NWSA focused on winning a U.S. Constitutional amendment for women while opposing the Fifteenth Amendment, but entertained other issues like divorce reform and women's property rights. The NWSA had initially sought to bar men from membership or office, but later softened its position.

The more inclusive AWSA had a larger membership initially, but attendance at conventions fell off after the first one. After its founding, it quickly began campaigning for state laws to grant the vote, while supporting the Fifteenth Amendment. It also set up a more formal structure of working with local auxiliaries and apportioning voting delegates for its conventions.

On February 3, 1870, the Fifteenth Amendment won ratification, and the AWSA could focus on the vote for women. The state approach was particularly difficult, because suffragists had to persuade male voters, but they would campaign in nearly sixty such referendums between 1867 and 1918. They had to travel long distances, often by horse, carriage, or buggy, in the days before modern transportation, and they lived under primitive conditions.

Had the two factions not split up, perhaps at this point the suffragists would have been in a stronger position to win a federal amendment, since the freedmen's voter issue was settled, and their allies were still in power. The state-by-state approach would be especially long and painful, and instead of having one strong organization, and perhaps their old male allies' help, they had two weakened and competing ones with few allies.

Breakthrough in Wyoming

A breakthrough came in late 1869 when the Wyoming Territory's legislature passed a bill giving women over twenty-one the right to vote in all elections, and Governor John A. Campbell quickly signed it. Wyoming women voted for the first time in September 1870.

William Bright, a saloon-keeper and Democrat elected to the legislature, had introduced the bill to give women the right to vote. No record of the debate exists, but articles at the time suggested that after the Gold Rush fizzled there, the population was thinning out, and lawmakers wanted some good publicity throughout the land to draw more settlers, especially women. The entire population of Wyoming was just over nine thousand in the 1870 census. The ratio of men to women who were not Native American in the territory was six to one. Democrats, who dominated the legislature, also expected that women who came to the territory would vote for the party that had given them the opportunity. Legend says the Democrats also hoped to put their Republican governor in a difficult spot. He had supported votes for the freedmen. How could he now turn down votes for women?

At the time, most Democrats remained adamantly opposed to the Reconstruction reforms, opposing full citizenship and voting rights for black men. President Ulysses S. Grant, a Republican elected in 1868, had appointed Campbell and other officials, including Attorney General Joseph A. Carey, to run the Wyoming Territory created that July by act of Congress. Not long after taking office in May 1869, Carey issued an opinion that no one in the territory could be denied the right to vote based on race. Democrats suspected this was a move to win black votes for the Republicans, but Democrats took all twenty-two seats in the legislature in an election that October.

The new legislature passed a resolution allowing women to sit inside an area where members sat, a law guaranteeing male and female teachers equal pay, and a bill guaranteeing married women's property rights.

Finally, Bright and other legislators argued that women should have the vote if blacks and Chinese immigrants were going to have it under the attorney general's ruling.

Chinese men had trickled into Wyoming to work on the Union Pacific railroad, in the coal mines, and at other labor. They were the targets of extreme prejudice, but their numbers were small then, and they were not a large factor in elections. Native Americans who lived on reservations were considered citizens of their own tribes, rather than of the United States. They were denied the right to vote because they were not considered citizens by law and were thus ineligible. In 1924, many Native Americans became United States citizens, but many Western states disenfranchised them with some of the same tactics used against blacks in the South.

The woman suffrage sponsor's lovely wife, Julia Bright, twenty-one years his junior, might have persuaded her husband. Another resident, Esther Hobart Morris, a supporter of woman suffrage, might also have been influential. Soon after, she secured an appointment as justice of the peace, the first Wyoming woman to hold public office. The next legislature tried to repeal woman suffrage, but Governor Campbell vetoed the legislation and the legislature was unable to override the veto.

The Long Wait

Utah's territorial legislature also granted women the vote, in February 1870, for reasons that were less clear. Passage might have come from a desire to shore up the Mormon vote as new settlers were arriving. Lawmakers later revoked it and then restored it in 1896. Similar measures to enfranchise women in the territories of Washington, Nebraska, and Dakota failed.

The decade since the Civil War began had been a tumultuous one for the supporters of woman suffrage with the horrors of the conflict itself, the achievement of the abolition goal for which many of them had worked so long, and the emotional upheaval that had resulted in a catastrophic divide in the movement. Old friends were now rivals, and old alliances ended. The wounds would heal, but reunification and reconciliation were twenty years off.

The victories in the territories gave suffragists hope that the ballot would someday be in the hands of every American woman. In the next decade, new ideas, new strategies, and new leaders would emerge, but the suffragists who already had been pushing for the vote for more than twenty years by 1870 could not have imagined that victory would not come for another five decades.

★ Susan B. Anthony ★
The Drum Major for Suffrage

**Susan B. Anthony drafted what became
the Nineteenth Amendment.**
Library of Congress

Susan B. Anthony, motivated by a strong sense of justice, devoted the greater part of her life to securing the vote for women and became the most energetic and stalwart champion of the cause.

Anthony came to the women's rights movement a bit later than some of the other prominent figures but with perhaps more zeal than anyone, and she stayed on the battlefield the longest. For more than a half century, she *was* the movement.

Her alliance with Elizabeth Cady Stanton and their complementary skills would be the engine that drove the movement for decades. They formed a lifelong friendship and formidable working relationship as they counterbalanced each other's strengths and weaknesses. Their tools were petition drives, legislative testimony, lectures, newspaper articles, and, most important, the power of persuasion.

The History of *Woman Suffrage* incorporates an unnamed mutual friend's view:

> Mrs. Stanton is a fine writer, but a poor executant; Miss Anthony is a thorough manager, but a poor writer. Both have large brains and great hearts...Opposites though they be, each does not so much supplement the other's difficiencies as augment the other's eccentricities...These two women sitting together in their parlors, have for the last thirty years been diligent forgers of all manner of projectiles, from fire works to thunderbolts, and have hurled them with unexpected explosion into the midst of all manner of educational, reformatory, religious, and political assemblies, sometimes to the pleasant surprise and half welcome of the members, more often to the bewilderment and prostration of numerous victims; and in a few signal instances, to the gnashing of angry men's teeth. I know of no two more pertinacious incendiaries in the whole country! Nor will they themselves deny the charge. In fact this noise-making twain are the two sticks of a drum for keeping up what Daniel Webster called "the rub-a-dub of agitation."

Together, they would become a mighty force, and their strength was in their differences. When they needed to work on something—a call to a convention, legislative testimony, or a speech—Anthony would often settle in at Stanton's house and watch the children while Stanton wrote. They called her "Aunt Susan" and found her a little less indulgent than their mother was.

However, Anthony's feminism, unlike Stanton's, did not stem from anger or resentment. It came more from her conviction that all people were equal and from the humanitarianism implicit in her faith.

A "Mecca" for Reformers

Anthony drew her values from her upbringing in a home where the Quaker faith was an anchor, where she was encouraged to learn, and where being a reformer was an expectation. Her parents' home had been a gathering place for like-minded abolitionists and other reformers, including Frederick Douglass, on Sunday afternoons.

One historian described the home as a "mecca for fugitive slaves and abolitionists."

Almost every Sunday the antislavery Quakers met at the Anthony farm. The Posts, the Hallowells, the DeGarmos, and the Willises were sure to be there. Sometimes they sent a wagon into the city for Frederick Douglass and his family. Now and then famous abolitionists joined the circle when their work brought them to western New York—William Lloyd Garrison...Wendell Phillips, handsome, learned, and impressive; black-bearded, fiery Parker Pillsbury; and the friendly Unitarian pastor from Syracuse, the Reverend Samuel J. May. Susan, helping her mother with dinner for fifteen or twenty, was torn between establishing her reputation as a good cook and listening to the interesting conversa-

tion. She heard them discuss woman's rights, which had divided the antislavery ranks. They talked of their antislavery campaigns and the infamous compromises made by Congress to pacify the powerful slaveholding interests. Like William Lloyd Garrison, all of them refused to vote, not wishing to take any part in a government which countenanced slavery. They called the Constitution a proslavery document, advocated "No Union with Slaveholders," and demanded immediate and unconditional emancipation. All about them and with their help the Underground Railroad was operating, circumventing the Fugitive Slave Law and guiding Negro refugees to Canada and freedom. Amy and Isaac Post's barn, Susan knew, was a station on the Underground, and the DeGarmos and Frederick Douglass almost always had a Negro hidden away. She heard of riots and mobs in Boston and Ohio; but in Rochester not a fugitive was retaken and there were no street battles.

Anthony was born in Adams, Massachusetts, on February 15, 1820, the second eldest of seven children. Her father, Daniel, owned a small cotton factory. He later moved the family to Battenville, New York, where he ran a larger cotton mill, and after that to a farm near Rochester, New York. He had a mill and worked as an insurance agent.

Daniel had a long history of activism. His mother, Hannah Latham Anthony, was an elder in their meeting house in Adams, and his sister, Hannah Anthony Hoxie, a well-known preacher. His Friends' meeting rebuked him for marrying an outsider, Lucy Read Anthony, who was a Baptist and never converted.

Lucy's life was difficult, and her health was poor. In addition to caring for her husband and children, she did farm chores, ran a boarding house for the mill, and cooked for the workers. Still, she supported her husband's reformist spirit and encouraged it in her children.

Not only did Daniel Anthony, as a Quaker pacifist, not vote until later in life, he also refused to pay taxes that could support war. Susan recalled that he would let the tax collector in and place his pocketbook on the table, telling him, "I shall not voluntarily pay these taxes. If thee wants to rifle my pocketbook, thee can do so."

Nevertheless, Daniel was later "disowned" by his church, or "read out" of meeting, after he allowed a dancing school to use a former ballroom on his property. He had forbidden his children to take part, because Quakers frowned on dancing, as

well as singing, fancy clothing or furnishings, smoking, drinking, liquor, and just about every worldly pleasure. Such things might distract them from discerning the "inner light" of God. Daniel was active in the temperance movement and refused to sell liquor at a store he had started on his property. He attended the Friends' meetings for a while, despite his ouster, and then joined a new organization, the Congregational Friends.

Susan B. Anthony, unlike Lucy Stone and Elizabeth Cady Stanton, did not grow up in a home where the parents slighted or mistreated girls. Her upbringing was more like that of her fellow Quaker and women's rights leader Lucretia Mott. Like Mott, Daniel Anthony had studied at the Nine Partners School in Dutchess County, New York. He started out as a teacher and believed in giving all of his children a good, solid education. At first, they attended a district school, but when a schoolmaster told Susan that girls did not need to learn long division, her father started a school on the farm for his children. He hired teachers trained at the few female seminaries in existence, including Mary Perkins, who studied at Zilpah Grant's school in Ipswich, Massachusetts. Daniel also started an evening school for his cotton mill workers, mostly young women, and sometimes taught it himself.

He encouraged Susan to learn business principles and later encouraged her in her reform work, sometimes sending her money when she traveled.

"In Susan he saw ability of a high order and that same courage, persistence and aggressiveness which entered into his own character," her biographer wrote. "She received also the sympathy and assistance of her mother, who, no matter how heavy the domestic burdens, or how precarious her own health, was never willing that she should take any time from her public work to give to the duties of home, although she frequently insisted upon doing so."

Mr. Anthony sent three daughters, Guelma, Susan, and Hannah, to Quaker boarding schools. Susan attended Deborah Moulson's Female Seminary near Philadelphia, briefly. When her family fell on hard times in 1837, she returned home and started teaching to contribute her earnings, eventually becoming headmistress of the female department of the Canajoharie Academy.

While at Canajoharie, she often went to Albany, where she frequented the home of Abigail Mott and her sister, Lydia, a friend from boarding school. Abigail was a writer and an abolitionist who was a cousin to Lucretia Mott's husband, James. The Mott sisters' home was an Underground Railroad station, a boarding house for lawmakers, and a hub for reformers, according to biographical sketches of the sisters. Later, when Anthony was traveling often to Albany to lobby on temperance issues, the Motts' place became a second home.

After her school closed in 1849, Susan went back home to run the family farm so her father could spend more time in his insurance business. There, she also found her parents' home "a hotbed of discussion and fermentation," according to Ida Husted Harper's biography of Anthony. Two of Susan's brothers, Daniel and Merritt, moved to Kansas, where they worked in the "free soil" campaign to keep slavery out of that state. Merritt joined up with the rebellious John Brown and was active in the conflict between antislavery and proslavery forces in Kansas.

Susan's father introduced her to Frederick Douglass, who had started his newspaper in Rochester. She considered him a friend from then on, although they would have their differences later. A sculpture in a small park near Anthony's home in Rochester memorializes their friendship, depicting them having tea while seated at a small table.

Choosing a Cause

Anthony's family had begun attending the First Unitarian Church of Rochester, as their Quaker church was not friendly to the antislavery cause. First Unitarian was the church where her parents and sister Mary had attended the second women's rights convention in 1848 and signed the Declaration of Sentiments. Susan's cousin, Sarah Burtis Anthony, had been

Ida Husted Harper was Susan B. Anthony's biographer and worked on later volumes of History of Woman Suffrage.
Library of Congress

secretary of the convention. Mary also later became a suffragist and a school principal in Rochester.

Surprised by her family's enthusiasm about the women's meetings and the praise for the women who spoke, Susan was a little amused but longed to meet some of them. She had heard Lucretia Mott speaking at the Quaker meetings while attending school in Philadelphia. In September 1852, Susan Anthony had finally been able to attend the National Woman's Rights Convention in

Syracuse, New York, where she could meet the Motts and other leaders of this new movement. Thereafter, Anthony became a regular at the women's national and state meetings, rising through the leadership.

Around this time, Susan began attending antislavery meetings, and she traveled for a week with the abolitionist Abby Kelley Foster and her husband, Stephen.

In the spring of 1851, Anthony had met Elizabeth Cady Stanton in Seneca Falls, where Susan had gone to hear Garrison and George Thompson of Britain at an antislavery event. Stanton was escorting the speakers to her home when she ran into Amelia Bloomer and Anthony on a street corner, a scene immortalized in a sculpture on a sidewalk in Seneca Falls. Bloomer had recently started a women's temperance newspaper, the Lily, and had been at the Sen-

eca Falls Convention. Her husband ran the Seneca County Courier.

As Stanton later recalled the encounter with Anthony, "There she stood with her good earnest face and genial smile, dressed in gray silk, hat and all the same color, relieved with pale blue ribbons, the perfection of neatness and sobriety. I liked her thoroughly."

Not long after, Stanton invited Anthony to dinner at her home, along with Lucy Stone, the orator, and Horace Greeley, the editor, all of them in town to discuss a proposal to found a college. It was the first time Stone and Anthony had met. "These women who sat at the dinner table that day were destined to be recorded in history for all time as the three central figures in the great movement for equal rights," wrote Ida Husted Harper.

Exposed to these movements, Susan became active in reforms, especially temperance, and became a paid agent. She made her first speech to the Daughters of Temperance in Canajoharie in 1849, became president of a local society in Rochester, and organized societies in other locales. She went to Albany to attend the state convention of the Sons of Temperance, but when she rose to speak, the chairman scoffed, telling her, "The sisters were not invited here to speak, but to listen and to learn."

Some of the women walked out and called their own meeting for that evening. They made plans to call a state convention, and Susan invited Stanton to speak. The conventioneers formed the Women's State Temperance Society, electing Stanton president and Susan vice president. They petitioned the state government for a law allowing women to control their earnings, granting them guardianship of their children in the event of divorce, and establishing voting rights for women.

Anthony organized a petition drive, selecting sixty women to be captains, one for each county in the state, and in 1854 set out to get signatures against formidable obstacles and resistance as men and women slammed doors in their faces. Still they gathered six thousand signatures in ten weeks, and they used the petitions to gain a hearing in the legislature. Anthony planned a convention in Albany during the legislative session. Stanton appeared before the Joint Judiciary Committee. The bill failed, and in the winter of 1855, she set out to gather more petitions, traveling personally to fifty-four of the sixty counties of New York. A more sweeping bill did pass in 1860, extending women's property rights, giving them control of their own wages, and granting rights of inheritance from their husbands. (Lawmakers watered down the property rights law during the Civil War.)

In 1856, Anthony also became a paid agent for the American Anti-Slavery Society, traveling around New York to lecture and organize meetings throughout the state, and she aided the Underground Railroad. She noted tersely in her diary in 1861 that she had "fitted out a fugitive slave for Canada with the help of Harriet Tubman." The famed "conductor" had settled nearby in Auburn, New York, where she was friends with Martha Wright.

At the urging of Lucy Stone, who had been organizing the national women's rights conventions, Anthony also became more active in the suffrage campaign. She attended the state women's rights convention in New York City—the so-called mob convention—that was disrupted by hecklers and ruffians in 1853, following a debacle at the World's Temperance Convention after it ejected women delegates.

Anthony presided over a national women's rights convention for the first time in 1858. Stanton and Anthony were appointed to head a committee to plan future conventions. A decade had passed since the Seneca Falls Convention, but the team that would propel the movement forward was now in place.

Stanton was still somewhat tied to home with the work of raising seven children as her husband became more politically active, while Anthony emerged as a nearly full-time suffrage worker, traveling constantly on behalf of the movement. Her trademarks were an alligator-skin briefcase and a red shawl.

She never married but had at least one proposal. In later years, she purchased a modest brick home with her sister Mary near downtown Rochester, New York, and lived there until her death in 1906. She added a third floor that served as suffrage headquarters. While working on the History of Woman Suffrage, Anthony lived at Stanton's home, then in Tenafly, New Jersey. She also boarded with the Stantons in New York City while doing Loyal League work during the Civil War.

The interests of Anthony and Stanton diverged somewhat in later years, but the two remained close friends. Stanton said of their relationship:

It is often said by those who know Miss Anthony best, that she has been my good angel, always pushing and guiding me to work, that but for her pertinacity I should never have accom-plished the little I have; and on the other hand, it has been said that I forged the thunderbolts and she fired them. Perhaps all this is in a measure true...

Thus, whenever I saw that stately Quaker girl coming across my lawn, I knew that some happy convocation of the sons of Adam were to be set by the ears, by one of our appeals or resolutions. The little portmanteau stuffed with facts was opened, and there we had what the Rev. John Smith and the Hon. Richard Roe had said, false interpretations of Bible texts, the statistics of women robbed of their property, shut out of some college, half paid for their work, the reports of some disgraceful trial, injustice enough to turn any woman's thoughts from stockings and puddings. Then we would get out our pens and write articles for papers, or a petition to the

Legislature, letters to the faithful here and there, stir up the women in Ohio, Pennsylvania, or Massachusetts, call on The Lily, The Una, The Liberator, and The Standard, to remember our wrongs as well as those of the slave. We never met without issuing a pronunciamento on some question.

We were at once fast friends, in thought and sympathy we were one, and in the division of labor we exactly complemented each other. In writing we did better work together than either could alone. While she is slow and analytical in composition, I am rapid and synthetic. I am the better writer, she the better critic. She supplied the facts and statistics, I the philosophy and rhetoric, and together we have made arguments that have stood unshaken by the storms of thirty long years: arguments that no man has answered. Our speeches may be considered the united product of our two brains.

Anthony helped Stanton form the National Woman Suffrage Association after the Civil War, while Lucy Stone founded the American Woman Suffrage Association. When these two organizations merged in 1890, Anthony soon became president of the new National American Woman Suffrage Association. She presided over her last convention in 1900, but returned to speak at least six more times. She was a revered figure by then, and her eightieth birthday was celebrated in the White House when William McKinley was president. The country could not give her an amendment in her lifetime, but it could pay homage to the woman who had probably done the most and traveled the farthest to try to force the hand of government.

She continued working on issues and projects, including the final volumes of the *History of Woman Suffrage*, until her death in 1906. Her biographer, Ida Husted Harper, completed it.

Section 5

Resolved, That the women of this nation,
in 1876, have greater cause for discontent,
rebellion and revolution than the men of 1776.

Susan B. Anthony

A SQUELCHER FOR WOMAN SUFFRAGE.

How Can She Vote, when the Fashions Are so Wide, and the Voting Booths Are so Narrow?

*This print shows a woman being denied
the opportunity to vote because she is wearing a dress and a hat
that are too wide for the narrow booths labeled
"Ballots Must Be Prepared in These Booths."*

Library of Congress

A New Direction

A new star of the movement emerged, shining briefly before exploding. Victoria Woodhull, an iconoclastic free spirit with a controversial reputation, managed to get a hearing before the Judiciary Committee of the House of Representatives on January 11, 1871. Woodhull had declared her intention to run for president the year before and had been pursuing the suffrage issue on her own. She addressed a memorial, or written statement of facts accompanying a petition, to Congress. In it, she made the case that women were citizens—native born or naturalized—and that the Fourteenth and Fifteenth Amendments protected the right of citizens to vote. Therefore, women as citizens were already entitled to the vote.

The statement said in part:

Whereas, no distinction between citizens is made in the Constitution of the United States on account of sex, but the XIV Article of Amendments to it provides that "no State shall make or enforce any law which shall abridge the privileges and immunities of citizens of the United States," "nor deny to any person within its jurisdiction the equal protection of the laws:"

And whereas, Congress has power to make laws which shall be necessary and proper for carrying into execution all powers vested by the Constitution in the Government of the United States; and to make or alter all regulations in relation to holding election for Senators and Representatives, and especially to enforce, by appropriate legislation, the provisions of the said XIV Article:

And whereas, the continuance of the enforcement of said local election laws, denying and abridging the Right of Citizens to Vote on account of sex, is a grievance to your memorialist and to various other persons, citizens of the United States, being women,—

Therefore your memorialist would most respectfully petition your Honorable Bodies to make such laws as in the wisdom of Congress shall be necessary and proper for carrying into execution the right vested by the Constitution in the citizens of the United States to vote, without regard to sex.

Woodhull was a beautiful, engaging, and well-spoken woman with a questionable past. She appeared at the invitation of Representative Benjamin Butler of Massachusetts, whom she had met at the Willard Hotel in Washington. She had taken up residence there to lobby powerful people (in the hotel that gave rise to the term "lobby"), and had learned there that a proposed Sixteenth Amendment securing woman suffrage was stalled. Under congressional rules, new legislation was referred to a committee for consideration and for a vote on whether to send it to the whole body for passage. A committee can kill a bill by failing to act on it. In theory, a bill could remain in committee forever. The suffrage amendment was locked in committee with no one pleading the case to advance it.

Woodhull's charms had already made her a rich woman after Cornelius Vanderbilt set up her sister, Tennessee Claflin, and her in their own stock brokerage firm. With her sister, Woodhull also published a newspaper,

Victoria Woodhull ran for president and went to jail
for publishing an article about a scandal.
Library of Congress

Woodhull and Claflin's Weekly. Among other things, it promoted free love.

Her testimony before the committee made her the first woman to petition Congress in person, and her arguments impressed the lawmakers and the woman suffrage leaders who had come to hear her, including Susan B. Anthony. Anthony had come to Washington for a convention on woman suf-frage called by Isabella Beecher Hooker, a women's rights leader in New England. Hooker heard of Woodhull's pending appearance the day before, alerted Anthony, and postponed the meeting's opening to attend this unprece-dented hearing. Anthony was in awe. None of the other suffrag-ists had ever been able to get an audience in Congress.

"She presented her memorial to Congress, and it was a power,"

Victoria Woodhull reads her argument that the Fourteenth and Fifteenth Amendments gave women the vote before the Judiciary Committee of the House of Representatives.

Anthony said later. "It was a mighty effort, and one that any woman might be proud of...She is young, handsome and rich. Now if it takes youth, beauty, and money to capture Congress, Victoria is the woman we are after."

Isabella Hooker invited Woodhull to speak that afternoon at her convention, where Woodhull read her memorial to Congress. Anthony and Elizabeth Cady Stanton also invited her to speak at the National Woman Suffrage Association in New York in 1871.

The congressional committee rejected her argument, but the suffragists embraced her.

That is, until she made the mistake of trying to usurp the NWSA convention the following year to turn it into a nominating convention for her presidential race. Anthony was presiding and promptly had the gaslights shut off. As Woodhull stood in the dark, Anthony ruled her out of order.

★ *The Woodhull Scandal* ★

Victoria Woodhull and her supporters formed the Equal Rights Party, which ratified her presidential nomination on June 6, 1872. It nominated Frederick Douglass as vice president. His selection was apparently without his consent, and he never acknowledged it. Nevertheless, this made Victoria Woodhull the first American woman to win any party nomination to run for president. The fact that she was not old enough to serve does not seem to have fazed her. Born in 1838, she would not turn thirty-five until September 1873, six months after the inauguration date. For that reason, some people consider Belva Lockwood, a Washington, D.C., lawyer and suffragist who ran for president in 1884 and 1888, the first woman to mount a serious campaign for president. Lockwood reasoned that although she could not vote, the Constitution did not bar men from voting for her. She wanted to pave the way for women to get the vote and participate in politics.

Nothing came of the Woodhull campaign, partly because a few days before the election, Victoria Woodhull and her sister went to jail for mailing obscene materials—their newspaper. The *New York Times* of November 3, 1872, reported that an agent of the Society for the Suppression of Obscene Literature appeared before a U.S. Commissioner to request a warrant, which he promptly issued after seeing the previous day's edition of *Woodhull and Claflin's Weekly*. Deputy marshals appeared at their brokerage house at No. 48 Broad Street, the paper reported.

Belva Lockwood, a lawyer, ran for president.
Library of Congress

"At 12¼, they drove up in a carriage and were immediately arrested," the *Times* reported. "Three thousand copies of the newspaper containing the alleged obscene matter were found in their carriage."

After a brief appearance in court, with a large crowd trailing behind, they were taken to the Ludlow Street Jail, where they "received a great number of sympathizers," including the financier George Francis Train, the *Times* said.

Angered that Henry Ward Beecher was excoriating her from his pulpit for her free love philosophy, Woodhull had used her newspaper to expose an affair he was having with the wife of Theodore Tilton, an editor and woman suffrage activist. Both were members of Beecher's church. Accusations and denials flew back and forth.

*Henry Ward Beecher was the first president
of the American Woman Suffrage Association.*
Library of Congress

Elizabeth Cady Stanton eventually admitted to leaking it, plunging the women's movement into scandal. After Tilton sued Beecher for alienation of affection, the salacious case stayed in the papers for months. Because the case involved prominent leaders in the women's movement, the resulting publicity was a blow to progress. (Beecher was president of the AWSA, and Stanton was president of the NWSA.) In many minds, the women's rights campaign was already associated with free love, lax divorce laws, and loose women. A sordid scandal engulfing Beecher (who was also Isabella Beecher Hooker's half brother), Stanton, and Tilton, all pillars of the women's movement, was the last thing the movement needed.

The New Departure

The NWSA, awakened to the avenue Woodhull suggested, pursued the theory that the Fourteenth Amendment and Fifteenth Amendment, which they had opposed, already gave women the right to vote.

In 1871, the NWSA convention adopted a platform of encouraging women to vote, and if turned away, to file federal suits demanding their right to vote. The goal was to get a case through to the U.S. Supreme Court.

They called the strategy the New Departure. It was a brilliant epiphany. The language of the amendments was broad enough that they could make the case. Woodhull had not asked Congress to grant women suffrage. She insisted that they already had that right under the Fourteenth Amendment, which said in Section 1:

> All persons born or naturalized in the United States, and subject to the jurisdiction thereof, are citizens of the United States *and of the state wherein they reside.* No state shall make or enforce any law which shall abridge the privileges or immunities of citizens *of the United States; nor shall any state deprive* any person *of life, liberty, or property, without due process of law; nor deny to* any person *within its jurisdiction the equal protection of the laws.* [Emphasis added.]

Therefore states were denying women, as citizens, their right to vote.

The Fifteenth Amendment merely says, "The right of *citizens of the United States to vote shall not be denied or abridged* by the United States or by any State on account of race, color, or previous condition of servitude" (emphasis added).

Women in various places—Washington, D.C.; Michigan; and New Hampshire—had already begun testing the laws by registering and voting. Women in Vineland, New Jersey, had attempted it on the presidential Election Day, November 19, 1868, but had to cast ballots in a separate box. One hundred seventy-two women voted, including four black women, but the votes were not counted. The aging Grimké sisters led a similar voting effort in 1870, leading forty women through a snowstorm to cast ballots.

On November 5, 1872, Anthony led more than a dozen women, mostly Quakers, including her three sisters and friend Rhoda DeGarmo, to the polls in Rochester, after having registered a few days earlier at a barbershop. The ballot included election for members of Congress. A poll watcher challenged Anthony on her qualifications to vote. An inspector asked whether she was a citizen, lived in the district, and had accepted any bribes for her vote. She answered satisfactorily, and inspectors accepted her ballot. "Well, I have been & gone & done it!!" she wrote to Stanton that day. Anthony voted for Ulysses S. Grant for president and for two members of Congress.

Federal warrants for the arrest of Anthony and fourteen other women were issued nine days after the election, charging them with voting for members of Congress "without having a lawful right" to do so. On Thanksgiving Day, a U.S. Marshal showed up at Anthony's home to tell her that the commissioner wished to see her at his office. She told the story of that day often and the accounts vary, but she asked why he wanted to see her, and the officer told her that the commissioner planned to arrest her. "Is that the way you arrest men?" she asked. After he said no, she demanded that she "should be arrested properly" and, as one story goes, held out her hands, insisting on being handcuffed.

Officials arrested the other women as well but released them pending the outcome of Anthony's trial. Officials arrested three elections inspectors, too, for letting them vote. Anthony spent the time leading up to the trial lecturing in twenty-nine towns and villages in her county (Monroe), delivering a speech entitled, "Is It a Crime for a U.S. Citizen to Vote?" In it, she declared that if the Fourteenth Amendment "was meant to be a prohibition of the states to deny or abridge [the black man's] right to vote—which I fully believe—then it did the same for all persons, white women included, born or naturalized in the United States; for the amendment does not say all male persons of African descent, but all persons are citizens."

Noting that dictionaries defined "citizen" as a person in the nation entitled to vote and hold office, she said, "The only question to be settled now is: Are women persons?"

Prosecutors had the trial moved to federal court, which met in another county, because they feared they could not get an impartial jury. Anthony gave dozens more lectures in the other county, and her friend Matilda Joslyn Gage spoke in many places, too.

At the trial in June 1873, Henry R. Selden, former lieutenant governor of New York, represented Anthony, and their main argument was that she voted in good faith, without criminal intent, because she believed she was rightfully entitled to do so. The judge rejected that argument and ordered the jury to find her guilty based on his interpretation of the law. Anthony was convicted in a highly publicized trial in which she was not permitted to speak until after the verdict. When the judge asked if she had anything to say, she unleashed a jeremiad of complaint against the injustices brought upon her and womankind. The judge repeatedly tried to cut her off, but she kept on.

"When I was brought before your honor for trial, I hoped for a broad and liberal interpretation of the Constitution and its recent amendments...that should declare equality of rights the national guarantee to all persons born or naturalized in the United States. But failing to get this justice—failing, even, to get a trial by a jury *not* of my peers—I ask not leniency at your hands—but rather the full rigors of the law," Anthony said. Women generally did not serve on juries. In 1898, Utah would become the first state to permit them to do so.

After the judge sentenced her to pay a $100 fine, she responded, "May it please your honor, I shall never pay a dollar of your unjust penalty." She never did. Capitalizing on her martyrdom and fame to call attention to the cause, Anthony had three thousand copies of the trial proceedings printed and widely circulated.

Around the same time, Virginia Louisa Minor, who was president of the Missouri Woman Suffrage Association, and her husband, Francis Minor, a lawyer, filed suit against a registrar, Reese Happersett, in St. Louis. He had refused to allow Virginia to vote, invoking the Missouri state constitution, which specifically barred women from voting. The Minors argued that the Fourteenth Amendment in the federal Constitution allowed women to vote. The Minors lost in the lower courts and appealed to the U.S. Supreme Court, which ruled against them unanimously in October 1874, in *Minor v. Happersett*. The justices concluded that the states had a right to bar various classes of citizens from voting, including women. In 1869, Francis Minor had written resolutions presented to the Missouri association and later adopted by the NWSA arguing that while the U.S. Constitution left qualifications for voting to the states, it did not allow the states to deny the vote to citizens, including women.

In 1876, the NWSA asked to present a Declaration of Rights for women at the official ceremony celebrating the centennial of United States independence, but the officials in charge denied them. Anthony and four other women waited for a lull, walked up on the platform, and handed their declaration to the stunned presider. They exited quickly, handing out copies to bystanders. Outside, Anthony read the proclamation to a large crowd that gathered before leading a procession to attend a NWSA convention at a nearby Unitarian church.

Beginning in 1876, Anthony and Stanton also collaborated with Matilda Joslyn Gage to write the *History of Woman Suffrage*. Eventually, it grew to six volumes, the last of which Ida Husted Harper completed after their deaths. Some allies warned that it was too early to attempt such a history, and Lucy Stone, then still estranged, refused to cooperate. For that reason and others, the *History* is not as balanced as it could be, but historians have found it to be a rich source of narratives, convention proceedings, reminiscences, letters, and other documents. Stan-

ton's daughter Harriot insisted they include Stone's American Woman Suffrage Association and accepted the job of writing a chapter on it.

Stone was immersed in the AWSA and running the *Woman's Journal*. During this period, the AWSA pressed forward with its efforts to push for reform of the state constitutions that barred women from voting. Efforts in Massachusetts and New Jersey had failed, just as they had in Kansas, and woman suffrage had scored no victories since Wyoming and Utah granted it, in 1869 and 1870 respectively. Lucy Stone had built up a strong network of affiliates and close associations with women all over the country.

In 1877, Stone and her husband, Henry Blackwell, went to Colorado, which had just become a state, to campaign for woman suffrage. The effort failed when voters rejected it almost two to one, but Stone and Blackwell suspected tampering and fraud.

When the legislature in Nebraska agreed to put a referendum on woman suffrage to the voters, all male, in 1882,

Lucy and Henry traveled to Nebraska to support the work of the Nebraska Woman Suffrage Association, which had sought help from both the NWSA and the AWSA. Again, the referendum lost nearly two to one, and rumors of vote tampering and deception surfaced.

Despite the NWSA's concentration on a federal amendment, Susan B. Anthony had campaigned in Colorado and Nebraska, too. Both groups held their conventions in Omaha, two weeks apart, during the campaign, and Anthony attended the AWSA's convention. Those defeats just reinforced the NWSA leaders' conviction that they had to get Congress to advance an amendment.

The Susan B. Anthony Amendment

On January 10, 1878, Senator Aaron Augustus Sargent, Republican of California, introduced an amendment in Congress that would give women the vote. Sargent's wife, Ellen Clark Sargent, was a leading suffragist—president of the California Equal Suffrage Association, treasurer in the NWSA, and a friend of Anthony and Stanton. Ellen Sargent's husband enthusiastically supported her work in the movement.

The amendment, which declared, "The right of citizens of the United States to vote shall not be denied or abridged by the United States or by any state on account of sex," promptly failed in committee. Sympathetic lawmakers continued to introduce "the Susan B. Anthony Amendment" in each new Congress—every two years. Committees in both houses reported the bill favorably for the next three Congresses. Finally, on December 8, 1886, the bill made it to the Senate floor for debate. The debate resumed on January 25, 1887, and the bill was roundly defeated 34–16 (with 26 marked "absent").

Opponents argued that women should not vote because their intellectual capacity was less than men's, that women's domestic duties would not allow them time to vote, and that the vote should be reserved for men because only they did military service. One senator predicted that giving women the vote would destroy domestic bliss for every husband in the country, and another argued that essen-

Aaron Augustus Sargent of California
introduced a woman suffrage amendment in Congress.
Library of Congress

tially voting was an onerous duty for men that women should be spared.

"How is she, with all these heavy duties of citizen, politician, and officeholder resting upon her shoulders, to attend to the more sacred, delicate, and refining trust...for which she is peculiarly fitted by nature?" asked Senator Joseph E. Brown, Democrat of Georgia. "How is she, in connection with them, to discharge the more refining, elevating, and ennobling duties of wife, mother, Christian, and friend, which are found in the sphere where nature has placed her? Who is to care for and train the children while she is absent in the discharge of these masculine duties?"

Brown also opposed the amendment because it would enfranchise black women, whom he argued lacked the education to use their votes wisely.

Senator George Graham Vest,

Democrat of Missouri, took the same position. "It is a fact known to every intelligent man that in one single act the right of suffrage was given without preparation to hundreds of thousands of voters who today can scarcely read," Vest argued. "That Senator proposes now to double, and more than double, that illiteracy. He proposes to give the negro women of the South this right of suffrage, utterly unprepared as they are for it."

Southern lawmakers voted solidly against the amendment.

Senator Henry W. Blair countered each argument, declaring that voting "is the great primitive right...in which all freedom originates and culminates." He pointed out, for instance, that men who did not serve in the military were still permitted to vote and that women could decide for themselves if voting would take them away from their motherly and wifely duties.

"More men are kept from the polls by drunkenness, or, being at the polls, vote under the influence of strong drink...than all those who would be kept from any given election by the necessary engagements of mothers at home," Blair said.

Congress considered the amendment, and it failed, in nearly every session until 1896, when it dropped off the agenda until 1913.

The Mother Vote

Meanwhile, the AWSA had promoted "partial suffrage" in some areas—enfranchisement for school boards, municipal offices, or primary elections—which brought some success. In Massachusetts, for instance, the legislature passed a law in 1879 allowing women to vote for the school district committee. Supporters argued that mothers should have a say in school matters because they bore the main responsibility for child rearing.

Happy to be voting on something at last, Lucy Stone went to cast her ballot, but the registrar told her she could not vote "by any other name than that of her husband."

She protested that Stone was her name, not Blackwell, and that no law required a wife to take her husband's name. The registrar stood firm, and she did not vote. Soon after that, to avoid any future incident, the legislature enacted a law requiring married women to use their husband's name to vote. Since it was very rare for a married woman to keep her own name, the law was probably aimed solely at Stone. Unbent, Lucy tried unsuccessfully to get Massachusetts to expand voting rights to municipal elections or full suffrage for women.

Kentucky was the first state to give women the school vote, in 1838, but its law applied only to widows. Michigan and Minnesota gave women the school vote in 1875, and a total of nineteen states had done so by 1890. Three states granted suffrage on tax and bond issues.

The Opposition Forces

Around this time, organized opposition to the movement spread among men and women in the public, not just among lawmakers. As quickly as the suffragists presented petitions, the opponents, or "remonstrants," got up petitions against them and wrote lawmakers urging them to block state suffrage bills.

Among the leaders were Ellen Ewing Sherman and Elmira Phelps. Sherman was the wife of General William Tecumseh Sherman, a Civil War hero for the Union, and Phelps was the sister of the educator Emma Willard. The women were generally wealthy, privileged, and in fear of seeing their domestic role undermined. The *Woman's Journal* mocked them and their comfortable lives. Mrs. Sherman helped spearhead a campaign that gathered one thousand signatures on a petition in 1872 urging the U.S. Senate to block the Susan B. Anthony Amendment.

These antisuffrage women argued that an overwhelming majority of women did not want the right to vote, and it would be unfair to thrust the responsibility on them. Women distracted by politics would not be able to devote their full energies to domestic, religious, and civic duties, they reasoned. The women opposing suffrage also argued that their men represented them through their votes, and the women often hired men to speak for them in legislative hearings and public appearances.

Men were also organizing to

THE AGE OF BRASS

A Currier & Ives print depicts "the Triumphs of Women's Rights," including women smoking, voting, and making their husbands tend to babies as they turn out to see "the Celebrated Man Tamer."

Courtesy of Angela P. Dodson

oppose woman suffrage, and a multitude of opposition groups sprang up. The more victories the suffragists won, the greater the opposition seemed to be, and the suffragists were often unsure who was backing the "anti" elements who popped up to write letters, petition, buy votes, and sometimes steal elections.

Opposition was greatest in the South, from which few women had emerged to join the suffrage movement. White Southerners feared that expanding the black voting population would upset the social order. Southerners had largely nullified the black male vote through the use of poll taxes, tests for registrants, intimidation, and violence. In the Midwest and West, brewing interests were assumed to be behind the "anti" element, and in the East, it was largely corporate interests.

A Boston Committee of Remonstrants formed to fight suffrage interests in several states, and a newspaper, the *Remonstrance*, was founded in 1890. It was published quarterly by the Massachusetts Association Opposed to the Further Extension of Suffrage to Women.

In January 1909, the newspaper said:

> *The average woman...is already overburdened with duties which she cannot escape and from which no one proposes to relieve her. If she is given the suffrage, it is an added duty. Is it reasonable to suppose that, called upon to perform a duty which lies outside of the ordinary employments of her life, she would do it more wisely than the average man? Would she not inevitably act hastily, impulsively, spasmodically? And, in that case, would not the community as well as she herself suffer by the change?*

Similar associations operated in at least twenty-one states. The National Association Opposed to Woman Suffrage, headed by Josephine Jewell Dodge, known as Mrs. Arthur M. Dodge, formed in 1911 in New York.

In an article in the *Columbia Spectator* in 1915, she wrote, "Woman is not political minded, and she never will be if she is in politics for a thousand years."

These women's associations maintained close ties to the liquor lobbies that feared woman suffrage would embolden the temperance movement, and suffrage leaders came to believe that the antisuffrage groups were fronts for the brewers, distillers, saloons, and liquor retailers.

The women's movement had gained a new friend: Frances Willard, president of the Woman's Christian Temperance

Union (WCTU). The temperance movement—dedicated to abstinence from alcohol and tobacco—had grown up alongside the woman suffrage movement, and many women had been active in both. Its aims were compatible, as the temperance movement sought to protect women and children from the harm drunken men could cause—cruelty, wrecked homes, impoverishment, and abandonment. Now, Willard saw the vote as a way of empowering women and protecting families, and she was interested in broader social reform. For suffragists, it was clear that if men had absolute power over their wives and the family's money, and if women had no recourse, a drunkard was a grave threat to his family and society.

The WCTU officially endorsed woman suffrage in 1880 and established a Department of Franchise, headed by Zerelda Wallace and Dr. Anna Howard Shaw. It marshaled forces across the country to fight for suffrage. The association with the WCTU also brought new enemies for the movement, as the liquor lobby saw this marriage of causes as a greater threat than the WCTU alone had been. With the vote, women could kill their industry. Temperance women already had roamed through towns singing, praying, and invading saloons, forcing them to shut down, if only temporarily. Unleashed as a strong unified national force, the two movements could be a formidable opponent to the liquor industry.

Aside from the liquor lobby, opposition also came from big political machines that feared that they couldn't control women's votes and that women would make good on their intention to clean up politics. Other corporate powers also backed the antisuffragists and lobbied against the state woman suffrage amendments and the federal amendment out of similar fears that a flood of new voters might make laws that threatened their interests. Industries worried that enfranchised women would push for better working conditions for women. Some clergy, especially Roman Catholic leaders, warned that women's involvement in the political process would undermine morality, marriage, and the family, and would take women away from a higher calling.

Together these forces would prove to be formidable obstacles that would stall most state amendments and the federal amendment for years to come. The suffragists would need to reunify their forces and refine their strategies to overcome them.

Reunification

Together Again

With the dawn of the 1890s, the women's movement took another step forward with the reunification of its two largest organizations. Many overtures had been made over the years, by Lucretia Mott, Martha Wright, Elizabeth Cady Stanton, and others. The NWSA and the AWSA had operated independently for twenty years, occasionally working on the same state campaigns.

Now, the issues that divided them had diminished in importance. A younger generation of suffragists did not have the memories of what had caused the rift nor of the personal animosities and petty slights that had kept the rivalry going, and the new recruits were perhaps frustrated by the lack of progress toward suffrage.

The older generation had lost bitter battles and become increasingly aware of the need for strong coalitions. The suffragists had celebrated the thirty-year anniversaries of Seneca Falls in 1878 and of the first national convention in Worcester in 1880 separately, with the NWSA honoring the first and the AWSA honoring the latter. Many of their old friends had died, including Martha Wright in 1875 and her sister Lucretia Mott in 1880.

Most of the credit for initiating a reconciliation goes to Alice Stone Blackwell, daughter of Lucy Stone and Henry Blackwell. Most recently, Alice had worked alongside her parents to turn the *Woman's Journal* into an influential newspaper. Harriot

Stanton Blatch, Elizabeth Cady Stanton's daughter, who had become active in a number of women's causes, also played a role in the reconciliation. Negotiations took three years, culminating in a joint convention of the organizations in February 1890 and formation of the National American Woman Suffrage Association (NAWSA).

The reunification eliminated a duplication of efforts and dual expenses of keeping two organizations alive. It also allowed the movement to speak with one voice and stick to new strategies.

While the federal amendment remained the goal, the new organization would also work to build support for state amendments, simultaneously creating a base for ratification by three-fourths of the states once they could persuade Congress to pass an amendment.

Stanton accepted the presidency with Anthony as vice president and Stone as chair of the executive committee. Anthony actually took over daily operations and became president in 1892, holding the post until 1900. Lucy Stone withdrew from active participation after the 1892 convention and died in 1893.

Stanton immersed herself in her own projects, notably the first volume of a feminist critique of the Judeo-Christian scriptures that she called *The Woman's Bible*, after she (long disaffected with organized religion) became convinced that conservative interpretations of the scriptures were the main stumbling block to furthering women's rights. Her work challenged traditional religious orthodoxy that scriptures made it clear women should be subservient to men, an argument the suffragists had often heard and countered in debates and articles.

Her "bible" was so controversial that the NAWSA disavowed it in 1896 as potentially harmful to the movement. Impervious to the criticisms, which helped make it a best seller, Stanton published another volume in 1898 and worked on other writings until her death in 1902.

With the elevation of Susan B. Anthony, the national association began a new era under her more steady hand coupled with her talent for organization. While Stanton could fire up a crowd, Anthony could lead them more effectively to focus their energies on the long-sought goal. It would become less a movement of ideas and more a movement of action.

"Lifting as We Climb"

While the support of the temperance union and the reunification strengthened the movement, its leaders seemed intent on squandering another potential ally—the legion of black women, Northern and Southern, who were engaged in clubs and increasingly identifying with the suffrage cause.

While many antisuffragists used the argument that allowing women to vote would interfere with their role in the home, black women, many of whom worked outside the home out of necessity, especially challenged this notion. Alice Dunbar, a leader in the National Association of Colored Women (NACW) and wife of the poet Paul Laurence Dunbar, argued that voting would not interfere with the duties of wives and mothers any more than church activities did.

Toward the end of the nineteenth century, women all over the country were joining and forming clubs devoted to various purposes, social, literary, charitable, and educational. Most excluded black women, who formed their own clubs, often with a more aggressive political and reformist agenda. Black women's clubs dedicated themselves to educational and social uplift, antilynching campaigns, aid to the downtrodden, and justice.

While many people, black and white, think of the suffragist movement as merely a white women's cause, a few black women had been a part of the movement early on and attended the national conventions. Along with Sojourner Truth and Frances E. W. Harper, mentioned earlier, Harriet Forten Purvis and her sister Margaretta Forten participated in the conventions, according to the historian Rosalyn Terborg-Penn. The sisters were founders, along with Lucretia Mott, of the Philadelphia Female Anti-Slavery Society, which remained active after the Civil War, working for ratification of the Fifteenth Amendment.

A well-known abolitionist lecturer, Sarah Remond of Salem, Massachusetts, and Mary Ann Shadd Cary, a Washington, D.C., lawyer and former editor of an antislavery newspaper, were active in the suffragist movement.

Cary attended an NWSA convention in Washington while studying at Howard University Law School in 1871. She also wrote a statement to the House Judiciary Committee about black women's need for the vote in the District of Columbia, based on the argument Victoria Woodhull had made asserting that the Fourteenth and Fifteenth Amendments gave women the right to vote. Cary also successfully registered to vote that year in D.C. but was not allowed to cast a ballot. In 1876, Cary submitted the names of ninety-four black women to the NWSA for inclusion among the signers of the Women's Declaration of Rights for the 1876 centennial that demanded immediate enfranchisement of women.

Hattie Purvis, daughter of Harriet Forten Purvis and Robert Purvis, participated in the American Equal Rights Association that formed after the Civil War to fight for universal suffrage. (Black men were speakers and committee members in these conferences as well, including abolitionists like Hattie's father and William Still. In 1867, Robert Purvis presided over the AERA with Lucretia Mott.)

When the division over the Fifteenth Amendment split the movement, some black women joined the National Woman Suffrage Association, and some joined the American Woman Suffrage Association. Sojourner Truth divided her time between them.

Other black women became attracted to the cause, including

Caroline Remond Putnam, who helped to found the Massachusetts Woman Suffrage Association. Josephine St. Pierre Ruffin, described below, joined that society, and both of these women worked alongside Lucy Stone and Julia Ward Howe in the AWSA.

Fewer black Southern women were active during this period, but Charlotte "Lottie" Rollins chaired the founding meeting of the South Carolina Women's Rights Association and attended AWSA conventions. Her sisters, Louisa, Kate, and Frances, were activists as well. Mary McCurdy of Rome, Georgia, complained that Southerners had disenfranchised black men or bought their votes during Reconstruction. She championed the causes of temperance and woman suffrage through a newspaper she edited, the *National Presbyterian*.

Another writer, Gertrude Bustill Mossell, supported woman suffrage through her column in the *New York Freeman*, a black newspaper run by T. Thomas Fortune.

Soon, black women leaders were calling for formation of a national organization to solidify their efforts. Hallie Quinn Brown, a professor at and graduate of Wilberforce University, had begun pushing for formation of a national organization around 1890, and Ida B. Wells-Barnett, a journalist and antilynching lecturer, began helping to form clubs around the nation. With her help, Josephine St. Pierre Ruffin issued a call for a national meeting in August 1895 in Boston. Ruffin was founder of the New Era Club, along with her friend Mary Baldwin and daughter, Florida Ruffin Ridley.

More than fifty women met to form the National Federation of Afro-American Women. Among them were Frances Harper, Mary Church Terrell (an educator and reformer from Washington, D.C.), and Margaret Murray Washington (third wife of the educator Booker T. Washington). Most of the attendees were already suffragists, and they listened eagerly to William Lloyd Garrison Jr. speak on women's political equality. (The son of the great abolitionist was also the son-in-law of Martha Wright, a Seneca Falls organizer.)

Mary Church Terrell, president of the National Association of Colored Women, addressed several women's rights conventions.

Library of Congress

A year later, at a meeting in Washington, D.C., at the Nineteenth Street Baptist Church, the federation united with the Colored Women's League of Washington, D.C., to become the National Association of Colored Women with Terrell as president. Terrell, an eloquent speaker and Oberlin College graduate, addressed several of the national woman suffrage conventions and mesmerized the audience at an international women's conference in 1904 when she spoke in English, German, and French.

She attended every National American Woman Suffrage Association meeting that was held in Washington, D.C. In an address before the association on February 18, 1898, she recalled the progress made by women since Seneca Falls fifty years before and by black women since emancipation.

"Lifting as we climb, onward and upward we go, struggling and striving, and hoping that the buds and blossoms of our desires will burst into glorious fruition ere long," she concluded. "With courage, born of success achieved in the past, with a keen sense of the responsibility which we shall continue to assume, we look forward to a future large with promise and hope. Seeking no favors because of our color, nor patronage because of our needs, we knock at the bar of justice, asking an equal chance."

The NACW adopted "Lifting as We Climb" as a slogan. Mary McLeod Bethune, the educator, became president of the NACW in 1924. She later founded the National Council of Negro Women. *The Woman's Era*, the official publication of the NACW and the first periodical published by black women in the nation, gave them a forum for their views. Its editors were all suffragists, including Terrell, Margaret Murray Washington, Wells-Barnett, Fannie Barrier Williams, and Josephine Silone Yates. Anna Julia Cooper, an educator in Washington, D.C., wrote a feminist analysis of the condition of blacks and women and wrote many speeches supporting the rights of both. Her book, *A Voice from the South by a Black Woman from the South*, was published in 1892.

Prominent black suffragists also included Grace Baxter Fenderson, one of the founders of the National Association for the Advancement of Colored People (NAACP), and Florence Spearing Randolph, a minister. She was founder of the New Jersey Federation of Colored Women's Clubs, a lecturer for the Woman's Christian Temperance Union, and a board member of the New Jersey Woman Suffrage Association. Maggie Lena Walker of Richmond, Virginia, the first woman in the United States to be president of a charter bank, traveled the country giving speeches about women's rights and disenfranchisement, as well as financial issues.

White suffragists did not always welcome this progress by black women and their desire to be working partners in the drive for women's enfranchisement. The national leaders of the movement were willing to sacrifice black support to pacify Southerners and court their support for the ballot.

★ *Ida B. Wells-Barnett* ★

Ida B. Wells was born in 1862 in Holly Springs, Mississippi, to parents who were enslaved. Her parents, James and Lizzie Warrenton Wells, fared well after slavery ended with his earnings as a carpenter and hers as a cook. Ida became an orphan at the age of sixteen when her parents died of yellow fever in 1878. She studied at Rust College in Holly Springs, took a teaching job to help support her five siblings, and later moved to Memphis, Tennessee. She began writing under the name "Iola" for newspapers, becoming a prominent journalist in her twenties and owner of a Memphis newspaper, the *Free Speech and Headlight*. When she denounced the lynching of three prominent black businessmen, she had to leave town ahead of a mob that broke into her offices and smashed her presses. She undertook a lifelong campaign against lynching, lecturing and later writing for other newspapers, including the *New York Age*.

She met Frederick Douglass in 1892, and he became her mentor until his death in 1895. As an editor and orator fighting for justice and human rights like he was, she was often compared to Douglass.

Wells married Ferdinance Barnett, a black Chicago lawyer, in 1895, and became mother to two stepchildren and eventually to four of her own. She hyphenated her name—unlike

Ida B. Wells-Barnett, a newspaper editor and club woman,
started a woman suffrage organization in Chicago.
This image was published in **The African-American Mosaic:**
A Library of Congress Resource Guide for the Study
of Black History and Culture, *edited by Debra Newman Ham*
(Washington, D.C.: Library of Congress, 1993).

Library of Congress

most married women of her day, who took their husband's names—and gave herself away at her wedding.

Wells-Barnett helped found the NAACP in 1909 and the National Association of Colored Women. She became friends with Susan B. Anthony, who sponsored her lecture in Rochester, New York, in 1894, and stayed at Anthony's home. The suffrage leader fired her own secretary during the visit when she would not assist Wells-Barnett, refusing "to take dictation from a colored woman."

Anthony and Wells-Barnett clashed over Anthony's willingness to indulge the prejudices of white Southern women for the sake of expediency and the expansion of the woman suffrage movement, but they continued correspondence on the issues involved.

In 1913, after Illinois passed limited suffrage for women (in municipal and presidential elections), Wells-Barnett worked to organize black women to vote. She had been active in the Republican Party (see Section 4, "The Party of Lincoln") and had founded the Women's Second Ward Republican Club in 1910. With Belle Squire, a white columnist for the *Chicago Tribune*, she founded the Alpha Suffrage Club, which canvassed neighborhoods to get black women to register. The club had two hundred members by 1916, and helped to elect Chicago's first black alderman, Oscar De Priest, later a congressional representative.

The club raised money to send Wells-Barnett to the Washington suffrage parade in 1913. Illinois sent an integrated delegation, but its leader acquiesced to the national leaders' insistence that blacks march together in the rear of the parade. Wells-Barnett refused. Two white women, Squire and Grace Brooks, supported her, but lost the battle. Wells-Barnett left the delegation but stepped out of the crowd of onlookers to rejoin them when the delegation passed in front of her. The *Chicago Tribune* printed a picture of her marching triumphantly between Brooks and Squire. In later years, she continued her work for justice and civil rights and ran unsuccessfully for office. Before her death in 1931, she began an autobiography that was completed by her younger daughter, Alfreda Duster, and published in 1970 as *Crusade for Justice: The Autobiography of Ida B. Wells*.

The Southern Strategy

The NWSA was pursuing a "Southern strategy." Susan B. Anthony made appearances in the South, held conventions there to attract supporters and publicity for the cause, and tried to appease the segregationists. The suffragists needed Southern states to ratify a suffrage amendment if Congress ever passed it, and some Southerners were leery of adding black women to the voting population. The prospect of doubling the black vote struck fear in the hearts of the protectors of the whites-only power structure.

With the Fourteenth and Fifteenth Amendments enshrined in law, many of the suffragists ignored the fact that the South had managed to suppress the black vote almost entirely through intimidation, violence, poll taxes, and test requirements. They also faulted those black men who, when they could vote, accepted bribes for their ballots, instead of blaming the corrupt politicians who paid for them. Black leaders, including such prominent educators as Nannie Helen Burroughs and Anna Julia Cooper, were also critical of black men who sold their votes. Black suffrage clubs and voter-education efforts sprang up around the nation, partly to address that issue.

Southern women traditionally had not joined the suffrage organizations and had not organized on their own, with the exception of Kate Gordon of Louisiana, a former officer of the national association, who founded the Southern States Woman Suffrage Conference to work for suffrage for white women. Another Southerner, Laura Clay of Kentucky, left the prosuffrage movement to start an organization in opposition to it, the Citizens' Committee for a State Suffrage Amendment.

To attract support in the South, the NAWSA's strategy involved distancing itself from black supporters to avoid offending Southern sensibilities, while openly suggesting that woman suffrage, especially educated suffrage involving some literacy test, was a way to maintain white supremacy. (Laws had forbidden teaching black people to read under slavery, and the segregated schools provided for them after emancipation were generally inferior. An education requirement would exclude many African-Americans who remained undereducated. An English literacy test would block many of the new immigrants from voting as well at a time when anti-immigrant sentiments ran high.)

Paula Giddings, author of *When and Where I Enter*, argues that Anthony personally did not favor educated suffrage, held liberal views, and treated blacks with dignity and respect. She entertained African-Americans in her home and often had friendly exchanges about issues related to race and women's rights.

When Anthony turned down a request from black women to form their own chapter of NAWSA, Wells-Barnett criticized her, saying, "She might have made gains for suffrage, but she confirmed white women in their attitude of segregation." Similar snubs would arise later. (Other organizations discriminated against the black clubwomen as well.) Wells-Barnett later cofounded a black woman suffrage organization in Chicago, the Alpha Suffrage Club.

The NAWSA accepted black members but discouraged them from attending the organization's conventions in the South. Adella Hunt Logan, an educator at Tuskegee Institute, attended some anyway, possibly passing for white when she did so, according to her granddaughter and biographer, Adele Logan Alexander. Born in 1863, as the daughter of a white planter and a mixed-race mother in Sparta, Georgia, Logan was very fair-skinned. She lectured to women's clubs and wrote about suffrage for the *Crisis*, the NAACP's official publication. Alexander argued that if white women needed the vote, black women had a greater need of it. Logan became passionate about woman suffrage after hearing Susan B. Anthony speak at Atlanta University in 1895 and remained a supporter of hers despite her organization's Southern agenda.

More serious at this juncture was that the NAWSA released the state organizations to adopt whatever suffrage strategy they wished, and some states amended their constitutions to give the franchise only to white women, having already excluded black men. Even as late as 1919, white Southerners were also trying to modify the Anthony Amendment to restrict the vote to white citizens.

Although the Southern appeal did not prevail, the relationship between African-Americans and the suffragists remained a complex one in which friendships and alliances were strained, much as they are in families in which people love each other but often have to accept a relative's bad behavior for the sake of harmony.

The seeds of distrust planted in this era echoed in the strained relationships between white feminists and black women in the women's rights movement of the 1960s and '70s. Black women in the presuffrage era sometimes challenged the way the white leaders treated them, but for the most part they seemed very forgiving or simply accepting of the segregationist norms of the time. Mary Church Terrell once wrote about Anthony's role as an abolitionist, noting that "she had to work so much longer for the political emancipation of her sex than she did for the physical emancipation of an enslaved race...

"And yet Miss Anthony was one of the most earnest, most

courageous and most eloquent members of that immortal group who worked so hard and so successfully for the freedom of the slave," Terrell said in an undated article, "Susan B. Anthony, Abolitionist," found in her personal papers at Howard University. "Nobody labored with sublimer heroism and more ardent zeal than did that noble woman."

In a 1946 article, "Use the Franchise! An Appeal to Colored Women to Vote," she recalled how Douglass had defended Stanton's resolution for suffrage at Seneca Falls while "many good people" deemed it "untimely and unwise."

"The women of this country owe a great deal of gratitude to Frederick Douglass," she wrote. "At the risk of doing an irreparable injury to himself and to the cause of abolition which was so dear to his heart, he did everything in his power to secure the franchise for women, so that they would no longer be classed with infants and idiots and criminals. If Frederick Douglass had not had the courage to second Mrs. Stanton's motion...how long the franchise for women would have been delayed is anybody's guess."

She expressed the hope that the fact a black man had done so much to secure the vote for women would increase the determination of black women to use it and to do so wisely.

Despite the obstacles, black women and men continued to work for woman suffrage, within the NAWSA and on the outside, and white suffragist leaders would come looking for help from blacks near the end of the struggle. Giddings noted that most black male leaders, like W. E. B. Du Bois, editor of the *Crisis*, were strong advocates for giving women the vote. Du Bois covered the woman suffrage struggle heavily in his journal from 1910 to 1934. He wrote many editorials himself in favor of it and devoted special editions of the *Crisis* to woman suffrage in September 1912, August 1915, and November 1917. He and other black leaders who supported suffrage were motivated as much or more by the prospect of increasing the black vote as they were by the desire to see women get their just due.

Farewell to Douglass

To appease the Southern suffragists in 1895, Susan B. Anthony asked Frederick Douglass to skip the NAWSA's Atlanta convention and defended the decision to Ida B. Wells-Barnett. Anthony said that the sight of him, a black man sitting with white women on the platform, a place of honor he always held at the conventions, would upset their Southern hosts. (The NAWSA was eager to avoid any controversy, especially after the Woodhull scandal and the blowup over *The Woman's Bible*.)

Ironically, when Douglass was widely criticized for marrying a white woman in 1884 after his first wife, who was black, died, Elizabeth Cady Stanton was one of the few people who sent him well wishes and defended his choice. His second wife, Helen Pitts, was a feminist and daughter of an old abolitionist friend.

Douglass made his last appearance with the suffragists on February 20, 1895, at a triennial meeting of the National Council of Women in Washington, D.C., where Susan B. Anthony and Dr. Anna Howard Shaw escorted him to the platform. He bowed but declined to speak, then sat next to Anthony for the whole day of sessions. Soon after he returned home that evening, he died as he was preparing to go out again to speak.

"After dining, he had a chat in the hallway with his wife about the doings of the council. He grew very enthusiastic in his explanation of one of the events of the day, when he fell upon his knees, with hands clasped," the *New York Times* reported the following day. "Mrs. Douglass, thinking this was part of his description, was not alarmed, but as she looked he sank lower and lower, and finally lay stretched upon the floor, breathing his last."

The *Times* noted that he was a member of the NWSA and regularly attended its meetings.

"It is a singular fact, in connection with the death of Mr. Douglass, that the very last hours of his life were given in attention to one of the principles to which he has devoted his energies since his escape from slavery," the *Times* wrote.

Anthony was bereft. At his funeral at the Metropolitan African Methodist Episcopal Church in Washington, D.C., she read her "highly eulogistic" tribute and Elizabeth Cady Stanton's remarks, the *Times* reported on February 25. Anthony recalled

WASHINGTON, D. C.—THE NEW ADMINISTRATION—COLORED CITIZENS PAYING THEIR RESPECTS TO MARSHAL FREDERICK DOUGLASS, IN HIS OFFICE AT THE CITY HALL.—SKETCHED BY OUR SPECIAL ARTIST.

Black citizens pay their respects to Marshal Frederick Douglass, in his office at the city hall, 1877.

Library of Congress

that he had promised to speak at Stanton's eightieth birthday party the following week. Stanton's eulogy recalled various incidents in their long association.

Some Southern newspapers reported with derision on their display of respect for their fallen friend, and Carrie Chapman Catt, who had become one of Anthony's most promising deputies, commented that by paying Douglass such public homage, they had undone most of what they had accomplished in the South.

"The relationship of our leaders to the colored question at the Douglass funeral has completely taken the wind out of our sails. You should see some of the clippings I have from the Southern Press and some of the letters," she wrote to a fellow suffragist. "They were suspicious of us all along, but now they know we are abolitionists in disguise."

Changing of the Guard

Perhaps it was best that the movement was about to experience a historic change of leadership to usher it through its most tumultuous era yet. Long before she retired in 1900, Susan B. Anthony had been training younger women to take over the leadership. Among them were Carrie Chapman Catt and Dr. Anna Howard Shaw.

First, the leadership would fall to Catt, who had been active in the suffrage movement in Iowa, where she grew up, as early as 1887 and in the national organization since 1890.

Catt, a former teacher and journalist, had joined the movement as a county organizer and become a state leader, launching ten "political equality" clubs within a year. Her leadership and organizational skills emerged early, and she fine-tuned them as the suffrage department leader for a temperance society. In January 1890, she attended her first NAWSA convention in Washington, D.C., the historic meeting where the suffrage organizations reunited. There, she met the legendary leaders of the movement, Elizabeth Cady Stanton, Susan B. Anthony, and Lucy Stone, among others, and they took notice of the Iowa representative's speaking skills. (Soon after that meeting, she married George Catt, a prosperous engineer in Seattle, who encouraged and underwrote her activism. They later moved to New York as his bridge-building and harbor-dredging business grew.)

An engraving from the Graphic, *a British illustrated newspaper, depicts a speaker and audience at "the Congress of Representative Women of All Lands," part of the Columbian Exposition in Chicago in 1893, organized by May Wright Sewall and Rachel Foster Avery.*

Courtesy of Angela P. Dodson

She attended the 1892 convention, where Anthony began to put fresh leadership in place. Always in search of talent, Anthony tapped Catt early on to speak before a congressional committee on suffrage and to head the business committee, replacing the old executive committee.

In the decade after that, Catt worked on state campaigns, barely surviving a bout of typhoid after her first one in South Dakota. She built a network of lecturers and wrote many speeches and articles. She came to the NAWSA with a provincial outlook—later she mockingly termed her attitude "jingoist"—and grew into an international leader after undergoing a conversion at the Congress of Representative Women of All Lands, part of the Columbian Exposition in Chicago in 1893, organized by May Wright Sewall and Rachel Foster Avery.

As head of the business committee, she had established procedures and structures for keeping track of membership, supervising the work of state affiliates, controlling finances, and training members. Later, she formed and headed an organization committee to coordinate the work in all regions of the country and build suffrage clubs that could sustain themselves between campaigns for suffrage. Catt also created a course of study in political science for the local clubs. This helped to keep women engaged, even in states where women had already secured suffrage, so they could remain in place to lobby for the eventual federal amendment and ratification. She urged suffragists to raise funds, obtain tax lists, and compile data to document how much property tax was paid by women. This, she predicted, would underscore that they were citizens without representation and, as her biographer put it, "would instantly convert every believer in the Declaration of Independence to woman suffrage." A few women in the movement had withheld taxes as a protest in the past but not systematically.

She also urged them to keep high profiles in their respective states. They were to attend political conventions, make themselves known to lawmakers, and feed suffragist material to the press. She also expended much of the organization's energies and money on trying to organize the South—without much success.

★ *Carrie Chapman Catt* ★

Carrie Lane was born January 9, 1859, in Ripon, Wisconsin, to Lucius and Maria Louisa (Clinton) Lane. They later moved to Charles City, Iowa.

As an Iowa farm girl, Carrie was fortunate to have an educated mother who nourished her love of reading and curiosity about life. As she got older, she rode a horse five miles to attend a one-room school and begged her parents to let her go to the Iowa State Agricultural College, paying for most of it herself by teaching school during breaks. During the terms, she washed dishes and worked in the library. She entered with twenty-seven students, six of them women, but she was the only woman in her graduating class in November 1880.

This "100 Years of Progress" stamp features
Elizabeth Cady Stanton, Carrie Chapman Catt, and Lucretia Mott.
United States Postal Service

She became a teacher and principal. She honed her skills as a speaker after her first husband, Leo Chapman, a newspaper publisher, died of typhoid, forcing her to take to the lecture circuit to make more money. She was also a newspaper reporter in San Francisco. She remarried to George Catt, a successful San Francisco civil engineer and former schoolmate at Iowa State, who encouraged her work and her activism.

In 1887, she moved back to Charles City, Iowa, and became active in the temperance movement and then the suffrage movement. She began attending national suffrage meetings and moved up quickly in the National American Woman Suffrage Association, serving twice as president. She was valued as the consummate organizer. During her second stint, she led the organization to victory for the Nineteenth Amendment. With ratification nearly in hand, she founded the League of Women Voters and dissolved the NAWSA. She also founded the International Alliance of Women. Catt died March 9, 1947, in New Rochelle, New York.

The Doldrums

The movement Catt inherited had laid the groundwork but had not been having much success during the years that historians, beginning with Eleanor Flexner, called "the doldrums" of the movement, 1896 to 1910.

The period from 1870 to 1900 had been a tumultuous one for the movement, and the strategy to win amendments in the states for at least partial suffrage had consumed considerable energy with little to show for it.

The process required in some states that the legislature adopt a resolution calling for suffrage. Then a constitutional convention had to vote out an amendment. Then two-thirds of the electorate, all male by definition, had to approve it.

The only states to adopt woman suffrage amendments allowing women to vote in all elections were in the West: Colorado in 1893, and Idaho in 1896, plus Utah and Wyoming, which had adopted measures when they were territories and retained them when they were admitted as states. The states that would follow would also be in the West: Washington, 1910; California, 1911; Oregon, 1912; and Arizona, 1912. Yet no new suffrage states were won from 1896 to 1910.

Catt calculated that from 1870 to 1910, women waged 480 campaigns in thirty-three states to get referenda submitted to voters. Only seventeen of those resulted in a referendum, all but three in states west of the

Mississippi: Michigan, 1874; Rhode Island, 1887; and New Hampshire, 1902. The main enemy in many of these states was the liquor lobby, and the methodology involved was often old-fashioned vote stealing.

"During that time [the suffragists] were forced to conduct fifty-six campaigns of referenda to male voters; 480 campaigns to get Legislatures to submit suffrage amendments to voters; 47 campaigns to get State constitutional conventions to write woman suffrage into state constitutions; 277 campaigns to get State party conventions to include woman suffrage planks; 30 campaigns to get presidential party conventions to adopt woman suffrage planks in party platforms, and 19 campaigns with 19 successive Congresses," Catt said.

On the congressional front, hearings were held like clockwork when NAWSA met in Washington every other year, but no committee had reported out the Anthony Amendment, recommending a vote to either house, since 1893.

Perhaps the greatest accomplishment of this era was that the suffragists had raised the profile of their cause, though not always in a good way. They had also built extensive networks of supporters and left a strong nationwide organization in place with new leaders emerging. Now, it was up to Catt and the next generation to pick up where they had left off and carry the baton forward.

Woman suffrage parade, Washington, D.C., March 3, 1913.

Library of Congress

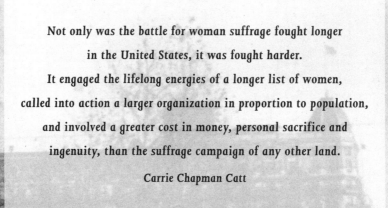

Not only was the battle for woman suffrage fought longer
in the United States, it was fought harder.
It engaged the lifelong energies of a longer list of women,
called into action a larger organization in proportion to population,
and involved a greater cost in money, personal sacrifice and
ingenuity, than the suffrage campaign of any other land.

Carrie Chapman Catt

How Long
Must
Women
Wait?

A New Era

One of the most iconic photographs of the woman suffrage movement shows Carrie Chapman Catt, a stout, strong-looking woman, dressed in a long white coat with a feathery white hat, carrying a flag and marching resolutely down Fifth Avenue in a parade on October 27, 1917, during the last, victorious campaign for suffrage in New York State.

The new century would require new tactics and new ideas, and the veterans of the movement would have to make way for and learn from a radical new element. Tired of waiting, suffragist women were ready to do battle as they never had before.

By the time Catt took over the NAWSA, her organizational skills were her trademark.

The movement had attracted wealthy, prominent women, like Millicent Willson Hearst, wife of the newspaper publisher William Randolph Hearst, and Jane Lathrop Stanford, wife of the railroad tycoon Leland Stanford, who contributed generously to the cause.

The NAWSA also had a younger core of members, many of whom were more highly educated than the previous generations of women. After Oberlin opened its doors to women in the 1830s and Mount Holyoke began as a college for women in the 1840s, more colleges permitted women to attend or were opened specifically for women. By the early twentieth century, it was more common for women to have graduate degrees and professional degrees in law or medicine. The new generation of women was the most highly educated ever of their sex. They had attended such colleges and universities as Vassar, Swarthmore, Penn, New York University, and Columbia. Most of them still faced tremendous barriers to working in their fields or to obtaining more advanced education, but exposure to higher education may also have emboldened them.

Many of the younger members, however, were not as socially conscious as the old alliance of abolitionists, radical Quakers, and human rights reformers. Quite a few of the newcomers espoused anti-immigrant views, resenting the fact that male immigrants from Europe and elsewhere could qualify for the franchise they coveted. Some jurisdictions allowed noncitizen residents to vote in local elections, and naturalized male immigrants would gain the vote within a few years of arrival. Millions of new immigrants—Italian, Polish, Russian, Asian, including many Jews and Catholics—poured into the country after the mid-1880s. They worked mainly as laborers and often lived in the slums of major cities.

Many Americans saw them as unequal and undeserving. It is likely that the more educated younger women especially resented male immigrants' access to the franchise denied them. Antisuffragists used immigration as an argument against expanding the vote, saying woman suffrage would give the ballot to foreign women who were unfit to vote. Suffragists increasingly argued that they should not be subject to the rule of ignorant men. It was similar to the arguments Southern women used against allowing black men to vote.

Catt had held similar views and had lectured on them in earlier years, but after the Chicago Exposition she had broadened her outlook and embraced the international suffrage movement. Susan B. Anthony suggested the idea of an international organization while visiting Elizabeth Cady Stanton in Britain (where she was living with her daughter, Harriot) in 1884. The International Council of Women they helped form held several congresses, but they abandoned it when they could not get the support they wanted for the suffrage cause. They were not enthusiastic when Catt sought support for the idea of an international suffrage organization, and told her she would have to proceed on her own. In 1902, Catt called an exploratory meeting to coincide with the NAWSA meeting in Washington that year. Women from seven countries attended. At that meeting on February 12, 1902, Catt helped launch the International Woman Suffrage Alliance. She became its president and would build it into an influential organization.

"Stirring Up the World"

The next couple of years were difficult ones for the NAWSA. First came the death of Elizabeth Cady Stanton on October 26, 1902, at her home in New York City. Susan B. Anthony had planned to visit her there in a little over two weeks to celebrate her eighty-seventh birthday. She drafted a birthday letter a few days before Stanton's death recalling their work together:

> It is fifty-one years since first we met and we have been busy through every one of them, stirring up the world to recognize the rights of women. The older we grow the more keenly we feel the humiliation of disfranchisement and the more vividly we realize its disadvantages in every department of life and most of all in the labor market.
>
> We little dreamed when we began this contest, optimistic with the hope and buoyancy of youth, that half a century later we would be compelled to leave the finish of the battle to another generation of women. But our hearts are filled with joy to know that they enter upon this task equipped with a college education, with business experience, with the fully admitted right to speak in public—all of which were denied to women fifty years ago. They have practically but one point to gain—the suffrage; we had all. These

strong, courageous, capable young women will take our place and complete our work. There is an army of them where we were but a handful. Ancient prejudice has become so softened, public sentiment so liberalized and women have so thoroughly demonstrated their ability as to leave not a shadow of doubt that they will carry our cause to victory.

And we, dear, old friend, shall move on to the next sphere of existence—higher and larger, we cannot fail to believe, and one where women will not be placed in an inferior position but will be welcomed on a plane of perfect intellectual and spiritual equality.

Catt labored that winter to win passage of a woman suffrage amendment in New Hampshire. She participated in two days of lively debates with the Reverend Lyman Abbott, speaking for the antisuffragists. He was a Congregationalist theologian based in Brooklyn, New York, who had spoken out against the movement for years, and his wife, known as Mrs. Lyman Abbott, was a prominent antisuffragist.

In any case, the amendment ultimately failed. Catt spent the next year or so traveling with and tending to her husband, who was ill, and she resigned as president of the NAWSA in 1904 to spend more time with him and devote more time to the international alliance.

Dr. Anna Howard Shaw succeeded Catt. It had been a difficult decision for Anthony to pass over her, because they were long-standing friends, but Catt was the better organizer, a skill much needed at the time. Dr. Shaw was a gifted orator, not a manager.

The doctor, who had first been a preacher, entered medical school at the age of thirty-five and graduated in 1886. She had worked as a minister and physician among women in Boston's slums and as a temperance advocate, heading the suffrage department of the Woman's Christian Temperance Union.

Despite her disappointment over not getting the job the first time around, she had continued working tirelessly and traveling widely for the movement during Catt's term. By the time she became president, she had made gaining suffrage for women her career, and Anthony secured donations to support her as she undertook the presidency so she would not need to earn money lecturing.

Dr. Shaw, who served eleven years as president, was devoted and hardworking, but her lack of organizing and communications skills soon became apparent, and the movement stalled. Her biggest achievement was initiating a petition to Congress asking it to pass the woman suffrage amendment. The goal was to get one million signatures, but the drive yielded a little more than four hundred thousand.

During her term, as before, the officers were scattered in different cities, and the organization had no central office. Face-to-face meetings were impractical, and communication by mail was cumbersome and subject to misunderstandings. The state of the movement was not good, but change was about to come from outside.

A Bolder Course

Inspiration would come from the British suffrage movement. First, Harriot Stanton Blatch, who had married an Englishman and lived in his country for twenty years, came home in 1902 to find the movement she had been born into in shambles, its members uninspired and uninspiring. Living in New York, where she also found the state organization stagnant, she called a meeting of forty women to form the Equality League of Self-Supporting Women in January 1907.

In Britain, she had witnessed the women's movement take their agitation to limits the Americans had never dared. British women had also been working actively since the 1860s to get the vote. The British

Parliament would not take up the issue of woman suffrage, as major parties blocked it from coming up for debate in the House of Commons. Advocates were tired of cajoling and petitioning its members. Led by Emmeline Goulden Pankhurst and her daughters, Sylvia, Christabel, and Adela, they held huge meetings outdoors, disrupted men's deliberations, and heckled speakers. They formed the Women's Social and Political Union and tried to organize factory workers to support them. When some women harassed a party leader, spectators and police attacked them, and police hauled them off to jail. The attention gained for the movement only encouraged them to do more and to provoke violence. Their intent was to embarrass leaders into addressing the woman suffrage issue. Some of them used violent means themselves to keep the nation focused on their cause. The more militant women were dubbed "suffragettes," a term used derisively by others before it was embraced by the British women. More arrests followed. In prison, they went on hunger strikes. When their jailers force-fed them—in a horrendous process—it only fanned the flames and attracted more attention.

This was still going on when Blatch returned to America after the turn of the century. Her new group set out to attract "industrial women"—the thousands laboring in factories—to join forces with the business and professional women. As immigration continued to swell, meeting a demand for cheap labor, the number of women in the workforce also mushroomed between 1880 and 1890, from 2.6 million to more than 4 million. Women in New York State and elsewhere were laboring under horrendous and often dangerous conditions in clothing manufacturing sweatshops, textile mills, millineries, laundries, and various kinds of factories, working long hours for the lowest possible wages. The number of women in the workforce rose from about 4 million in 1890 to nearly 7.5 million in 1910, according to census data. Women's greater participation in the workforce weakened arguments that women could be "covered," represented and protected by men.

Some women had begun to join or organize unions, and Blatch's group got union workers to testify before the legislature on behalf of suffrage. The Equality League worked with the New York Collegiate Equal Suffrage League to hold big public meetings. By October 1908, the Equality League had nineteen thousand members.

"Outdoor Warfare"

The most visible innovation was the introduction of the suffrage parade. Blatch's group led the first major one in New York in 1910. In a statement for the *New York Tribune* in 1912, she said her group had organized the parades, held annually through 1913, because "men and women are moved by seeing marching groups of people and by hearing music far more than by listening to the most careful argument."

Blatch envisioned the parade, a distinctly ceremonial performance, as a bold gesture taking the demand for woman suffrage out of sequestered spaces into the street—using public space to make a public demand for public rights.

Americans were accustomed to seeing men marching boldly in parades as soldiers, members of fraternal organizations, or band members, but not women like their mothers, daughters, and sisters.

"The parades of the woman suffrage movement appropriated this public expression of solidarity—a symbolic form traditionally employed by men to proclaim their collective agency—as a conscious transgression of the rules of social order," Jennifer L. Borda explained in a journal article. "Suffrage women's very presence in the city streets decisively challenged traditional notions of femininity and subsequent restrictions on women's conduct."

A more radical New York

In the woman suffrage procession in Washington, D.C., on March 3, 1913, a crowd surrounds a Red Cross ambulance.

Library of Congress

group, the American Suffragettes, led by Bettina Borrman Wells, also had begun staging open-air meetings and parades. Like the British women, American women were growing bolder.

By the time of the 1913 parade, the *New York Times* of May 4, 1913, noted that women had won significant victories since the previous parade and had the "full franchise" in nine states. Oregon, Kansas, and Arizona had adopted suffrage within the year (following California in 1911). The legislatures of five more states had put forth amendments, and in four more the legislatures had adopted amendments that required reenactment in the next session.

The article said that versus the radical British tactics the "pleasanter methods of the American suffragists have led them on in the twelvemonth from victory to victory."

They too had changed strategies, moving from "indoor tactics to outdoor warfare," the *Times* said.

"You have seen almost the end in most places of the indoor parlor meeting," a suffragist told the reporter at the national association headquarters. "Instead of holding meetings and talking mostly among themselves, the suffragists were taking their message to legislative meetings, party conventions, women's associations, and city clubs, as well as to the streets."

Meanwhile, Carrie Chapman Catt had also seen the British suffrage protestors in action during her travels on behalf of the international suffrage organization. While she remained unconvinced the more militant tactics would work at home, she came home in November 1912 convinced the United States movement could use some new vigor.

That same month, she addressed several large meetings in New York City and attended the forty-fourth annual convention of the National American Woman Suffrage Association in Philadelphia.

In 1910, Alice Paul had attended the NAWSA convention for the first time. At the 1912 convention, Lucy Burns and she reported on the forced feedings in the British prisons that they had experienced firsthand. Paul, a Quaker from Mount Laurel, New Jersey, had gone to England for graduate studies in economics and politics and became a social worker in the slums of London. She joined the radical suffragettes of Britain and like them was arrested, jailed, and force-fed. She met Burns, an American already involved in the protests, while there. Burns had worked as an organizer in Scotland before and had just returned home to the United States in time for the 1912 convention. Paul and Burns approached NAWSA leaders about working on passage of the federal suffrage amendment, and the board appointed them to NAWSA's Congressional Committee. First introduced in 1878 and unchanged, it was still known as

President Woodrow Wilson changed his
opposition to woman suffrage to support.
Library of Congress

the Susan B. Anthony Amendment. It would no longer be the
Sixteenth Amendment, as three
others had been added; now it
was slated to be the nineteenth.
With the help of Jane Addams,
the social reformer and NAWSA
vice president, Paul and Burns
persuaded the organization to
let them organize a parade.

Paul and Burns came to
Washington in January 1913
to work on it, and within two
months, they and a few other
women—Crystal Eastman Ben-

edict, Mary Beard, and Dora
Lewis—had organized the parade of up to eight thousand
women.

To draw attention to the
cause, the parade was to be the
day before Woodrow Wilson's inauguration, when Washington's
population would swell with
many visitors arriving for the
ceremonies for the first Democratic president elected in a
quarter century. The Democrats
had also won control of both
houses of Congress. Wilson sub-

scribed to the notion that the suffragists had long fought, that women should remain in their domestic "sphere." Although he had taught at a women's college, Bryn Mawr, he disdained his students, writing in his diary that "lecturing to young women of the present generation on the history and principles of politics is about as appropriate and profitable as would be lecturing to stone-masons on the evolution of fashion in dress."

He thought women were unfit for voting because, in his view, they let emotion, rather than reason, rule them, and he was on record as opposed to woman suffrage. In 1912, he told an aide that he was "definitely and irreconcilably opposed to woman suffrage; woman's place was in the home, and the type of woman who took an active part in the suffrage agitation was totally abhorrent to him."

Welcoming Wilson

little after three o'clock in the afternoon of March 3, 1913, on horseback, Jane Burleson, the grand marshal, kicked off the parade of thousands. Behind her was Inez Milholland, a Vassar alumna and recent law graduate from New York University. Riding a white horse and wearing a long, flowing white dress, Milholland was a striking figure. Hoisting a huge flag, Carrie Chapman Catt led the first section of the parade in Washington, D.C., followed by units from all over the country, representing homemakers, professionals, collegiate women, states, male supporters, and others. They carried before them a yellow banner with the words WE DEMAND AN AMENDMENT TO THE CONSTITUTION ENFRANCHISING THE WOMEN OF THE COUNTRY.

In spite of the inclusive language, Paul had first tried to exclude black women and then insisted that black women march as a unit in the rear, claiming Southern women would not accept integrated units. Hearing of the plans for a segregated parade, Adella Hunt Logan had stirred up Mary Church Terrell and other black women to take part. The participants that day included members of the Delta Sigma Theta Sorority, then newly formed at Howard University, just weeks after dissolving their affiliation with the Alpha Kappa Alpha Sorority. The crusading journalist Ida B. Wells-Barnett, president of the Alpha Suffrage Club of Chicago,

*A German actress, Hedwiga Reicher, wearing the costume
of "Columbia" as other suffrage pageant participants stand in
the background in front of the Treasury Building,
March 3, 1913, Washington, D.C.*

Library of Congress

had wanted to march with her state unit instead of in the rear with other black women. She pretended to comply but stepped out of the crowd once the march was under way and joined her state unit flanked by white supporters.

All the marchers headed downhill from the U.S. Capitol to make a mile-and-a-half journey down Pennsylvania Avenue to the White House. Women staged a spectacular allegorical pageant simultaneously on the plaza of the Treasury Building. As the women pushed forward, crowds of rowdy, often drunken men heckled and pushed, yelling obscenities, insulting, groping, and yanking banners from them. The throngs pressed against the

WOMAN'S JOURNAL
AND SUFFRAGE NEWS

VOL. XLIV. NO. 10 — SATURDAY, MARCH 8, 1913 — FIVE CENTS

PARADE STRUGGLES TO VICTORY DESPITE DISGRACEFUL SCENES

Nation Aroused by Open Insults to Women—Cause Wins Popular Sympathy—Congress Orders Investigation—Striking Object Lesson

AMENDMENT WINS IN NEW JERSEY

Easy Victory in Assembly 46 to 5—Equal Suffrage Enthusiasm Runs High

MICHIGAN AGAIN CAMPAIGN STATE

Senate Passes Suffrage Amendment 26 to 5 and Battle Is Now On

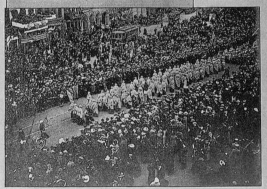

General Rosalie Jones in Pilgrim Costume; Miss Inez Milholland on White Steed Leading the Parade; One of the Scores of Imposing Floats; One View of the Procession.

Front page of the Woman's Journal and Suffrage News *with the headline: "Parade Struggles to Victory Despite Disgraceful Scenes." The parade took place in Washington, D.C., on March 3, 1913.*

Library of Congress

marchers, separating the divisions, and making it impossible to proceed at some points. As many as one hundred to two hundred people were injured. Police had done little to stop the attacks. Finally, the U.S. cavalry charged in from Fort Myer, the army post across the Potomac River near Arlington National Cemetery, to press back the riotous attackers. A Senate investigation of the police role in the fiasco resulted in the suspension of the police chief.

The episode drew widespread coverage, making the parade a public relations success. That experience heightened Catt's interest in the British protest tactics, and she returned to London as the violence had increased. She was determined to study this phenomenon more closely that April, attending meetings, going to jails, attending the gallery of the House of Commons, and observing protests before traveling on to preside over the seventh and last congress of the International Woman Suffrage Alliance before World War I broke out. By the time the alliance met again in 1920, the women of the United States could report that they had won suffrage.

Catt came home inspired but still unconvinced that the British-style militancy would work. The suffrage movement faced challenges and opportunities. A victory came in Illinois, where women gained partial suffrage, the right to vote in presidential races. By 1915, referenda for full suffrage were pending in Pennsylvania, New Jersey, New York, and Massachusetts.

The campaign to win suffrage in New York was in full swing. Victory in New York, with the largest population of any state and the largest representation in Congress, could build the momentum for a national victory. Under Catt's leadership, suffrage societies organized from top to bottom with leaders in each election district under the slogan of "Victory in 1915." One hundred thousand women joined the Woman Suffrage Party in New York City, headed by Mary Garrett Hay.

Another Split

Meanwhile, the NAWSA it-self was in a battle over methods. Alice Paul had been head of the Congressional Committee, which had the job of lobbying Congress for the federal amendment. The committee members now included Paul's friends, but previously its work had consisted of preparing for the annual congressional hearings on the Susan B. Anthony Amendment. Her predecessor had a budget of $10, returned some of it, and reported its activity as one appearance before the Senate Judiciary Committee and a tea given for congressional wives. Paul had formed an organization to support the committee, the Congressional Union for Woman Suffrage, and questions soon arose over money raised for the NAWSA committee but used under auspices of the union. Those questions were never quite resolved. The biggest split, however, was over Paul's insistence on targeting the party in control, the Democrats, in the way the British suffrage movement did to the ruling party, to fight their reelection. The NAWSA leadership insisted that the organization should remain nonpartisan, because it had supporters in both parties. Paul also wanted to direct all the national organization's efforts to the federal amendment, while NAWSA leaders thought they still needed to win some major state contests. The NAWSA also supported a new, weakened federal amendment that would make it easier to call for state referenda but still require a pro-tracted state-by-state offensive. Paul refused to acquiesce, and the two groups split. The NAWSA had hoped to retain Paul and Burns for their organizing talent and to rein them in.

Alice Paul had led a delegation of women to meet with Woodrow Wilson in the White House shortly after his first inauguration. He had been non-committal on suffrage, using the excuse that no one had ever brought it to his attention and so he did not know where he stood. Paul's organization began sending delegations of women to the White House, representing various constituencies—collegiate women, New Jersey women, working women, and others—to meet with the president or his secretary, Joseph Tumulty. The White House received them po-litely and gave them nothing.

Paul's organization under-took other attention-getting actions, including a cross-country caravan of suffragists to deliver a petition with a million signa-tures to Congress and the un-furling of a banner demanding suffrage during Wilson's second inaugural speech. They raised thousands of dollars and started a newspaper, the *Suffragist*. Paul wrote editorials, hired a cartoonist to mock Wilson, and dispatched women to sell the newspaper on the street as major dailies did. Their efforts did not move Wilson on the issue.

No suffrage amendment had made it out of a congressional committee since 1896. The Senate had last voted one down in 1887. The House had never voted on it.

Women's suffrage had few friends in Congress and no enthusiastic champions. The suffrage movement was simply still not a popular one. The same attitudes espoused by oppo-nents for a half century—that women were happiest in the home and men were happiest if they stayed there, that women were disinterested in voting and unfit to do so—still prevailed among the vast majority of men and possibly most women, as the antisuffragist elements claimed. Moreover, the powerful lobbies

*Julia Emory and Bertha Graf, with luggage and flags,
leave Washington, D.C., for a suffrage demonstration
at the home of Warren Harding in Marion, Ohio.*
Library of Congress

of liquor and big business were more resistant than ever, and the specter of huge numbers of women added to the electorate discouraged political powers from taking up the cause. Southerners especially still did not want to see black women added to those numbers.

Northern political machines did not want a new voting bloc that might attack vested interests. Women might vote for things like tougher child-labor laws, better working conditions, and prohibition.

The NAWSA continued working with state organiza-

tions to pass amendments at
that level.

The New York amendment
was defeated in 1915, as were
initiatives in Massachusetts,
New Jersey, and Pennsylvania,

but leaders vowed to try again,
especially in New York in 1917.

Not long after the 1915 election, Dr. Shaw announced plans
to retire as NAWSA president,
tired of the administrative work

Members of the Congressional Union for Woman Suffrage
gather outside its National Summer Headquarters
at 128 Bellevue Avenue, Newport, Rhode Island.
Library of Congress

that was never her forte, but she was willing to continue lending her oratorical skill to the cause. The national convention that December drafted Catt to replace her, and Catt accepted reluctantly. The organization also rescinded support for the new amendment in favor of the original Susan B. Anthony Amendment.

Alice Paul formed the National Woman's Party in 1916 to fight for women's suffrage nationally. It worked to defeat Wilson for reelection and Democratic congressional candidates, even supporters of suffrage.

★ *Alice Paul* ★

Alice Paul was born January 11, 1885, into a prominent Quaker family from Mount Laurel, New Jersey. Her parents were William Mickle Paul and Tacie Parry Paul, and she was a descendant of William Penn, the founder of Pennsylvania.

Paul was brilliant, aloof, and well educated. She studied at Swarthmore College, where her mother's relatives had been among the founders, then went on to earn a master's and a doctoral degree in sociology from the University of Pennsylvania. After laboring as a social worker among the poor in New York City, she moved to England to study economics and politics at the Woodbrooke Quaker Study Centre and the London School of Economics (and later earned law degrees from American University's Washington College of Law). She worked in a Quaker settlement house in Birmingham and then in the slums of London.

While in Britain she joined the women's movement and became one of its most militant activists. She came home and became active in the National American Woman Suffrage Association. With her friend Lucy Burns, she helped organize a major parade to greet Woodrow Wilson before his inaugural.

Alice Paul, chairman, and officers of the National Woman's Party in front of its Washington headquarters before leaving for the Republican Party Convention in Chicago. From left: Sue White of Nashville, Tennessee; Benigna Green Kalb of Houston, Texas; Jas Rector of Columbus, Ohio; Mary Dubrow of New Jersey; Alice Paul of Washington, D.C.; and Elizabeth Kalb of Texas.

Library of Congress

Lucy Burns, shown in 1913, was the organizer behind many of Alice Paul's activities.

Library of Congress

tional Woman's Party, which began a relentless campaign of silent picketing outside the White House gates. After the 1920 suffrage victory, Paul went to law school to learn more about women's rights and their legal deprivations. She wrote the Equal Rights Amendment in 1923 and began working for its passage. Most of her supporters faded away to other causes and private pursuits. She later revised the amendment and was still alive in 1972, when the ERA was passed by both houses in Congress and submitted to the state legislatures for ratification. She worked to get the states to ratify it, and she enjoyed a period of rediscovery by feminists and the media. Alice Paul died July 9, 1977, without seeing the outcome. Only thirty-five states voted to ratify the ERA, three short of the necessary thirty-eight needed before the 1982 deadline.

Onlookers bombarded the women until the U.S. cavalry came to restore order. Paul and Burns soon broke with the NAWSA in a dispute over use of funds and tactics. Paul founded the Congressional Union for Woman Suffrage and then the Na-

"The Winning Plan"

eanwhile, the NAWSA tried to get both parties to add a suffrage plank to their platforms in 1916. The association organized a huge parade outside the Republican convention in Chicago on June 7, where thousands of women marched through a rainstorm. They poured into the convention halls drenched but in high spirits, just as an antisuffrage speaker was making the charge that women didn't want to vote.

Later that month, six thousand suffragists in white dresses with yellow sashes and yellow parasols lined the Democratic delegates' route into their meeting hall. Both parties adopted planks. The Republicans watered theirs down with a states' rights provision, at the urging of antisuffrage delegates led by Senator Henry Cabot Lodge of Massachusetts, whose concern was that women would oppose preparations for war then under way. The Democrats weakened theirs with support for extending suffrage only by state action. Catt complained that while the Democrats were under pressure to put something about woman suffrage in the platform, "they thought to hoodwink the women with a jumble of words."

Catt called an emergency convention of the NAWSA for September 1916 in Atlantic City, where she addressed the body on the odds they faced and reiterated the grueling difficulty of winning suffrage state by state, a task made more difficult by the fraud they had witnessed. She told them this was "the woman's hour," but seizing it would demand immediate, uncompromising, unrelenting effort in all forty-eight states to win as many referenda as possible and lay the groundwork to win ratification of a federal amendment by the states if Congress submitted it.

To the executive council (the national officers and state presidents), she laid out what became known as "the Winning Plan." They were to direct every resource toward the plan, and begin work immediately.

- States where women already had suffrage would get their legislatures to send resolutions to Congress asking for a federal amendment.
- States that stood a chance of getting an amendment through would push for a referendum. If one were already scheduled in 1916 or 1917, members in those states would work to win the popular vote.
- Other states would push their legislatures to adopt

suffrage to the greatest extent possible, preferably for presidential races.
- Southern states should seek woman suffrage in primary elections.

Catt insisted on complete authority for the NAWSA board to act, cooperation from everyone, and support from at least thirty-six state affiliates pledged to the plan. She asked them to sign a compact, and they did, but the plan was to remain their secret. She had also asked the convention for one million dollars for the year's work and got $818,000 in pledges on the spot (about $18 million in 2016 dollars, according to the Bureau of Labor Statistics calculator, bls.gov).

On its final night in session and in the middle of his reelection campaign, President Wilson addressed the NAWSA convention. Women wearing blue-and-gold sashes and holding banners with their states' names and suffrage flags lined his way to the stage. Wilson's position on suffrage had been shifting from outright opposition and derision to resignation that he could not act unless Congress did, nor intervene to urge its committees to act. In October 1915, he announced he would go home to Princeton, New Jersey, to vote in favor of the state referendum. As the former governor of New Jersey and former president of Princeton University, he was making a strong statement by his actions.

His remarks at the women's convention seemed to signal that victory for woman suffrage by federal action was inevitable, as "the movement was coming to a full tide," and his remarks were complimentary. However, he did not clearly endorse the federal amendment, nor did he make any promise that he would.

"I have not come to ask you to be patient, because you have been," said Wilson, "but I have come to congratulate you that there was a force behind you that will...be triumphant and for which you can afford a little while to wait."

At Catt's request, Dr. Shaw responded on behalf of the organization, telling him pointedly, "We have waited long enough for the vote. We want it now."

Turning to look at him, she said, "And we want it to come in your administration."

The president smiled, bowed, and said nothing before departing the stage. The audience rose and women waved handkerchiefs in a traditional suffragist salute.

The women were not the only people tired of waiting. That fall, W. E. B. Du Bois wrote an open letter to Wilson in the NAACP official publication, the *Crisis*, to express disappointment over his racial policies. He reminded the president that he and other leaders had worked hard to direct black votes to him because they felt the Republican Party had failed them. Upon taking office, Wilson promptly segregated government offices and enforced strict segregation in Washington. "We have waited for some time to gather from your writings and speeches something of your present attitude toward colored people," Du Bois wrote.

Du Bois, a strong supporter of woman suffrage, added, "A republic must be based on universal suffrage, or it is not a republic; and yet, while you seem anxious to do justice toward women, we scarcely hear a word concerning those disenfranchised masses of the South."

"War Work"

Wilson won reelection in November 1916, despite the National Woman's Party's efforts, on a slogan of "He kept us out of war." Now the United States was about to be drawn into World War I, and he was advocating "preparedness."

Carrie Chapman Catt was a pacifist who pondered what role the NAWSA should play in the war, but called a meeting of her executive council to discuss it. The council ultimately agreed to pledge the organization to whatever "war work" women could undertake, if the nation declared war. In a letter to Wilson, they pledged loyalty to the nation and offered to coordinate women's efforts. Unlike the women's rights advocates during the Civil War, they did not agree to set aside their work for suffrage. Dr. Shaw chaired the Women's Committee of the Council of National Defense, while Catt primarily stuck to carrying out the Winning Plan for suffrage. The National Woman's Party, dominated by Quakers devoted to pacifist principles, did not pledge to take a role or work as a group to aid the war effort.

In fact, as the NAWSA was gearing up for its final offensive, the NWP had begun its own.

The party organized a card file on lawmakers to raise lobbying efforts to new heights, and Paul set up headquarters across Lafayette Park where its flag was visible from the White House.

In early January 1917, representatives of the NWP began

showing up outside the White House gates daily, standing, no matter the weather, as silent pickets holding various suffrage signs: MR. PRESIDENT, WHAT WILL YOU DO FOR WOMAN SUFFRAGE? and HOW LONG MUST WOMEN WAIT FOR LIBERTY? On Inauguration Day, March 4, the silent pickets circled the White House. Picketing the White House was unheard of, but at first officials ignored the demonstrations. Crowds gathered but were generally just curious or even sympathetic. President Wilson would tip his hat as he came and went through the gates.

The Congresswoman
Votes "No"

Wilson asked Congress to declare war, and it met in special session to consider it on April 2, 1917. The Senate adopted the war resolution on April 4, and the House followed on April 6.

The election in 1916 was important for another reason. Jeannette Pickering Rankin of Montana, a NAWSA lobbyist who had been instrumental in securing woman suffrage in her home state two years earlier, won election to Congress. She took her seat on April 2, 1917, and cast her vote four days later as one of fifty against the war resolution. "I want to stand for my country, but I cannot vote for war," she said. "I vote no."

To welcome her to Congress, the NAWSA and the NWP collaborated to give her a luncheon earlier that day, with Catt seated on one side of her and Paul on the other. Two hundred women dined with her at the Shoreham Hotel. The NAWSA had opened an impressive new headquarters in Washington in December 1916, and Rankin was staying in one of its several guest rooms. After the lunch, she went to the headquarters to deliver a speech from a balcony. Suffragists accompanied her in a motorcade to the House office building, and a delegation escorted her to the Capitol.

After her vote against the resolution, Rankin faced tremendous criticism, unlike the forty-nine men who voted with her, but she defended her position. She served in the House from 1917 to 1919 and again from 1941 to 1942, and she voted against entry into World War II as well. A pacifist, she was the only member of Congress to vote against entering both world wars.

Jail and Hunger Strikes

After the war declaration, Alice Paul's picketers began to include signs that offended onlookers caught up in the patriotic, prowar spirit. Mobs attacked them for holding signs calling the president "Kaiser Wilson" and suggesting the nation was a democracy in name only (DEMOCRACY SHOULD BEGIN AT HOME) because it did not allow women to vote. On June 20, as the White House received a Russian delegation, signs appealed to the Russians to help make American women free. Plainclothesmen tore down their banners, and mobs attacked the pickets. The District chief of police visited Paul at her party headquarters to warn that police would arrest them if they insisted on picketing. Paul insisted their picketing was legal.

On June 22, 1917, a mob attacked the pickets and police began arresting the women on charges of obstructing the sidewalks. No one arrested the attackers. Initially, the officials dismissed the women without sentence, and they continued their demonstrations. More arrests followed, and the courts began to sentence women to a few days, then weeks, then months in jail. Police arrested 218 women that year, and 97 went to prison in the D.C. jail or the Occoquan Workhouse in northern Virginia. Some of the women went on hunger strikes. When officials began force-feeding them, as the British authorities had done to demonstrators there, the resulting publicity increased the women's notoriety and made them martyrs.

The brutal process described by Paul after her British experiences called for prison officials to restrain the women as a doctor inserted a tube through their nostrils and shoved it down into their stomachs, often requiring repeated attempts as the women gagged. Then the jailers poured milk and liquefied food down the tubes.

The jailed women included respected professionals and wives and daughters of wealthy people, and Wilson's supporters warned him of the consequences of the publicity.

Denied basic civil liberties, the jailed women lived in horrendous conditions.

Women who weren't in jail continued picketing. Those jailed returned to the lines as soon as jailers released them. When they continued picketing, police arrested them again.

The authorities rearrested Paul in October 1917, and denied her a jury trial and counsel. Jailers treated her harshly and sent her off to a psychiatric ward. She was in danger of being sent to a psychiatric hospital, where she could be detained indefinitely.

"Night of Terror"

A group of women, including Paul's associate Lucy Burns and Dorothy Day, the social reformer, were arrested on November 14–15, 1917, and sent to the Occoquan Workhouse, where guards subjected them to various tortures, assaults, threats, and atrocities during what they called the Night of Terror. Jailers dragged them, handcuffed some to bars, pummeled them, and hurled them into cells. All of them went on a hunger strike and endured the horrid forced feedings. News of the horrors and maltreatment leaked to the press, and protests poured into the Congress and the White House.

Wilson at first defended the arrests and washed his hands of them by saying he had no juris- diction over public gatherings or obstruction of sidewalks. He accepted assurances from District commissioners that the treatment of the women was not out of line and that they were merely publicity seekers.

Then, suddenly, on November 27, a week before Congress was to reconvene, Wilson pardoned all the jailed women. Paul went back to work, asking her fellow prisoners to write affidavits about their experiences, as she planned to demand an investigation. After their release, Paul staged a ceremony where she gave each a "jail pin" in the shape of a prison door with a chain across it and a heart-shaped padlock. Paul also organized a national train tour of the "Suffrage Prison Squad," featuring women in jail uniforms. A few months later, the D.C. Court of Appeals invalidated the arrests and prison sentences of all of the women.

The prison episode had inspired some women to join Paul's party, while others were appalled at the radical tactics, including the NAWSA. It made every effort to distance itself from the National Woman's Party, courted Wilson's favor, and kept silent about the abuses of the sister suffragists. The NAWSA had done nothing to seek their release and complimented Wilson on his handling of the situation. Still, he refused to act on women's suffrage and did not mention it in his recommendations to Congress when it reconvened in December of that year.

New York
Victory in 1917

Suffragists received good news that November as New York finally passed a suffrage amendment, after the Tammany Hall Democratic political machine decided not to make any effort to stop it. The Democrats calculated that votes for women, including their own mothers, wives, sisters, and daughters, could add to their own voting strength. In spite of the optimism in 1915, suffragists initially had found it difficult to persuade the legislature to put the referendum on the ballot, and it stayed bottled up in committee. The women leaned on the lawmakers, intimating that they now had the clout in Washington to block any ambitions holdouts might have to federal office. The measure passed the legislature.

Carrie Chapman Catt spoke of the amendment as a war measure in the way the Emancipation Proclamation had been, arguing that women's votes were necessary to prevent such wars. The treasurer of the New York State Woman Suffrage Party (NYSWSP), Helen Rogers Reid, wife of the publisher of the *New York Herald*, and Vira Boarman Whitehouse, the chairman of the NYSWSP, set a fund-raising goal of a half million dollars for the New York campaign.

Catt personally had earlier received an unexpected bequest of $2 million from Mrs. Frank Leslie, as she was known (Miriam Florence Follin Squier Leslie), who had taken over her husband's failing newspaper, then known as *Frank Leslie's*

Illustrated Newspaper, and made a fortune. Catt knew Mrs. Leslie socially but had spoken to her at length only once. It took Catt years to fight off attempts to break the will that whittled down the estate. She began receiving some of the money in 1917. Catt gave Whitehouse $10,000 for the state campaign and Mary Garrett Hay $15,000 for work in New York City.

New York suffragists collected more than a million signatures on petitions appealing for the vote and displayed them in the last major suffrage parade in New York on October 27, 1917, in which twenty thousand women marched up Fifth Avenue from Washington Square to Sixty-Second Street in a three-hour-long procession. They marched in divisions: farmers, factory workers, doctors, nurses, social workers, teachers, artists, writers, and so on.

Before Election Day on November 6, the suffragists learned of the Tammany Hall pledge to keep hands-off, responding to appeals from members with wives and other relatives who were workers in the Woman Suffrage Party. Suffrage leaders waited for returns at New York headquarters. The first inkling of victory came from returns showing woman suffrage was carrying every borough in the city. When final confirmation came before midnight that it had won across the state, shouts of joy went up.

Victories had also come that year in North Dakota (presidential and primary suffrage) and Ohio, Indiana, and Arkansas (primary suffrage). Rhode Island, Nebraska, and Michigan also passed presidential suffrage.

The tide seemed to be turning, probably for a variety of reasons. The softening stance of the political machine in its own self-interest was a major factor in New York. There and elsewhere, some men voted out of prejudice, expressing the sentiment that their wives and female kinfolk deserved the vote at least as much as black and immigrant men. During World War I, thousands of women took up jobs men had held, and men became conditioned to seeing women as equals. The emboldening of women because of their greater workforce participation and increased educational opportunities was another force at work. More men probably had to hear suffrage arguments in their own homes.

The fact that the women's organizations were better financed than ever and finally organized behind specific, sound strategies went a long way toward explaining their successes. This gave them a fighting chance against the well-heeled lobbies of liquor and other industries. The spectacle of the parades after years of relying on intellectual argument, as well as the two-pronged "good cop versus bad cop" approaches of the traditional suffragists and the more radical activists, no doubt was somewhat effective in changing public opinion. Finally, the sight of white middle- and upper-class American women being dragged off to jail and reports of them being tortured began to wear on the consciences of some lawmakers and provoke outrage among women and men alike. Others were appalled that the pickets were attacking a president in time of war, but both factions gained followers during this period. The NAWSA's solid, nationwide organization had two million members, compared to an estimated ten thousand in the more fluid National Woman's Party, and growing numbers of women seemed to identify with the suffrage aims in general.

A Vote in Congress

President Woodrow Wilson had signaled his evolving position when he voted for the New Jersey referendum in 1915 and in his remarks at the Atlantic City convention in 1916. Carrie Chapman Catt continued to court his favor for the suffrage cause and stayed in close communication with him, often bombarding him with facts about the difficulties of gaining suffrage state by state. She seemed to follow the adage "Keep your friends close and your enemies closer." In fact, Catt turned an enemy into an ally. Her ability to deliver women's loyalty and hard work during World War I no doubt impressed him and won favor.

Alice Paul's faction, of course, had done its part to confront him with consciousness-raising tactics, and the horrific reports of how she and her followers were treated in jail may have worn him down or seeped into his conscience. At one point, he had sent his own emissary to investigate the conditions where they were detained, and the District of Columbia officials briefed him regularly. Both suffrage factions took credit for the president's reversal on this issue. Wilson also was one of those men who probably endured suffragist rhetoric at home. At least one of his three daughters, Jessie Woodrow Wilson Sayre, was active in the movement.

Beth A. Behn, in her 2012 dissertation, "Woodrow Wilson's Conversion Experience," argued that he was most persuaded by the steady work of the NAWSA to build a case for suffrage and create a climate in which it could win passage. Catt's organization "was decisive in Wilson's conversion to the cause of the federal amendment because its approach mirrored his own conservative vision of the appropriate method of reform: win a broad consensus, develop a legitimate rationale, and make the issue politically valuable."

Whatever the reason, he seems to have concluded that it was an idea whose time had come, and that it might be a winnable cause. With women winning the vote in more states, more congressional representatives came from states where women already had the vote. They were part of the electorate that would decide which party remained in power.

"Not out of a sense of justice or any wholesale feminist conversion, but out of knowledge of political reality, Wilson came to support the federal amendment. The degree to which he grew to personally regard women as deserving members of the franchise is difficult to discern," Behn concluded.

She pointed out that previous historians had done little analysis of his reasons for supporting the amendment and had devoted little if any of their accounts of his presidency to his accomplishments in enfranchising women.

"Sadly, one could browse through shelves of monographs on Wilson's foreign and domestic policy and not realize that one-half of the nation's population gained the right to vote during his administration. The presence of an organized suffrage movement of more than two million women, not to mention more than 700,000 organized anti-suffragists, is notably absent from these accounts," Behn said.

This is part of a pattern in which women's history and women individually are ignored in histories primarily written by men.

In September 1917, the U.S. Senate Committee on Woman Suffrage favorably reported out the amendment, and the House formed a similar committee for the first time. In December, the House of Representatives scheduled a vote on suffrage for January 10, 1918. The day before the vote, Wilson declared his support to the committee chair and encouraged members to vote for it, citing women's service during the war still in progress. He told a delegation of Democratic representatives that although he believed state-by-state action was the proper course, "all the conditions under which we are living have changed, and the world is a different place."

Representative Jeannette Rankin opened the debate on the measure to send the amendment to the states for ratification. It passed 274 to 136, with exactly the two-thirds majority required, after four supporters left their sickbeds to vote. One of them was carried in a stretcher, and another member left his wife's deathbed to be there.

With the House vote in hand, suffragists assumed the Senate vote could not be far behind, but it would be nine months before that body took it up for a vote.

More Delays, More Arrests

Despite Wilson's apparent change of heart, he did not publicly declare support for the amendment immediately, and some suffragists doubted that his conversion was sincere. Displeased with his efforts, Paul returned with her forces to picketing the White House in the summer of 1918, taking more strident actions, including setting bonfires outside the White House gates. This drew more arrests and more publicity. Paul was rearrested twice but "temporarily" released before she would need force-feeding.

The amendment remained stalled in the Senate, but opponents suddenly cleared the way for consideration, confident it would lose. On September 30, 1918, on the eve of the vote in the Senate, Wilson took the unusual step of appearing before the Senate to urge passage. He asked the lawmakers to adopt suffrage as a necessary war measure. The president declared that the amendment was "vital to winning the war" and to setting an example as a democracy. Women in twenty-six countries, including Russia, Germany, and England, had gained the right to vote, most of them within the previous two years.

Wilson also asked the senators to reward women's sacrifices in the war.

We have made partners of the women in this war; shall we admit them only to a partnership of suffering and sacrifice and toil and

*not to a partnership of priv-
ilege and right? This war
could not have been fought,
either by the other nations
engaged or by America,
if it had not been for the
services of the women—
services rendered in every
sphere—not merely in the
fields of effort in which we
have been accustomed to
see them work, but wherever
men have worked and upon
the very skirts and edges of
the battle itself.*

Nevertheless, the following
day, the Senate rejected the
amendment 62 to 34, two votes
short of the necessary two-
thirds.

Disappointed but freshly
motivated, the NAWSA immediately made plans to work against
the reelection of its enemies,
as it had vowed in its last convention. Two powerful senators
lost their elections in November 1918, enough to shift the
winning margin. A prosuffrage
senator had also been appointed
to fill the seat of a deceased

opponent, Ben Tillman of South
Carolina.

Opponents blocked efforts
to have the Senate debate the
amendment and vote in a lame-
duck session of Congress after
the election. World War I had
ended with the armistice of November 11, 1918, and suffragists
feared losing momentum in the
postwar era.

Wilson called a special session of the new Congress for
May 20, 1919. While attending
the Peace Conference in Paris, he
cabled an address to Congress,
again recommending passage.
The House passed it May 21—304
to 89, with 42 more than the
two-thirds needed. The Senate
debated for two days, with opponents doing most of the talking,
with a final vote on June 4 of 56
to 25 (out of a possible 96 votes
from the forty-eight states then
in the nation).

When he had appealed to the
Senate the previous year, Wilson credited women's sacrifices
in the war, giving support to
the idea that the NAWSA's loyal
stand had carried the day. How-

ever, many believe that the less ladylike tactics of Alice Paul and her National Woman's Party had politicized the issue and forced Wilson's hand. He rejected the notion that the "voices of the foolish and intemperate agitators" had swayed him. As the efforts were simultaneous, it is hard to say if one way would have won without the other. However, the NAWSA would now take the lead to win ratification. Paul also traveled to states to work in the ratification efforts.

Dr. Anna Howard Shaw welcomed the victory but would not see ratification. She died July 2, 1919.

Battle for Tennessee

Ratification required victory in the legislatures of thirty-six states. The suffragists would no longer have to persuade a majority of the male voting population, just a relatively small group of men whom they could easily identify and to whom they could appeal directly.

The first state votes came within a week of the Senate vote. Wisconsin was the first to file its ratification resolution with the U.S. secretary of state. Illinois came second, Michigan third. Then, the pace slowed and ratifications drifted in through the next spring. Some governors were reluctant to call special sessions of their legislatures to consider the amendment, citing costs or legal arguments. When it appeared that Tennessee was the last hope for ratification in time for the 1920 election, President Wilson prevailed upon its governor to call a special session.

Lobbyists from all manner of opposition forces, including well-organized women's anti-suffrage groups, and from all over the country, including the National Association Opposed to Woman Suffrage, the American Constitutional League, and the Southern Women's Rejection League, took up residence in Nashville. The "anti" groups were closely aligned with and sometimes actually married to the old enemies of women's suffrage—liquor, railroad, and business interests. They threatened the governor with defeat in the next election if he called a special session, and the pro-suffrage forces threatened him if he didn't. The antisuffrage leaders sent out appeals to women across Tennessee to give them moral support, warning that the Nineteenth Amendment would lead to "surrender of state sovereignty, Negro woman suffrage and race equality." They brought in antisuffrage leaders from around the country, wrote letters to the newspapers, and buttonholed lawmakers at garden parties, as well as at the capitol.

Catt and other NAWSA leaders and the National Woman's Party, represented by Sue White, crisscrossed the state, holding rallies, issuing press releases, and polling legislators on their intentions. Alice Paul asked the NAACP in Tennessee for help winning over legislators. Leaders reminded her of her treatment of blacks but gave aid by urging black male voters to lobby lawmakers.

The suffragists made the Hermitage Hotel their headquarters, as did their opponents. Supporters they had counted on began to backslide under a barrage of threats and bribes. Lobbyists plied lawmakers with liquor, and suffragists hoping to talk to them one last time found most of them drunk the night before the vote.

The next morning, antisuffragists passed out red roses for their supporters to wear, and the prosuffragists passed out yellow roses.

The Senate convened and voted 25 to 4 in favor. Action in the House met with one postponement after another, and the suffragists were uncertain of how many votes they had. They despaired of predicting the outcome. An unexpected tie on a motion to table allowed the amendment to come up, after Representative Banks Turner, a friend of the governor's, sided with the women. When the clerk called the roll, they still did not know how Turner would vote on the amendment itself. Before his name came up, it was Harry T. Burn's turn. Leaders in his district in McMinn County in southeast Tennessee opposed ratification, but he had said he would vote for it if women needed his vote. When his name came up, he voted yes.

 He had received a letter that morning from his widowed mother, Febb Ensminger Burn of Niota, Tennessee, an educated woman who had quietly supported woman suffrage. She had urged him to "be a good boy" by voting for suffrage. Turner also voted for it, and it carried, 49 to 47. Further attempts to undo the vote or prevent its certification failed. The governor of Tennessee signed it and sent the certification to Washington by train.

★ *The League of Women Voters* ★

As victory for the Nineteenth Amendment seemed imminent in early 1919, suffragists held a "Jubilee Convention" to celebrate the fiftieth anniversaries of the National and the American Woman Suffrage Associations and of the woman suffrage victory in Wyoming.

Disappointed that the goal of winning a federal suffrage amendment had eluded them, they were still confident that victory was at hand.

When the Jubilee Convention convened on March 24, 1919, in St. Louis, Carrie Chapman Catt unveiled a plan to dissolve the National American Woman Suffrage Association and form a League of Women Voters. The NAWSA executive council passed a resolution to create it.

In October 1919, Catt went on a "Wake Up America" tour to push for ratification of the Susan B. Anthony Amendment and to explain the concept for the league. Several committee heads for the new organization accompanied her.

Catt's vision was that once the ballot was secured for legions of women, the suffragists would continue to be a force for reform, working for extension of women's rights, good government, and other issues.

The NAWSA claimed a membership of two million women, and by 1919, seven million women in fifteen states had secured full or partial voting rights. If the federal amendment passed, twenty-seven million women would have full voting rights. As Catt's biographer, Jacqueline Van Voris, put it, this would be "the largest extension of the franchise by a government not in the throes of a revolution."

In a way, this was a revolution. Opponents of suffrage for women had argued that they were ill prepared to use the vote wisely, and Catt had seen for herself that women in the suffrage movement often lacked basic information about parliamentary or legislative procedures. Early women's rights advocates had been hampered by a lack of experience at even attending meetings,

let alone addressing them, and the suffrage movement had long suffered from lack of organization and divisiveness.

Catt was the consummate organizer, and among her first acts as a suffrage leader had been to set up mechanisms to educate and train workers in the movement in political science.

She intended the League to work for "the education of women citizens, piloting them through the first years of political participation, and removing relics of discrimination against women." She thought that its work might be accomplished quickly and that it could dissolve as the NAWSA would, but that its leaders might find it worth perpetuating. The League remained a part of the NAWSA for a year, and then was formally organized in 1920 at a "Victory Convention" in Chicago, February 12–18.

Catt explained that the

new organization would "be allied with and support no party" but its members would be encouraged to register to vote and work within the parties of their choice. She declined the presidency, and the convention elected Maud Wood Park, a Bostonian who had organized college women to support the suffrage amendment, to lead the new organization. Now the League could stand on its own as a nonpartisan activist organization that educated citizens about government and social reform and lobbied government on issues. Nearly a century later, the League works in fifty state organizations and seven hundred communities to provide information to voters.

"The Last Step"

Not long after it reached him early on the morning of August 26, 1920, Secretary of State Bainbridge Colby issued a proclamation making the Nineteenth Amendment, Susan B. Anthony's amendment, part of the Constitution. He acted quickly after verifying with legal counsel that everything was in proper order, because antisuffrage forces were still looking for ways to block or delay it. None of the women's leaders was there to witness the signing, but when Catt called to see if the certification had arrived that day, the secretary invited her and others to see it.

"So quietly as that, we learned that the last step in the enfranchisement of women in the United States had been taken and the struggle of more than seventy years brought to a successful end," Catt recalled.

On August 26, 2016—Women's Equality Day—the city of Nashville unveiled a monument featuring five women who were instrumental in the struggle for woman suffrage in Tennessee. They are Anne Dallas Dudley of Nashville; Abby Crawford Milton of Chattanooga; J. Frankie Pierce of Nashville; Sue Shelton White of Jackson; and Carrie Chapman Catt, the NAWSA president. The Tennessee Woman Suffrage Monument organization commissioned the sculpture by Alan LeQuire of Nashville.

Two more states ratified after the amendment was adopted. Ten states, mostly Southern and border states, did not ratify:

*This stamp commemorates
the woman suffrage amendment.*
United States Postal Service

Delaware, Virginia, Maryland, North Carolina, South Carolina, Georgia, Alabama, Louisiana, Mississippi, and Florida. In the Southern states, most black women, like black men, would still face impediments to voting well through the 1960s, but it did not stop them from trying.

It had been seventy years since the first National Woman's Rights Convention was held, seventy-two years since the meeting at Seneca Falls, and the leaders of the movement then probably could not have predicted how long it would take, nor how bitter the contest would be. The early twentieth-century years had been chaotic ones for the movement, requiring iron will and dogged determination to reach victory.

"Hundreds of women gave the accumulated possibilities of an entire lifetime, thousands gave years of their lives, hundreds of thousands gave constant interest, and such aid as they could. It was a continuous, seemingly endless chain of activity," Carrie Chapman Catt wrote later. "Young suffragists who helped forge the last links of that chain were not born when it began. Old suffragists who forged the first links were dead when it ended."

★ *Equal Rights Amendment* ★

Under the headline WAIT, WOMEN DON'T HAVE EQUAL RIGHTS IN THE UNITED STATES? in 2014, Tabby Biddle, an author and women's rights advocate, wrote:

> I'm part of Generation X—the generation where girls and young women were taught that we could be anything, do anything and, if we worked hard enough, could have it all.
>
> We saw women go into space, run for Congress, be appointed to the Supreme Court, anchor the news, break Olympic records, be "bionic" women, lead billion dollar companies, become successful lawyers, doctors, writers, journalists, artists and rock the world with their music and dance.
>
> I, like many of the young women of my generation, assumed that we had equal rights with men under the law of our Constitution. We lived in the United States of America, the strongest democracy in the world. Why wouldn't we?

Why indeed?

Alice Paul wrote an Equal Rights Amendment with fellow suffragist Crystal Eastman, a lawyer, in 1923, three years after passage of the Nineteenth Amendment.

Her goal was to grant women equality in everything "the government could touch." While she pushed for it, her supporters had mostly moved on, or as she put it, "Everybody just went back to their respective homes" after the Nineteenth Amendment ratification.

The ERA was reintroduced in Congress in every session for nearly fifty years with no success. No hearings were held on it in that time. Supporters had been trying to get any action on it in Congress ever since 1923, with the biggest push in the 1970s and early 1980s. Without it, the Constitution provides no guarantee that the rights of all citizens are protected regardless of sex.

The U.S. House of Representatives approved the ERA, voting 354 to 23, after it was introduced by Representative Martha Griffiths of Michigan on October 12, 1971. Senator Birch Bayh of Indiana introduced it in the Senate, and it passed 84 to 8 on March 22, 1972, sending it to the states for ratification.

The amendment said:

> Equality of rights under the law shall not be denied or abridged by the United States or by any State on account of sex.

Congress set a ratification deadline of March 22, 1979. States began ratifying it almost immediately, and by the end of 1977, thirty-five of the needed thirty-eight states had done so. The amendment seemed well on its way to be-coming part of the Constitution with little opposition. Then, five states rescinded their ratifications before the 1979 deadline. In 1978, Congress extended the deadline to June 30, 1982, but no more states ratified, killing the amendment.

Biddle said she discovered "I was not alone in assuming my equal rights. According to the Equal Rights Coalition, 96 percent of Americans think the Equal Rights Amendment (ERA) has passed."

Perhaps that is because the logic that women's rights should be protected seems so clear and because the last great battle for the ERA loomed so large in our collective memories. Advocates lobbied, petitioned, demonstrated, held rallies, and even went on hunger strikes like their sisters in the suffrage movement. Some wore ERA bracelets, vowing to wear them until the amendment won ratification. (It was a takeoff on the then-popular prisoner-of-war bracelets, which people were meant to wear until the soldiers named on them came home.)

Supporters who lived through it recall that the opposition was formidable, especially from women who rose up against the amendment, the same way the anti-suffragists organized to fight the suffrage amendment. Led by the infamous Phyllis Schlafly, they used arguments that were eerily similar. Schlafly organized the "STOP ERA" campaign. STOP stood for "Stop Taking Our Privileges."

Among the arguments used by its supporters were that women would lose benefits under their husband's Social Security, separate restrooms for males and females, and exemption from the military draft. Divorced women would lose rights to alimony and custody of their children, they argued.

Although feminists at the time were dismissive of the opposing arguments and defended the ERA as a question of justice and fairness, the anti-ERA arguments were persuasive to many conservatives and evangelical Christians.

The amendment has continued to be reintroduced in each session of Congress.

Pantsuit Nation

In the final days of the 2016 election for president of the United States, a social media phenomenon allowed women to air their stories about past discrimination, personal triumphs, and angst over the presidential race. Its stated purpose was to celebrate Hillary Rodham Clinton, the Democratic nominee. It was an invitation-only "secret" Facebook page called Pantsuit Nation, a reference to her signature fashion choice, and many women used it to post pictures of themselves in pantsuits like hers. A former college classmate and fellow journalist invited me to the page.

The founder of the group, Libby Chamberlain, told the *New York Times* that on Election Day, members were posting their pantsuit pictures at the rate of twenty thousand a minute.

The next day, after Hillary Clinton's defeat for the presidency, the mood was decidedly more somber. Some women posted pictures of themselves wearing mournful black pantsuits.

A young woman wrote, "I'm 18 and cast my first vote ever for HRC. When I met Hillary, I shared with her my goal to run for public office. Last night I attended Hillary Clinton's official election night event. The glass ceiling was so close we could almost touch it. You are all so brave and bold. I know we will break the glass ceiling soon. I'm going to run for office and be part of it."

In the three weeks after the page started, 2.5 million people

House Speaker Nancy Pelosi addressed the Democratic National Convention in Denver, Colorado, in August 2008.

(Photo by Carol M. Highsmith) Library of Congress

had joined, and many donated to the Clinton campaign for a total of $216,000.

So, if Clinton evoked such a response, why didn't she win?

For one thing, the majority of white women did not vote for her. According to CNN exit polls, 53 percent of white women voted for her opponent, Donald Trump.

(Only 4 percent of black women and 26 percent of Latinas voted for the Republican candidate, the polls showed.)

Angela Rye, a CNN commentator and former staffer for the Congressional Black Caucus, noted those figures, saying, "This is a swath of voters I have talked about at least on

Twitter. They can't see a woman being the head of a household. They can't see a woman being the head of a church without it being a co-pastor or in a co-pastoring role with their husband. And they can definitely not see a woman being the head of the nation. And I think that's something we really have to talk about."

Why couldn't we elect a woman president in 2016, ninety-six years after the ratification of the Susan B. Anthony Amendment?

Historians and political scientists will probably have to ponder that for many years to come, but contrary to the predictions of the suffragists and the fears of their opponents, women have generally not voted as a bloc. It turns out they have divergent interests and ideologies just like men.

Women have proved, however, that they wanted the vote and were willing to use it, and women have had many victories in politics.

Elle.com pointed out after the Clinton defeat, "Tucked into [the] horrific results [were] harbingers of hope" for women and for diversity in general.

On the same day Clinton was defeated:

- Tammy Duckworth defeated incumbent senator Mark Kirk of Illinois.
- Kate Brown, interim governor of Oregon, became the first openly LGBT person elected governor.
- Kamala Harris became the first black politician to represent California in the Senate and only the second black woman ever elected to that chamber of Congress.
- Catherine Cortez Masto became the first Latina ever elected to the Senate.
- Pramila Jayapal of Seattle, Washington, became the first ever Indian-American woman elected to Congress.
- Ilhan Omar of Minneapolis, Minnesota, became the first Somali-American to be elected to Congress and one of the few Muslims.

Their election indicates that women will continue to be a force in politics and will have many victories in the future, maybe even a presidency. The suffragists would like that. Women have come so far, and yet the ultimate political prize our country has to offer remains outside our grasp. The glass ceiling is the cruelest of all. You can see victory, but you can't wrest it from whatever the force is that maintains it as the sole purview of males. The suffragists witnessed that many times. Perhaps the knowledge gained from the experiences of these previous leaders will help us break that cycle.

Acknowledgments

Researching and writing *Remember the Ladies* has been a blessing, and I credit the Almighty for its completion. I would like to thank my editor, Adrienne Ingrum, at Center Street/Hachette Book Group, for planting the idea and shepherding the project with her steady hand and keen insights. I am also indebted to others at Hachette, including Grace Tweedy, the editorial assistant; Carolyn Kurek, the production editor; Melissa Mathlin, the production associate who hired designer Fearn Cutler de Vicq; Mark Steven Long, the copy editor; and Barbara Nelson, the contracts manager, for their hard work on the project.

I am also grateful to my husband, Michael I. Days, for his support and his wisdom in pushing me to explore the lives of the leaders in the woman suffrage movement to learn what motivated them. What gave them the courage to persist in defying the norms of their time and to insist on having a civic voice?

I also want to thank the "team" of professionals who helped me through various phases of the project: Lynn Suzette Price, Esq., who provided guidance on my contract; Michele Washington of Washington Design, who researched and gathered photographs, illustrations, and graphics; and Charles Morris of SKM Business Solutions LLC, who obtained licenses for the artwork. For the manuscript, I thank Betty Anne Williams, who assisted in the research on women in politics; Tracy Days, my daughter-in-law, who cross-checked women's history time lines; Woodrow Berry, Esq. and Geraldine Eure, Esq., who answered questions about constitutional law; and Ingrid Sturgis, who obtained documents from Howard University's Moorland-Spingarn Research Center and who enthusiastically accompanied me on my road trip to Seneca Falls and Rochester, New York.

Appendices
Firsts: A Woman's Place

★★★

We shall someday be heeded,
and . . . everybody will think it was always so, just exactly as
many young people think that all the privileges, all the freedom,
all the enjoyments which woman now possesses always were
hers. They have no idea of how every single inch of ground
that she stands upon today has been gained by the hard
work of some little handful of women of the past.

Susan B. Anthony

A mob surrounded and jostled marchers in the woman suffrage procession in Washington, D.C., on March 3, 1913, the day before Woodrow Wilson's inauguration. More than one hundred people were injured.
Library of Congress

Congressional Women's Caucus

A group of fifteen congresswomen met on April 19, 1977, in a small room in the Capitol known then as the Congresswomen's Reading Room, to convene for the first time as a bipartisan caucus. Known then as the Congresswomen's Caucus, its founding cochairs were Representative Elizabeth Holtzman, a New York Democrat, and Representative Margaret Heckler, a Massachusetts Republican. The caucus worked on such issues as Social Security and private pension reform, child care, job training, and welfare. They lobbied to have hearings on federal contracts for woman-owned businesses.

In 1981, the caucus invited men to join and changed its name to the Congressional Caucus for Women's Issues. In 1992, in what became known as the "Year of the Woman," twenty-four new congresswomen were elected to the House, nearly doubling the caucus membership then.

After the House of Representatives cut funding for caucus offices and staff in 1995, the women's issues caucus reformed as a membership organization without men. It is made up of all woman members of the House—eighty-four representatives for 2015–2016, or 20 percent of the body.

In the 114th Congress, its cochairs were Representative Kristi Noem, Republican of South Dakota; and Representative Doris O. Matsui, Democrat of California.

Appendix 2

Women in Congress

The following women were "firsts" in some respect regarding their service in Congress or in politics:

Carol Moseley Braun
Democrat of Illinois

She was born Carol Elizabeth Moseley in Chicago, on August 16, 1947, and served in the U.S. Senate one term, 1993–1999. She was the only female African-American senator, the first African-American senator for the Democratic Party, the first woman to defeat an incumbent U.S. senator in an election, and the only female senator from Illinois.

An attorney and then a federal prosecutor (1973–1977), she won a seat in the Illinois House of Representatives in 1978 and rose to assistant majority leader. A champion of social causes, she spearheaded a successful lawsuit against Democrats on behalf of black and Hispanic Illinois citizens in a significant reapportionment case. Her term ended in 1999 when she lost her reelection bid. She ran unsuccessfully for the Democratic presidential nomination in 2004 and served as ambassador to New Zealand and ambassador to Samoa.

Shirley Chisholm
Democrat of New York

The first black congresswoman, Shirley Anita St. Hill Chisholm (November 30, 1924, to January 1, 2005) was born in Brooklyn, New York, to parents who were immigrants from the

A poster for Shirley Chisholm's presidential campaign.
Library of Congress

Caribbean. She served in the House of Representatives from 1969 to 1983. After a career as a teacher and education consultant, she won election to the New York State Legislature in 1964 as the second African-American woman to serve in the legislature. When a federal court in 1968 mandated creation of a new congressional district that included her Bedford-Stuyvesant neighborhood, she decided to run for the seat. She defeated two African-Americans in the Democratic primary and beat back an overtly sexist challenge from James Farmer, a cofounder of the Congress of Racial Equality and organizer of the Mississippi Freedom Rides who was running on the Republican-Liberal ticket. Their views were similar on major issues. "Farmer hammered away, arguing that 'women have been in the driver's seat' in black communities for too long and that the district needed 'a man's voice in Washington,' not that of a 'little schoolteacher,'" according to her biography on the

Shirley Chisholm was the first woman to seek
the Democratic Party's presidential nomination.
Library of Congress

U.S. House of Representatives history website. Her slogan was "Unbought and Unbossed," which she subsequently used as the title of her autobiography, published in 1970.

Always outspoken, Chisholm didn't alter her style in this new arena. She got an assignment to the House Agriculture Committee, not directly relevant to her urban district's interests, as punishment for one of her early challenges of the Democratic leadership. Instead of backing down, she took her protest to the House leadership, resulting in a change in assignment to the Veterans Affairs Committee. She never changed, fighting for the causes she believed in and the people who otherwise did not have a voice, rather than compiling a reputation as a conciliator, dealmaker, or legislative strategist. She was a founding member of the Congressional Black Caucus in 1969 and the Congresswomen's Caucus in 1977.

In 1972, she became the first

African-American to seek a major party nomination for president, running as a Democrat. She also was the first woman to seek the Democratic nomination. Her pioneering footprint was highlighted in 2008 when Barack Obama and Hillary Clinton faced off in pursuit of the Democratic nomination. Each could cite Chisholm as their precursor. Chisholm was awarded the Presidential Medal of Freedom posthumously in 2015.

"I ran because someone had to do it first," she wrote in *The Good Fight*, her book about the campaign. "In this country everybody is supposed to be able to run for President, but that's never been really true. I ran *because* most people think the country is not ready for a black candidate, not ready for a woman candidate. Someday..."

Rebecca Latimer Felton

Democrat from Georgia

Rebecca Felton (June 10, 1835, to January 24, 1930) was the first woman appointed to the U.S. Senate and served only one day after being sworn in in 1922. Born Rebecca Ann Latimer in DeKalb County, Georgia, she married William Harrell Felton, a physician and Methodist preacher who served in Congress and in the Georgia State Legislature. She was an integral part of his political life—sometime campaign manager, congressional secretary, and all-around political aide.

A prolific writer, Rebecca Felton was the author of three books and served as a newspaper columnist for the *Atlanta Journal* for more than twenty years. She supported woman suffrage, prohibition, public education, and vocational training for girls. She also was considered virulently racist even for her time, as a crusader against the perceived threats to Southern white womanhood.

Her prominent role in statewide politics and her journalistic writing led to her largely symbolic appointment to the U.S. Senate by a governor who wanted to deflect attention from the fact that he had opposed the Nineteenth Amendment giving women the right to vote. Her

Geraldine Ferraro ran as Walter Mondale's running mate.

Library of Congress

appointment followed the death of a popular senator and preceded the seating of the successor chosen in a special election. She effectively served for one day.

Geraldine Ferraro
Democrat of New York

Geraldine Anne Ferraro (August 26, 1935, to March 26, 2011) was born in Newburgh, New York. An elementary school teacher turned lawyer, she married a real estate broker, John Zaccaro, the week after graduating from law school. She kept her maiden name as a tribute to her mother, a widow who struggled to raise three children on her own.

As an assistant district attorney for Queens County (appointed by a cousin), she led a unit that specialized in child welfare and domestic abuse cases. The problems she encountered led her to consider entering politics, which she viewed as an avenue for making a greater difference. She became active in local Democratic circles and developed a bond with Mario Cuomo, a party leader who became her mentor.

She won election to the House in 1978, initially beating the machine candidate and another candidate in the primary. She quickly adapted, made powerful friends (as a protégé of House Speaker Thomas "Tip" O'Neill of Massachusetts), and began moving up the ladder. She joined the House leadership by being elected secretary of the House Democratic Caucus in her second and third terms. Her alliances in the House led to choice committee assignments. She persuaded O'Neill to give better assignments to other women members as well.

"Male colleagues viewed her with respect as someone who was tough and ambitious," and in turn she was, as the *New York Times* later wrote, "comfortable with the boys." Taking an interest in national party politics, she played significant roles at the 1980 party convention.

She became the first woman ever to run on a major party's national ticket when Walter Mondale chose her as his vice presidential running mate in 1984. The ticket was decisively defeated, capturing only thirteen electoral votes, and few analysts felt that Ferraro's presence had a strong impact—positive or negative—on the outcome. Ferraro later ran for the U.S. Senate twice but was unsuccessful. She practiced law, public relations, and corporate strategy.

Barbara Jordan
Democrat of Texas

Barbara Jordan was the first African-American congresswoman from the Deep South and the first woman ever elected to the Texas Senate. Born on February 21, 1936, to Benjamin and Arlyne Jordan, in Houston, Texas, she was a lawyer and educator. The daughter of a Baptist minister and a maid, she became known as an outstanding debater and orator in high school. She graduated from Texas Southern University in 1956, and later from Boston University Law School. She set up

Representative Barbara Jordan of Texas delivers the keynote address at the Democratic National Convention, July 12, 1976.
Library of Congress

a law practice in her hometown and won her seat in the legislature in 1966, after two previous tries. In 1972, she was elected president pro tem of the Texas State Senate, becoming the first African-American woman in the post. Jordan also won election to the U.S. House of Representatives in 1972, where she became a member of the Judiciary Committee. She became nationally known as the committee held hearings during the Watergate scandal and supported the impeachment of President Richard Nixon.

Jordan gave the keynote address at the 1976 Democratic National Convention, where she told the crowd that her presence there was "one additional bit of evidence that the American dream need not forever be deferred." Jordan did not seek reelection in 1978 and began teaching at the University of Texas at Austin. She suffered from multiple sclerosis. She died January 17, 1996, of pneumonia, a complication of her later battle with leukemia.

Nancy Landon Kassebaum
Republican of Kansas

Nancy Landon Kassebaum, a Kansas Republican, was the first woman to have been elected to the Senate without having previously filled an unexpired congressional term. She was born in Topeka, Kansas, on July 29, 1932, into a life of privilege and politics. Her father was Alfred Mossman Landon, a two-term Kansas governor and the 1936 Republican presidential nominee. He was an oil man. Her mother, Theo Cobb Landon, was an accomplished pianist and harpist.

Nancy Landon Kassebaum was a member of the local school board and vice president of Kassebaum Communications, a family-owned company that operated several radio stations. In Washington, she worked as a caseworker for Senator James

B. Pearson of Kansas. When he decided not to seek reelection in 1978, she chose to run for his open seat. Her wide, deep family-based connections helped her to beat a field of eight candidates. "It has been said I am riding on the coattails of my dad," she admitted, "but I can't think of any better coattails to ride on." Her campaign slogan was "A Fresh Face: A Trusted Kansas Name."

She was the only woman among one hundred senators. She notably kept her sense of humor about it: "There's so much work to do: the coffee to make and the chambers to vacuum. There are Pat Moynihan's hats to brush and the buttons to sew on Bob Byrd's red vests, so I keep quite busy." According to her biography on the House history website, she earned "a reputation as a moderate who supported the broad outlines of Republican budget and defense programs but remained independent on social issues. For instance, she supported a woman's right to have an abortion. She also backed programs for international family planning, which again brought her into conflict with conservative Republicans. In 1992, she cofounded the Republican Majority Coalition, a group that sought to counter the rise of the religious right in the party."

She declined to run for re-election in 1996.

Patsy Mink
Democrat of Hawaii

Born Patsy Matsu Takemoto on December 6, 1927, in Paia, Maui County, Hawaii, she was a lawyer. She served in Hawaii's territorial House and Senate. She won election to two tours in Congress: 1965–1977 and 1989–2002 (she was reelected posthumously).

A supporter of the Great Society programs that Congress enacted during her first years in Congress, she became a vocal defender of the social safety net, which was unraveling during her second period in the House. She was a forceful advocate of women's rights and an author of the Women's Educational Equity Act, which was intended to

promote gender equity, increase educational and job opportunities, and excise stereotypes from books and curricula. She was also a promoter of Title IX of the Education Amendments of 1972, which prohibits discrimination based on sex in education programs or activities that receive federal financial assistance.

"Mink's legislative approach was premised on the belief, 'You were not elected to Congress, in my interpretation of things, to represent your district, period. You are national legislators,'" reads her biography on the House history website.

Nancy Pelosi
Democrat of California

Nancy Pelosi is to date the only woman to have served as speaker of the House of Representatives (2007–2011). She then served as House minority leader. As speaker, the third in the line of succession to the presidency, Pelosi arguably was (and still is) the most powerful woman ever to serve in elective office in the United States.

Nancy Patricia D'Alesandro

Nancy Pelosi attended the unveiling of the bust of Sojourner Truth, donated by the National Congress of Black Women, at the U.S. Capitol in April 2009.

Kristie Boyd / House of Representatives Photographer / Creative Commons

was born March 26, 1940, in Baltimore into a political family. Her father, Thomas D'Alesandro Jr., was a U.S. representative from Maryland and mayor of Baltimore. A brother, Thomas D'Alesandro III, also was mayor of Baltimore (1967–1971). She married Paul Pelosi in 1963.

In Congress, she was more of a legislative tactician and strategist, serving mostly in leadership roles, than a legislative draftswoman. A liberal, she has been regularly reelected from a safe district that includes most of San Francisco.

**Margaret Chase Smith of Maine
served in both the House and the Senate.**
Library of Congress

Margaret Chase Smith
Republic of Maine

Margaret Madeline Chase Smith (December 14, 1897, to May 29, 1995) was born in Skowhegan, Maine. She served in both the House (1940–1949) and the Senate (1949–1973), the first woman elected to the Senate without having first been appointed to serve.

She was a teacher, newspaperwoman, and manufacturing manager/executive before moving to Washington with husband, Clyde Smith, after he was elected to the House of Representatives, where she became his legislative secretary.

Margaret Smith ran for Congress at the suggestion of her husband, who became too ill to serve after suffering a heart attack in 1940. He produced a testimonial letter supporting her candidacy before he died (April 1940), and she went on to win the special election (June 1940) to fill his unexpired term; she later won three full terms.

She was the first member of Congress to condemn the anticommunist, witch-hunting tactics of her fellow Republican, Senator Joseph McCarthy, in a speech that has become famous, the Declaration of Conscience in 1950.

"The American people are sick and tired of being afraid to speak their minds lest they be politically smeared as 'Communists' or 'Fascists' by their opponents," she said. "The American people are sick and tired of seeing innocent people smeared and guilty people whitewashed."

She was an unsuccessful candidate for the GOP nomination for president in 1964. Still, she was the first woman to see her name placed in nomination for president at a major party convention. She served in the Senate until 1972, when she was defeated by Democrat Bill Hathaway.

Sources: U.S. Senate, Art and History, Senate.gov; Excerpt from Shirley Washington, *Outstanding Women in Congress* (Shirley Chisholm) (Washington, D.C.: U.S. Capitol Historical Society, 1995), 17; History.com; U.S. House of Representatives History, Art and Archives, House.gov; *Biographical Directory of the United States Congress*, Bioguide, Congress.gov; Jack Germond and Jules Witcover, *Wake Us When It's Over: Presidential Politics of 1984* (New York: Macmillan, 1985), 372; Douglas Martin, "Geraldine A. Ferraro, 1935–2011: She Ended the Men's Club of National Politics," *New York Times*, March 26, 2011, A1; *Working Woman* (Nancy Kassebaum), October 4, 1979, 62; Oral History Interview (Patsy Mink) March 6, 1979, March 26, 1979, and June 7, 1979, U.S. Association of Former Members of Congress; Brittanica.com.

Women as Governors

Thirty-seven women have served as governors, in twenty-seven states; twenty-two were Democrats and fifteen were Republicans, according to the Center for American Women and Politics. The following women represent "firsts" in some respect.

Ella Grasso

Democrat of Connecticut

Ella Grasso (May 10, 1919, to February 5, 1981) was the first woman elected governor in her own right. She served as governor from January 8, 1975, to December 31, 1980, when she resigned for health reasons.

Born Ella Rose Tambussi in Windsor Locks, Connecticut, she served in the Connecticut House of Representatives (1952–1957), as secretary of state of Connecticut (1958–1966), and in the U.S. House of Representatives.

A standout moment occurred during the Blizzard of 1978, which dumped thirty inches of snow on Connecticut. She ordered the closing of all roads and businesses, allowing emergency workers to perform essential services without worrying about stranded motorists, automobile accidents, and other issues. As a result, the state was able to get back to business in a few days' time.

Nikki Haley

Republican of South Carolina

Nikki Haley was born Nimrata Nikki Randhawa on January 20, 1972, in Bamberg, South Carolina, to Indian Sikh parents.

She and Susana Martinez were the first women of color to be elected governors of states; she began her term as governor of South Carolina in 2011.

Periodically in the national spotlight whenever questions are raised about diversity in the GOP, Haley drew national praise for her empathy and calm in 2015 after nine churchgoers were slain by a white supremacist in Emanuel Church in Charleston. The shock of the slayings led the South Carolina legislature to agree to remove the Confederate flag from the Statehouse grounds, long a source of contention in the state.

After the 2016 presidential election, Donald Trump nominated her to be the United States ambassador to the United Nations.

Susana Martinez
Republican of New Mexico

Susana Martinez was born July 14, 1959, in El Paso, and she and Nikki Haley were the first women of color elected governors of states. Martinez, who is also the first Hispanic governor of a state and the first woman governor of her state, began her term in 2011. She is chair of the Republican Governors Association. A lawyer, she held posts as assistant district attorney and district attorney for twenty-five years before her election.

During the 2016 presidential campaign, Martinez's name came up repeatedly in speculation about vice presidential running mates for the seventeen initial GOP candidates, but she was said not to be interested. She engaged in a widely publicized tiff with Donald Trump, who came to her state and insulted her after she declined to endorse him before he clinched the GOP nomination.

Sarah Palin
Republican of Alaska

Sarah Palin was the first Republican woman nominated for the vice presidency, as the running mate for Senator John McCain in 2008. Two years earlier, she had become the youngest and first female governor of

Alaska. After the GOP ticket lost the 2008 presidential election, Palin returned to Alaska but resigned as governor in July 2009 without completing her term. She pursued a career as a Fox News contributor, wrote books, and campaigned on behalf of other conservative Republicans.

She was born Sarah Louise Heath on February 11, 1964, in Sandpoint, Idaho. Her family soon moved to Alaska, where her father taught and her mother was a school secretary.

Her political career began when she won a seat on the Wasilla City Council in 1992; she became mayor of Wasilla in 1996. In 2003, she served as chair of the Alaska Oil and Gas Conservation Commission, which oversees the state's oil and gas fields, but resigned a year later.

Nellie Tayloe Ross
Democrat of Wyoming

The first woman governor in the United States, Nellie Tayloe Ross won the election to replace her husband, William Ross, who had died while running for re-election as governor. She served from 1925 to 1927 and did not win reelection.

Later, she became vice chair of the Democratic National Committee and director of the U.S. Mint. At the 1928 Democratic National Convention, she received thirty-one votes on the first ballot for vice president. She was born November 29, 1876, in Saint Joseph, Missouri, and died December 19, 1977, at the age of 101.

Lurleen Wallace
Democrat of Alabama

Lurleen Wallace served as governor of Alabama in 1967–1968, elected as a surrogate for her segregationist husband, George Wallace, who could not succeed himself.

Lurleen Brigham Burns Wallace was born September 19, 1926, in Tuscaloosa, Alabama, and died May 7, 1968. She met her future husband in the dime store where she worked, and they were married when she was sixteen. She spent the next twenty years as a homemaker and mother and then as First Lady of Alabama.

George Wallace failed in an attempt to get the legislature to amend the constitution and make it possible for a governor to serve consecutive terms so he could use that position as a base as he sought the presidency in 1968. Instead, the Wallaces announced that Lurleen would run to succeed him, freely acknowledging that George would continue to make the administrative decisions if she won.

Lurleen Wallace is recognized for at least two initiatives she undertook as governor without her husband's input: strengthening the state's residential hospital for disabled children and improving the state's parks.

Sources: Connecticut Women's Hall of Fame; ConnecticutHistory.org; Biography .com; South Carolina governor's office, governor.sc.gov; New Mexico governor's office, governor.state.nm.us/; Ashley Parker and Jonathan Martin, "Donald Trump Gives Gov. Susana Martinez a Poor Performance Review," *New York Times*, May 25, 2016; Alabama Department of Archives and History, www.archives.alabama.gov/govs_list/g_wallu.html; encyclopediaofalabama.org/; pbs.org/wgbh/.

Women Representatives and Senators by State and Territory, 1917–Present

This table is based on information drawn from the *Biographical Directory of the United States Congress*. States are listed in alphabetical order. Names are followed by the session of Congress in which the representative or senator first took office.

The following states and territories have never elected or appointed a woman to Congress: Mississippi, Northern Mariana Islands, Vermont.

Alabama

Name	Took Office	First Term	Body
Graves, Dixie Bibb	75th	1937–1939	Senate
Andrews, Elizabeth Bullock	92nd	1971–1973	House
Allen, Maryon Pittman	95th	1977–1979	Senate
Roby, Martha	112th	2011–2013	House
Sewell, Terri	112th	2011–2013	House

Alaska

Name	Took Office	First Term	Body
Murkowski, Lisa	107th	2001–2003	Senate

American Samoa

Name	Took Office	First Term	Body
Radewagen, Aumua Amata Coleman	114th	2015–2017	House

Arizona

Name	Took Office	First Term	Body
Greenway, Isabella Selmes	73rd	1933–1935	House
English, Karan	103rd	1993–1995	House
Giffords, Gabrielle	110th	2007–2009	House
Kirkpatrick, Ann	111th	2009–2011	House
Sinema, Kyrsten	113th	2013–2015	House
McSally, Martha	114th	2015–2017	House

Arkansas

Name	Took Office	First Term	Body
Oldfield, Pearl Peden	70th	1927–1929	House
Wingo, Effiegene Locke	71st	1929–1931	House
Caraway, Hattie Wyatt	72nd	1931–1933	Senate
Norrell, Catherine Dorris	87th	1961–1963	House
Lincoln, Blanche Lambert[1]	103rd	1993–1995	House

California

Name	Took Office	First Term	Body
Nolan, Mae Ella	67th	1921–1923	House
Kahn, Florence Prag	69th	1925–1927	House
Douglas, Helen Gahagan	79th	1945–1947	House
Burke, Yvonne Brathwaite	93rd	1973–1975	House
Pettis, Shirley Neil	94th	1975–1977	House
Fiedler, Bobbi	97th	1981–1983	House
Boxer, Barbara[2]	98th	1983–1985	House
Burton, Sala Galante	98th	1983–1985	House
Pelosi, Nancy	100th	1987–1989	House
Feinstein, Dianne	102nd	1991–1993	Senate

Waters, Maxine	102nd	1991–1993	House
Eshoo, Anna Georges	103rd	1993–1995	House
Harman, Jane L.	103rd	1993–1995	House
Roybal-Allard, Lucille	103rd	1993–1995	House
Schenk, Lynn	103rd	1993–1995	House
Woolsey, Lynn C.	103rd	1993–1995	House
Lofgren, Zoe	104th	1995–1997	House
Millender-McDonald, Juanita	104th	1995–1997	House
Seastrand, Andrea	104th	1995–1997	House
Bono, Mary	105th	1997–1999	House
Capps, Lois	105th	1997–1999	House
Lee, Barbara	105th	1997–1999	House
Sanchez, Loretta	105th	1997–1999	House
Tauscher, Ellen O'Kane	105th	1997–1999	House
Napolitano, Grace Flores	106th	1999–2001	House
Davis, Susan A.	107th	2001–2003	House
Solis, Hilda L.	107th	2001–2003	House
Watson, Diane Edith	107th	2001–2003	House
Sánchez, Linda T.	108th	2003–2005	House
Matsui, Doris	109th	2005–2007	House
Richardson, Laura	110th	2007–2009	House
Speier, Karen Lorraine Jacqueline (Jackie)	110th	2007–2009	House
Chu, Judy	111th	2009–2011	House
Bass, Karen	112th	2011–2013	House
Hahn, Janice	112th	2011–2013	House
Brownley, Julia	113th	2013–2015	House
Negrete McLeod, Gloria	113th	2013–2015	House
Torres, Norma Judith	114th	2015–2017	House
Walters, Mimi	114th	2015–2017	House
Barragán, Nanette Diaz	115th	2017–2019	House
Harris, Kamala Devi	115th	2017–2019	Senate

Colorado

Name	Took Office	First Term	Body
Schroeder, Patricia Scott	93rd	1973–1975	House
Degette, Diana	105th	1997–1999	House
Musgrave, Marilyn N.	108th	2003–2005	House
Markey, Betsy	111th	2009–2011	House

Connecticut

Name	Took Office	First Term	Body
Luce, Clare Boothe	78th	1943–1945	House
Woodhouse, Chase Going	79th	1945–1947	House
Grasso, Ella Tambussi	92nd	1971–1973	House
Kennelly, Barbara Bailey	97th	1981–1983	House
Johnson, Nancy Lee	98th	1983–1985	House
DeLauro, Rosa L.	102nd	1991–1993	House
Esty, Elizabeth	113th	2013–2015	House

Delaware

Name	Took Office	First Term	Body
Blunt Rochester, Lisa	115th	2017–2019	House

District of Columbia

Name	Took Office	First Term	Body
Norton, Eleanor Holmes	102nd	1991–1993	House

Florida

Name	Took Office	First Term	Body
Owen, Ruth Bryan	71st	1929–1931	House
Hawkins, Paula	96th	1979–1981	Senate
Ros-Lehtinen, Ileana	101st	1989–1991	House
Brown, Corrine	103rd	1993–1995	House
Fowler, Tillie Kidd	103rd	1993–1995	House
Meek, Carrie P.	103rd	1993–1995	House
Thurman, Karen L.	103rd	1993–1995	House

Brown-Waite, Virginia (Ginny)	108th	2003–2005	House
Harris, Katherine	108th	2003–2005	House
Wasserman Schultz, Debbie	109th	2005–2007	House
Castor, Kathy	110th	2007–2009	House
Kosmas, Suzanne M.	111th	2009–2011	House
Adams, Sandra (Sandy)	112th	2011–2013	House
Wilson, Frederica	112th	2011–2013	House
Frankel, Lois	113th	2013–2015	House
Graham, Gwendolyn (Gwen)	114th	2015–2017	House
Demings, Valdez Butler	115th	2017–2019	House
Murphy, Stephanie	115th	2017–2019	House

Georgia

Name	Took Office	First Term	Body
Felton, Rebecca Latimer	67th	1921–1923	Senate
Gibbs, Florence Reville	76th	1939–1941	House
Mankin, Helen Douglas	79th	1945–1947	House
Blitch, Iris Faircloth	84th	1955–1957	House
McKinney, Cynthia Ann	103rd	1993–1995	House
Majette, Denise L.	108th	2003–2005	House

Guam

Name	Took Office	First Term	Body
Bordallo, Madeleine	108th	2003–2005	House

Hawaii

Name	Took Office	First Term	Body
Farrington, Mary Elizabeth Pruett	83rd	1953–1955	House
Mink, Patsy Takemoto	89th	1965–1967	House
Saiki, Patricia	100th	1987–1989	House
Hirono, Mazie	110th	2007–2009	House
Hanabusa, Colleen	112th	2011–2013	House
Gabbard, Tulsi	113th	2013–2015	House

Idaho

Name	Took Office	First Term	Body
Pfost, Gracie Bowers	83rd	1953–1955	House
Chenoweth-Hage, Helen P.	104th	1995–1997	House

Illinois

Name	Took Office	First Term	Body
Huck, Winnifred Sprague Mason	67th	1921–1923	House
McCormick, Ruth Hanna	71st	1929–1931	House
Sumner, Jessie	76th	1939–1941	House
Douglas, Emily Taft	79th	1945–1947	House
Church, Marguerite Stitt	82nd	1951–1953	House
Simpson, Edna Oakes	86th	1959–1961	House
Reid, Charlotte Thompson	88th	1963–1965	House
Collins, Cardiss	93rd	1973–1975	House
Martin, Lynn Morley	97th	1981–1983	House
Moseley Braun, Carol	103rd	1993–1995	Senate
Biggert, Judy Borg	106th	1999–2001	House
Schakowsky, Janice D.	106th	1999–2001	House
Bean, Melissa L.	109th	2005–2007	House
Halvorson, Deborah L.	111th	2009–2011	House
Bustos, Cheri	113th	2013–2015	House
Duckworth, Tammy[3]	113th	2013–2015	House
Kelly, Robin L.	113th	2013–2015	House

Indiana

Name	Took Office	First Term	Body
Jenckes, Virginia Ellis	73rd	1933–1935	House
Harden, Cecil Murray	81st	1949–1951	House
Hall, Katie Beatrice	97th	1981–1983	House
Long, Jill Lynette	101st	1989–1991	House
Carson, Julia May	105th	1997–1999	House

Brooks, Susan	113th	2013–2015	House
Walorski, Jackie	113th	2013–2015	House

Iowa

Name	Took Office	First Term	Body
Ernst, Joni	114th	2015–2017	Senate

Kansas

Name	Took Office	First Term	Body
O'Loughlin McCarthy, Kathryn Ellen	73rd	1933–1935	House
Keys, Martha Elizabeth	94th	1975–1977	House
Kassebaum, Nancy Landon	95th	1977–1979	Senate
Meyers, Jan	99th	1985–1987	House
Frahm, Sheila	104th	1995–1997	Senate
Boyda, Nancy	110th	2007–2009	House
Jenkins, Lynn	111th	2009–2011	House

Kentucky

Name	Took Office	First Term	Body
Langley, Katherine Gudger	70th	1927–1929	House
Northup, Anne Meagher	105th	1997–1999	House

Louisiana

Name	Took Office	First Term	Body
Long, Rose McConnell	74th	1935–1937	Senate
Edwards, Elaine Schwartzenburg	92nd	1971–1973	Senate
Boggs, Corinne Claiborne (Lindy)	93rd	1973–1975	House
Long, Catherine Small	99th	1985–1987	House
Landrieu, Mary L.	105th	1997–1999	Senate

Maine

Name	Took Office	First Term	Body
Smith, Margaret Chase[4]	76th	1939–1941	House
Snowe, Olympia Jean[5]	96th	1979–1981	House

Collins, Susan Margaret	105th	1997–1999	Senate
Pingree, Chellie	111th	2009–2011	House

Maryland

Name	Took Office	First Term	Body
Byron, Katharine Edgar	77th	1941–1943	House
Holt, Marjorie Sewell	93rd	1973–1975	House
Spellman, Gladys Noon	94th	1975–1977	House
Mikulski, Barbara Ann[6]	95th	1977–1979	House
Byron, Beverly Barton Butcher	96th	1979–1981	House
Bentley, Helen Delich	99th	1985–1987	House
Morella, Constance A.	100th	1987–1989	House
Edwards, Donna F.	110th	2007–2009	House

Massachusetts

Name	Took Office	First Term	Body
Rogers, Edith Nourse	69th	1925–1927	House
Heckler, Margaret M.	90th	1967–1969	House
Hicks, Louise Day	92nd	1971–1973	House
Tsongas, Nicola S. (Niki)	110th	2007–2009	House
Clark, Katherine M.	113th	2013–2015	House
Warren, Elizabeth	113th	2013–2015	Senate

Michigan

Name	Took Office	First Term	Body
Thompson, Ruth	82nd	1951–1953	House
Griffiths, Martha Wright	84th	1955–1957	House
Collins, Barbara-Rose	102nd	1991–1993	House
Rivers, Lynn Nancy	104th	1995–1997	House
Kilpatrick, Carolyn Cheeks	105th	1997–1999	House
Stabenow, Deborah Ann[7]	105th	1997–1999	House
Miller, Candice S.	108th	2003–2005	House
Dingell, Debbie	114th	2015–2017	House
Lawrence, Brenda L.	114th	2015–2017	House

Minnesota

Name	Took Office	First Term	Body
Knutson, Coya Gjesdal	84th	1955–1957	House
Humphrey, Muriel Buck	95th	1977–1979	Senate
McCollum, Betty	107th	2001–2003	House
Bachmann, Michele	110th	2007–2009	House
Klobuchar, Amy	110th	2007–2009	Senate

Missouri

Name	Took Office	First Term	Body
Sullivan, Leonor Kretzer	83rd	1953–1955	House
Horn, Joan Kelly	102nd	1991–1993	House
Danner, Patsy Ann (Pat)	103rd	1993–1995	House
Emerson, Jo Ann	104th	1995–1997	House
McCarthy, Karen	104th	1995–1997	House
Carnahan, Jean	107th	2001–2003	Senate
McCaskill, Claire	110th	2007–2009	Senate
Hartzler, Vicky	112th	2011–2013	House
Wagner, Ann	113th	2013–2015	House

Montana

Name	Took Office	First Term	Body
Rankin, Jeannette	65th	1917–1919	House

Nebraska

Name	Took Office	First Term	Body
Abel, Hazel Hempel	83rd	1953–1955	Senate
Bowring, Eva Kelly	83rd	1953–1955	Senate
Smith, Virginia Dodd	94th	1975–1977	House
Fischer, Debra (Deb)	113th	2013–2015	Senate

Nevada

Name	Took Office	First Term	Body
Vucanovich, Barbara Farrell	98th	1983–1985	House
Berkley, Shelley	106th	1999–2001	House
Titus, Alice (Dina)	111th	2009–2011	House
Cortez Masto, Catherine Marie	115th	2017–2019	Senate
Rosen, Jacklyn Sheryl	115th	2017–2019	House

New Hampshire

Name	Took Office	First Term	Body
Shea-Porter, Carol	110th	2007–2009	House
Shaheen, Jeanne	111th	2009–2011	Senate
Ayotte, Kelly	112th	2011–2013	Senate
Kuster, Ann McLane	113th	2013–2015	House
Hassan, Margaret (Maggie)	115th	2017–2019	Senate

New Jersey

Name	Took Office	First Term	Body
Norton, Mary Teresa	69th	1925–1927	House
Dwyer, Florence Price	85th	1957–1959	House
Fenwick, Millicent Hammond	94th	1975–1977	House
Meyner, Helen Stevenson	94th	1975–1977	House
Roukema, Margaret Scafati	97th	1981–1983	House
Watson Coleman, Bonnie	114th	2015–2017	House

New Mexico

Name	Took Office	First Term	Body
Lusk, Georgia Lee	80th	1947–1949	House
Wilson, Heather	105th	1997–1999	House
Lujan Grisham, Michelle	113th	2013–2015	House

New York

Name	Took Office	First Term	Body
Pratt, Ruth Sears Baker	71st	1929–1931	House
Clarke, Marian Williams	73rd	1933–1935	House
O'Day, Caroline Love Goodwin	74th	1935–1937	House
Stanley, Winifred Claire	78th	1943–1945	House
St. George, Katharine Price Collier	80th	1947–1949	House
Kelly, Edna Flannery	81st	1949–1951	House
Weis, Jessica McCullough	86th	1959–1961	House
Chisholm, Shirley Anita	91st	1969–1971	House
Abzug, Bella Savitzky	92nd	1971–1973	House
Holtzman, Elizabeth	93rd	1973–1975	House
Ferraro, Geraldine Anne	96th	1979–1981	House
Slaughter, Louise McIntosh	100th	1987–1989	House
Lowey, Nita M.	101st	1989–1991	House
Molinari, Susan	101st	1989–1991	House
Maloney, Carolyn Bosher	103rd	1993–1995	House
Velázquez, Nydia M.	103rd	1993–1995	House
Kelly, Sue W.	104th	1995–1997	House
McCarthy, Carolyn	105th	1997–1999	House
Clinton, Hillary Rodham	107th	2001–2003	Senate
Clarke, Yvette Diane	110th	2007–2009	House
Gillibrand, Kirsten[8]	110th	2007–2009	House
Buerkle, Ann Marie	112th	2011–2013	House
Hayworth, Nan	112th	2011–2013	House
Hochul, Kathleen C.	112th	2011–2013	House
Meng, Grace	113th	2013–2015	House
Rice, Kathleen Maura	114th	2015–2017	House
Stefanik, Elise M.	114th	2015–2017	House
Tenney, Claudia	115th	2017–2019	House

North Carolina

Name	Took Office	First Term	Body
Pratt, Eliza Jane	79th	1945–1947	House
Clayton, Eva M.	102nd	1991–1993	House
Myrick, Sue	104th	1995–1997	House
Dole, Elizabeth Hanford	108th	2003–2005	Senate
Foxx, Virginia Ann	109th	2005–2007	House
Hagan, Kay	111th	2009–2011	Senate
Ellmers, Renee	112th	2011–2013	House
Adams, Alma	113th	2013–2015	House

North Dakota

Name	Took Office	First Term	Body
Burdick, Jocelyn Birch	102nd	1991–1993	Senate
Heitkamp, Mary Kathryn (Heidi)	113th	2013–2015	Senate

Ohio

Name	Took Office	First Term	Body
Bolton, Frances Payne	76th	1939–1941	House
Oakar, Mary Rose	95th	1977–1979	House
Ashbrook, Jean Spencer	97th	1981–1983	House
Kaptur, Marcia Carolyn (Marcy)	98th	1983–1985	House
Pryce, Deborah D.	103rd	1993–1995	House
Jones, Stephanie Tubbs	106th	1999–2001	House
Schmidt, Jean	109th	2005–2007	House
Fudge, Marcia L.	110th	2007–2009	House
Sutton, Betty	110th	2007–2009	House
Kilroy, Mary Jo	111th	2009–2011	House
Beatty, Joyce	113th	2013–2015	House

Oklahoma

Name	Took Office	First Term	Body
Robertson, Alice Mary	67th	1921–1923	House
Fallin, Mary	110th	2007–2009	House

Oregon

Name	Took Office	First Term	Body
Honeyman, Nan Wood	75th	1937–1939	House
Green, Edith Starrett	84th	1955–1957	House
Neuberger, Maurine Brown	86th	1959–1961	Senate
Furse, Elizabeth	103rd	1993–1995	House
Hooley, Darlene	105th	1997–1999	House
Bonamici, Suzanne	112th	2011–2013	House

Pennsylvania

Name	Took Office	First Term	Body
Boland, Veronica Grace	77th	1941–1943	House
Buchanan, Vera Daerr	82nd	1951–1953	House
Granahan, Kathryn Elizabeth	84th	1955–1957	House
Margolies-Mezvinsky, Marjorie	103rd	1993–1995	House
Hart, Melissa A.	107th	2001–2003	House
Schwartz, Allyson Y.	109th	2005–2007	House
Dahlkemper, Kathleen A. (Kathy)	111th	2009–2011	House

Puerto Rico

Name	Took Office	First Term	Body
González-Colón, Jenniffer	115th	2017–2019	House

Rhode Island

Name	Took Office	First Term	Body
Schneider, Claudine	97th	1981–1983	House

South Carolina

Name	Took Office	First Term	Body
Gasque, Elizabeth Hawley	75th	1937–1939	House
McMillan, Clara Gooding	76th	1939–1941	House
Fulmer, Willa Lybrand	78th	1943–1945	House
Riley, Corinne Boyd	87th	1961–1963	House
Patterson, Elizabeth J.	100th	1987–1989	House

South Dakota

Name	Took Office	First Term	Body
Pyle, Gladys	75th	1937–1939	Senate
Bushfield, Vera Cahalan	80th	1947–1949	Senate
Herseth Sandlin, Stephanie	108th	2003–2005	House
Noem, Kristi	112th	2011–2013	House

Tennessee

Name	Took Office	First Term	Body
Eslick, Willa McCord Blake	72nd	1931–1933	House
Reece, Louise Goff	87th	1961–1963	House
Baker, Irene Bailey	88th	1963–1965	House
Lloyd, Marilyn Laird	94th	1975–1977	House
Blackburn, Marsha	108th	2003–2005	House
Black, Diane	112th	2011–2013	House

Texas

Name	Took Office	First Term	Body
Thomas, Lera Millard	89th	1965–1967	House
Jordan, Barbara Charline	93rd	1973–1975	House
Hutchison, Kathryn Ann Bailey (Kay)	103rd	1993–1995	Senate
Johnson, Eddie Bernice	103rd	1993–1995	House
Jackson Lee, Sheila	104th	1995–1997	House
Granger, Kay	105th	1997–1999	House
Sekula Gibbs, Shelley	109th	2005–2007	House

Utah

Name	Took Office	First Term	Body
Bosone, Reva Zilpha Beck	81st	1949–1951	House
Shepherd, Karen	103rd	1993–1995	House
Greene Waldholtz, Enid	104th	1995–1997	House
Love, Ludmya Bourdeau (Mia)	114th	2015–2017	House

Virgin Islands

Name	Took Office	First Term	Body
Christensen, Donna Marie	105th	1997–1999	House
Plaskett, Stacey E.	114th	2015–2017	House

Virginia

Name	Took Office	First Term	Body
Byrne, Leslie Larkin	103rd	1993–1995	House
Davis, Jo Ann	107th	2001–2003	House
Drake, Thelma D.	109th	2005–2007	House
Comstock, Barbara J.	114th	2015–2017	House

Washington

Name	Took Office	First Term	Body
Hansen, Julia Butler	86th	1959–1961	House
May, Catherine Dean	86th	1959–1961	House
Unsoeld, Jolene	101st	1989–1991	House
Cantwell, Maria E.[9]	103rd	1993–1995	House
Dunn, Jennifer Blackburn	103rd	1993–1995	House
Murray, Patty	103rd	1993–1995	Senate
Smith, Linda	104th	1995–1997	House
McMorris Rodgers, Cathy	109th	2005–2007	House
Delbene, Suzan K.	112th	2011–2013	House
Herrera Beutler, Jaime	112th	2011–2013	House
Jayapal, Pramila	115th	2017–2019	House

West Virginia

Name	Took Office	First Term	Body
Kee, Maude Elizabeth	82nd	1951–1953	House
Capito, Shelley Moore[10]	107th	2001–2003	House

Wisconsin

Name	Took Office	First Term	Body
Baldwin, Tammy[11]	106th	1999–2001	House
Moore, Gwendolynne S. (Gwen)	109th	2005–2007	House

Wyoming

Name	Took Office	First Term	Body
Cubin, Barbara L.	104th	1995–1997	House
Lummis, Cynthia M.	111th	2009–2011	House
Cheney, Elizabeth (Liz)	115th	2017–2019	House

Source: History, Art and Archives, U.S. House of Representatives, http://history.house.gov/Exhibitions-and-Publications/WIC/Historical-Data/Women -Representatives-and-Senators-by-State-and-Territory/.

1 Served as a senator starting in the 106th Congress (1999–2001).
2 Served as a senator starting in the 103rd Congress (1993–1995).
3 Served as a senator starting in the 115th Congress (2017–2019).
4 Served as a senator starting in the 81st Congress (1949–1951).
5 Served as a senator starting in the 104th Congress (1995–1997).
6 Served as a senator starting in the 100th Congress (1987–1989).
7 Served as a senator starting in the 107th Congress (2001–2003).
8 Served as a senator starting in the 111th Congress (2009–2011).
9 Served as a senator starting in the 107th Congress (2001–2003).
10 Served as a senator starting in the 114th Congress (2015–2017).
11 Served as a senator starting in the 113th Congress (2013–2015).

Appendix 5

Woman Suffrage Time Line
1756–2016

1756 Lydia Taft, a widow, votes in town meetings in Uxbridge, Massachusetts.

1776, March 31 Abigail Adams writes to her husband, John Adams, at the Continental Congress in Philadelphia, asking him to "Remember the Ladies" in the new code of laws.

1776 New Jersey state constitution grants the vote to "all inhabitants" with property, including single women. (Married women cannot own property.)

1787 The U.S. Constitutional Convention leaves voting qualifications up to the states.

1792 Mary Wollstonecraft publishes *A Vindication of the Rights of Woman* in England.

1807 Women lose the right to vote in New Jersey.

1820, February 15 Susan B. Anthony is born in Adams, Massachusetts.

1831 Maria W. Stewart becomes the first American woman to speak before an audience of men and women on political issues and the first to leave texts of her speeches.

1833, December 9 Lucretia Mott and twenty-one other women found the interracial Philadelphia Female Anti-Slavery Society.

1836 Angelina Grimké appeals to Southern women to speak out against slavery.

1837 The "Pastoral Letter of the General Association of Massachusetts to the Congregational Churches Under Their Care" chastises women speaking in public against slavery; it is a veiled reference to the Grimké sisters, Angelina and Sarah.

1838 In Kentucky, widowed mothers win the right to vote in school board elections.

1840 The World Anti-Slavery Convention in London denies seats to Lucretia Mott and other women delegates. Mott meets the newlywed Elizabeth Cady Stanton, whose husband is a delegate.

1848, July Lucretia Mott; her sister, Martha C. Wright; Elizabeth Cady Stanton; and Mary Ann M'Clintock attend Jane Hunt's tea in Waterloo, New York. They decide to convene a meeting to discuss women's rights while Mott, a well-known Quaker preacher, is still in the area visiting her sister in Auburn, New York. A few days later, Stanton visits the M'Clintock home in Waterloo to help draw up the Declaration of Sentiments to present at the meeting. The women send a notice to the local paper, the *Seneca County Courier*.

1848, July 19–20 Three hundred people attend the first convention held to discuss women's rights at the reformist Wesleyan Chapel in Seneca Falls. James Mott presides.

1848, July 20 As Elizabeth Cady Stanton reads the declaration and resolutions, Frederick Douglass defends the inclusion of a formal demand for women's right to vote. The assembly adopts the resolution along with others urging equal treatment of women and men. Sixty-eight women and thirty-two men sign the Declaration of Sentiments, which includes the demand for the vote.

1848, August 2 Some women who attended the Seneca Falls meeting, including Amy Post, Sarah D. Fish, Sarah C. Owen, and Mary H. Hallowell, convene a women's rights convention in Rochester, New York. Abigail Bush chairs the public meeting, a first for American women.

1850 Sojourner Truth, the formerly enslaved preacher and lecturer, begins attending and speaking out at meetings on women's rights.

1850, April 19–20 In Salem, Ohio, women hold a women's rights convention in which they bar men in attendance from speaking. Emily Robinson calls the meeting to order. Mariana W. Johnson serves as president pro tem and Sarah Coates serves as secretary pro tem.

1850, October 23–24 The first National Woman's Rights Convention is held in Worcester, Massachusetts, with about one thousand people in attendance. Paulina Kellogg Wright Davis, of Rhode Island, organized the meeting. Frederick Douglass, Abby Kelley Foster, William Lloyd Garrison, Lucy Stone, and Sojourner Truth, all abolitionist leaders, attend.

National women's rights conferences continue to be held annually, except in 1857, until the Civil War begins.

1851 Elizabeth Smith Miller, daughter of a leading abolitionist, Gerrit Smith, and cousin of Elizabeth Cady Stanton, apparently imports a new style of dress that was popularized by Amelia Jenks Bloomer's publication, the *Lily*. Many of the women's rights leaders adopt the "Bloomer" as a "dress reform" for women. They soon have to abandon it because of ridicule and hazing.

1851 Amelia Bloomer introduces Susan B. Anthony and Elizabeth Cady Stanton on a street corner in Seneca Falls, New York, where Anthony is attending an abolitionist lecture. Anthony and Stanton soon begin working together in temperance groups.

1851, May 28–29 Sojourner Truth attends and addresses the woman's rights convention in Akron, Ohio.

1852 Susan B. Anthony attends the National Woman's Rights Convention for the first time, in Syracuse, New York.

1853, February Paulina Kellogg Wright Davis publishes the *Una*, the first newspaper devoted to the women's rights movement.

1853, September The World's Temperance Convention held in New York City bars women delegates, including the Reverend Antoinette Brown, from participation. Protestors gather for the Whole World's Temperance Convention. That same week, the New York State women's rights convention meet at the Broadway Tabernacle but are disrupted by a mob and disbanded. Lucretia Mott chairs.

1855 Lucy Stone, an abolitionist lecturer and one of the earliest female college graduates in the United States, marries Henry Blackwell and keeps her birth name. At the wedding, they issue a declaration of protest against laws and customs that are unfair to women. It is widely publicized. Married women who keep their own names are often called "Lucy Stoners."

1856 Susan B. Anthony becomes a paid lecturer for the American Anti-Slavery Society.

1861 Women in Kansas gain the vote in school board elections.

1861, February The last national women's rights convention before the Civil War is held in Albany, New York.

1861–1865 Women suspend the national conventions during the Civil War and work on wartime projects.

1863, May 14 Elizabeth Cady Stanton and Susan B.

Anthony call a meeting of the Loyal Women of the Nation and found the Women's Loyal National League. It gathers four hundred thousand signatures on petitions to Congress in support of the Thirteenth Amendment to abolish slavery permanently.

1865, May Wendell Phillips, a white Bostonian, assumes leadership of the American Anti-Slavery Society and declares that the women's vote issue must wait until voting rights for black men are secured because it is "the Negro's hour."

1865, December Elizabeth Cady Stanton, Susan B. Anthony, and Lucy Stone petition Congress for a constitutional amendment that would prohibit states from interfering with the franchise of citizens on account of sex.

1866, May 1 At the eleventh National Woman's Rights Convention, women and men agree to found the American Equal Rights Association, to work for suffrage for both women and black Americans.

1867 A woman suffrage amendment proposal is defeated in Kansas.

1867 The Fourteenth Amendment passes Congress; it includes the first use of the word "male" in the Constitution.

1868, January 8 Elizabeth Cady Stanton, Susan B. Anthony, and Parker Pillsbury publish the first edition of the *Revolution*, a women's rights newspaper, funded by George F. Train, under the motto "Men, their rights and nothing more; women, their rights and nothing less!"

1868, July The Fourteenth Amendment is ratified and becomes effective.

1868, November 19 In Vineland, New Jersey, 172 women cast ballots in the presidential election, but must place them in a separate box from the men's.

1868, December Senator S. C. Pomeroy of Kansas introduces the first federal woman suffrage amendment in Congress.

1869 The Fifteenth Amendment passes Congress, reinforcing the voting rights of black men.

1869, May 12 The American Equal Rights Association meets in New York City as the ratification process for the Fifteenth Amendment is taking place. Elizabeth Cady Stanton faces a challenge to her leadership over her statements opposing black male suffrage.

1869, May 14 Elizabeth Cady Stanton and Susan B. Anthony invite selected women to form the National

Woman Suffrage Association to work for woman suffrage under a new proposed federal amendment.

1869, November 24–25 Lucy Stone, Henry Blackwell, and Julia Ward Howe convene the first convention of the American Woman Suffrage Association in Cleveland to support the Fifteenth Amendment and work for woman suffrage by amending state constitutions. Leading abolitionists William Lloyd Garrison, Amelia Bloomer, Gerrit Smith, Abby Kelley Foster, and Lydia Mott join the call for the meeting. A leading minister, Henry Ward Beecher, becomes AWSA's first president.

1869 Wyoming Territory grants women the vote in all elections.

1870 The Utah Territory grants suffrage to women.

1870 The elderly Grimké sisters and forty-two other women cast ballots in Massachusetts, but they are ignored.

1870, January 8 The *Woman's Journal*, edited by Lucy Stone, Henry Blackwell, and Mary Livermore, makes its debut in Boston as the official organ of the American Woman Suffrage Association.

1871 Victoria Woodhull, a stockbroker and publisher, argues before the Judiciary Committee of the U.S. House of Representatives that the Fourteenth Amendment also gave women the right to vote. Woodhull does not belong to any of the suffrage groups but has announced plans to run for president.

1872, May 10 Victoria Woodhull becomes a presidential candidate.

1872, November Susan B. Anthony and a group of other women register and vote in Rochester, New York, using Woodhull's argument that the Fourteenth Amendment gave them that right. However, they are arrested a few days later and brought to trial. The following year, Anthony is denied a trial by jury and loses her case, but she refuses to pay a fine.

1874 Annie Wittenmyer founds the Woman's Christian Temperance Union (WCTU). Later headed by Frances Willard, the WCTU emerges as an ally to the suffragists, but the liquor lobby, fearing women may vote to prohibit liquor sales, becomes a nearly invincible opponent to the state and federal efforts.

1874 The Supreme Court rules in *Minor v. Happersett* that the Fourteenth Amendment did not grant women the right to vote.

1875 Michigan and Minnesota give women the right to vote in school elections.

1876 Susan B. Anthony, Matilda Joslyn Gage, and others disrupt the official U.S. Centennial celebration at Independence Hall in Philadelphia to present a "Declaration of Rights for Women." Anthony reads the Declaration in front of the Liberty Bell, and the suffragists meet later at the First Unitarian Church.

1878 Senator Aaron Augustus Sargent, Republican of California, introduces a woman suffrage amendment, the Susan B. Anthony Amendment. The wording remains unchanged until it is finally passed by Congress in 1919.

1880 In New York State, women gain school suffrage.

1880 Lucretia Mott, born in 1793, dies.

1883 Women in the Washington Territory win full voting rights.

1884 The House debates woman suffrage.

1884 Belva Lockwood, a Washington, D.C., lawyer and suffragist, runs for president.

1885, January 11 Alice Paul is born.

1887 The U.S. Senate defeats the suffrage amendment by two to one.

1887 Women in Utah lose the right to vote.

1887 Kansas women win the vote for municipal elections.

1887 Elizabeth Cady Stanton, Susan B. Anthony, and Matilda Joslyn Gage publish three volumes of the *History of Woman Suffrage*. The work will grow to six volumes.

1888, August 14 The Supreme Court strikes down the law that enfranchised women in the Washington Territory in the case of Nevada Bloomer.

1890 The American Woman Suffrage Association and the National Woman Suffrage Association merge, becoming the National American Woman Suffrage Association (NAWSA) to focus on state-by-state campaigns for suffrage. Elizabeth Cady Stanton is its first president.

1890, July 23 Wyoming is admitted as a state and becomes the first since New Jersey in 1776 to grant women full voting rights.

1892 Susan B. Anthony becomes president of the NAWSA.

1893 Colorado adopts a woman suffrage amendment after a campaign led by Carrie Chapman Catt.

1893 Lucy Stone, born in 1818, dies.

1895 Frederick Douglass, born in 1818, dies on the same day he attends a women's rights convention.

1895 Elizabeth Cady Stanton

publishes *The Woman's Bible*, but the NAWSA condemns it.

1896 Utah gains statehood with full suffrage for women.

1896 Idaho women win suffrage.

1896 Black women found the National Association of Colored Women (NACW), uniting more than one hundred clubs. Leaders include Josephine St. Pierre Ruffin, Mary Church Terrell, Anna Julia Cooper, Ida B. Wells-Barnett, and Frances E. W. Harper. The NACW endorses the woman suffrage effort.

1900 Carrie Chapman Catt becomes president of the NAWSA after Susan B. Anthony steps down.

1902 Elizabeth Cady Stanton, born in 1815, dies.

1904 The NAWSA adopts the Declaration of Principles.

1904 Carrie Chapman Catt resigns as president of the NAWSA to attend to her dying husband and devote time to international suffrage work. Dr. Anna Howard Shaw succeeds her.

1906 Susan B. Anthony, born in 1820, dies.

1907 Elizabeth Cady Stanton's daughter, Harriot Stanton Blatch, forms the Equality League of Self-Supporting Women to involve working women in reforms. It evolves into the Women's Political

Union in 1910. Blatch, who had lived in Britain for years, introduces some tactics used by suffragists there, including parades, pickets, and open meetings.

1910 The Women's Political Union organizes the first New York City suffrage parade.

1910 Washington State women win the right to vote.

1911 Women win suffrage in California.

1911 Three thousand people march in the second New York City suffrage parade.

1911 Alice Paul and Lucy Burns conduct the first-ever open-air suffrage meeting in Philadelphia.

1912 Theodore Roosevelt's Progressive Party endorses woman suffrage in its platform, the first time a major political party does so.

1912 Oregon women win the vote.

1912 Arizona women win suffrage.

1912 Kansas adopts a constitutional amendment for woman suffrage.

1912 Twenty thousand suffrage supporters join a New York City parade.

1913 Alice Paul and Lucy Burns found the National Woman's Party to secure passage of a federal amendment.

1913 Women win suffrage

in Alaska's territorial legislature.

1913, March 3 Alice Paul's organization stages a parade the day before President Woodrow Wilson's inauguration in Washington, D.C. As many as eight thousand to ten thousand suffragists march, but they are mobbed by hecklers, drunks, and hoodlums. Many people are injured. The U.S. cavalry restores order.

1913 Women win municipal and presidential election voting in Illinois.

1913, May 10 Ten thousand march in the largest suffrage parade down Fifth Avenue in New York City with as many as a half million onlookers.

1914 Women win suffrage in Nevada and Montana.

1914, September A bequest from Mrs. Frank Leslie, publisher of *Frank Leslie's Illustrated Weekly Newspaper*, nets Carrie Chapman Catt a million dollars for "the furtherance of the cause of woman suffrage."

1915 Dr. Anna Howard Shaw resigns as NAWSA president, and Carrie Chapman Catt replaces her.

1915 Forty thousand people march in a New York City suffrage parade with many of the women dressed in white.

1916 Jeannette Rankin of Montana, a suffrage activist, wins election to the House of Representatives.

1916, August The NAWSA endorses Carrie Chapman Catt's "Winning Plan" to win as many state campaigns for suffrage as possible, get the federal amendment through Congress, and get it ratified by legislatures.

1917, January 10 The National Woman's Party posts Silent Sentinels at the White House. They return daily, rain or shine. They carry banners saying, MR. PRESIDENT, WHAT WILL YOU DO FOR WOMAN SUFFRAGE? and HOW LONG MUST WOMEN WAIT FOR LIBERTY? With World War I under way, official tolerance evaporates. In June, arrests begin on charges of obstructing sidewalk traffic. Nearly five hundred women are arrested, and 168 serve up to six months' jail time. Many go on hunger strikes and are force-fed. Jailers deny civil liberties, brutalize, and injure many of the women. In November, President Woodrow Wilson pardons the picketers in response to public outcry and allows them unconditional release.

1917 New York State, Oklahoma, and South Dakota women secure full voting rights; North Dakota, Nebraska, Indiana, Michigan, and Rhode Island secure presidential suffrage for women; Arkansas women get the vote in primary elections.

1917, April 2 Jeannette Rankin of Montana is formally seated in the U.S. House of Representatives and votes against a resolution to enter World War I four days later.

1917 As the U.S. enters World War I, Carrie Chapman Catt, a pacifist, aligns the NAWSA with the war effort, pledging its support to gain favor for woman suffrage.

1917 Rearrested, Alice Paul, leader of the National Woman's Party, is in solitary confinement in the mental ward of a prison.

1918 Jailers release the suffragists from prison and an appellate court later rules all the arrests illegal.

1918 President Wilson declares support for suffrage and addresses the Senate in support of it. Jeannette Rankin opens debate in the House, and the suffrage amendment passes there, 274 to 136, with exactly a two-thirds vote but loses by two votes in the Senate.

1918 Michigan, South Dakota, and Oklahoma adopt full suffrage amendments for women; Texas secures primary suffrage by legislative enactment.

1919 January In front of the White House, the National Woman's Party builds a perpetual "Watchfire for Freedom," burning Woodrow Wilson's speeches in an urn. They maintain the fire until the suffrage amendment passes the U.S. Senate on June 4.

1919 Maine, Missouri, Iowa, Minnesota, Wisconsin, and Tennessee secure presidential suffrage by legislative enactment.

1919, March 24 The NAWSA convenes in St. Louis, where Carrie Chapman Catt lays out plans to transform the association into the League of Women Voters.

1919, Spring Former prisoners, including L. W. E. Havemeyer, Elizabeth S. Rogers, Vida Milholland, and Mabel Vernon, tour the country on a train, the "Prison Special," on behalf of the National Woman's Party.

1919, May 21 The House passes the woman suffrage amendment, 304 to 89, a margin of 42 votes over the required two-thirds majority.

1919, June 4 The Senate passes the Nineteenth Amendment 56 to 25, with just two votes to spare. It goes to the states for ratification. At least thirty-six states are needed for it to become part of the United States Constitution. The wording, "The right of citizens of the United States to vote shall not be denied or abridged by the United States or by any State on account of sex" is exactly as submitted by Susan B. Anthony in 1878.

1920, August 18 Tennessee becomes the thirty-sixth state to ratify the amendment. Secretary of State Bainbridge Colby certifies it.

1923 Alice Paul proposes the Equal Rights Amendment.

1925, January 5 Nellie Tayloe Ross of Wyoming is inaugurated as the first woman governor in the United States.

1968 Shirley Chisholm becomes the first black woman elected to the House.

1972, March 22 The Equal Rights Amendment is passed by Congress and sent to the states for ratification.

1982 The Equal Rights Amendment fails ratification by the states.

1984 Geraldine Ferraro becomes the first woman nominated by a major party for vice president.

1992 A record-breaking number of women, twenty-four, is elected to Congress.

2007, January Hillary Rodham Clinton announces her candidacy for the Democratic presidential nomination.

2008, June Hillary Rodham Clinton concedes to Senator Barack Obama, Democrat of Illinois, who wins the party's nomination and the 2008 presidential election.

2016, July 27 The Democratic National Convention nominates Hillary Rodham Clinton for president, as the first woman to head a major party ticket.

2016, November 8 Hillary Rodham Clinton loses the Electoral College vote to Donald Trump, 306 electoral votes to 232, but wins the popular vote by 2.6 million.

Sources: National Women's History Museum, "Woman Suffrage Timeline (1840–1920)," https://www.nwhm.org/education-resources/history/woman-suffrage-timeline; The Woman Suffrage Timeline, The Liz Library, http://www.thelizlibrary.org/suffrage/; Important Dates in U.S. Women's History, Scholastic.com, http://www.scholastic.com /teachers/article/important-dates-us-womens-history; Women's Rights Movement in the U.S., http://www.infoplease.com/spot/womenstimeline1.html; Women's Suffrage Time Line, About.com, http://womenshistory.about.com/od/suffrageoverview/a/suffrage _timeline.htm; Timeline of Women's Suffrage in the United States, http://www.dpsinfo .com/women/history/timeline.html; SeekingMichigan.org, http://seekingmichigan.org /look/2011/03/08/woman-suffrage.

Votes for Women — Progress in States

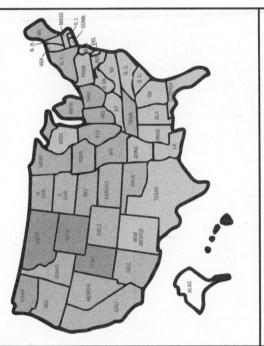

● could vote for president before the 19th Amendment

● gained voting rights with the passage of the 19th Amendment

Could vote for president prior to the 19th Amendment
Illinois 1913
Indiana 1917
Nebraska 1917
North Dakota 1917
Ohio 1917
Rhode Island 1917
Iowa 1919
Maine 1919
Minnesota 1919
Missouri 1919
Tennessee 1919
Wisconsin 1919

Gained voting rights after the passage
Vermont
New Hampshire
Massachusetts
Connecticut
Pennsylvania
New Jersey
Delaware
Maryland
West Virginia
Virginia
North Carolina
South Carolina
Georgia
Alabama
Florida
Mississippi
Louisiana
Arkansas
Texas
New Mexico
Kentucky

● had full voting rights before the 19th Amendment

● had full voting rights before the 19th Amendment and before statehood

States granting women the right to vote prior to the 19th Amendment
Wyoming 1890
Colorado 1893
Utah 1896
Idaho 1896
Washington 1910
California 1911
Arizona 1912
Kansas 1912
Oregon 1912
Montana 1914
Nevada 1914
New York 1917
Michigan 1918
Oklahoma 1918
South Dakota 1918

Full voting rights before 19th Amendment and before statehood
Territory of Wyoming 1869
Territory of Utah 1870
Territory of Washington 1883
Territory of Montana 1887
Territory of Alaska 1913

Source: Centuries of Citizenship: http://constitutioncenter.org/timeline/html/cw08_12159.html.

Notes

Section 1: A Long Silence

Tobias Salinger, "Susan B. Anthony's Grave Decorated with 'Thank You' Sign Celebrating Hillary Clinton's Nomination," *New York Daily News*, July 28, 2016.

Rochester, City of, "Office of the Mayor," http://www.cityofrochester.gov /article.aspx?id=8589934829 (accessed August 17, 2016).

Associated Press, "Steady Crowd Marks Election Day at Susan B. Anthony's Grave," Lexis-Nexis, November 9, 2016.

Eleanor Flexner, *Century of Struggle: The Woman's Rights Movement in the United States* (Cambridge, MA: Belknap Press of Harvard University Press, 1966).

Amanda Marcotte, "Trying to Make America Male Again: Women Control the Ballot Box—and Angry, Sexist Trump Voters Can't Deal," *Salon*, August 9, 2016, http://www.salon.com/2016/08/09/trying-to-make -america-male-again-women-control-the-ballot-box-and-angry-sexist -trump-voters-cant-deal/ (accessed August 18, 2016).

Abigail Adams, "Letter from Abigail Adams to John Adams, 31 March–5 April 1776," Massachusetts Historical Society, Adams Family Papers, http://www.masshist.org/digitaladams/archive /doc?id=L17760331aa&bc=%2Fdigitaladams%2Farchive% 2Fbrowse%2Fletters_1774_1777.php (accessed June 22, 2016).

Charles W. Akers, *Abigail Adams: An American Woman* (Boston and Toronto: Little, Brown, 1980).

Merrill D. Peterson, *Thomas Jefferson and the New Nation* (London, Oxford, and New York: Oxford University Press, 1970), 87–90.

Joseph J. Ellis, *American Creation: Triumphs and Tragedies at the Founding of the Republic* (New York: Random House, 2007), 84–91.

University of Chicago Press, "Representation: John Adams to James
 Sullivan, May 26, 1776," *The Founders' Constitution*, vol. 1, chapter 13,
 document 10, http://press-pubs.uchicago.edu/founders/documents
 /v1ch13s10.html (accessed October 25, 2016).

Henry Chapin, *Address Delivered at the Unitarian Church, in Uxbridge,
 Mass., in 1864: With Further Statements, Not Made a Part of the
 Address, But Included in the Notes* (Worcester, MA: Press of Charles
 Hamilton, 1881). Available at https://books.google.com/books?id
 =ua-pgcKRY2QC&pg=PA172#v=onepage&q&f=false (accessed
 June 23, 2016).

"The Constitution of 1776," Section IV, Official Website for the State of New
 Jersey, http://www.state.nj.us/njfacts/njdoc10a.htm (accessed June
 30, 2016).

Heritage Foundation, "New Jersey Recognizes the Right of Women to Vote:
 February 22, 1797," First Principles Series, http://origin.heritage.org
 /initiatives/first-principles/primary-sources/new-jersey-recognizes
 -the-right-of-women-to-vote (accessed July 1, 2016).

Judith Apter Klinghoffer and Lois Elkis, "'The Petticoat Electors': Women's
 Suffrage in New Jersey, 1776–1807," *Journal of the Early Republic* 12,
 no. 2 (Summer 1992), 159–193, http://www.jstor.org/stable/3124150
 (accessed July 1, 2016).

William Blackstone, *Commentaries on the Laws of England,* book 1, chapter
 15, University of Adelaide, Ebooks@Adelaide, https://ebooks.adelaide
 .edu.au/b/blackstone/william/comment/book1.15.html (accessed June
 23, 2016).

Ron Chernow, *Alexander Hamilton* (New York: Penguin, 2004).

Sibyl A. Schwarzenbach and Patricia Smith, eds., *Women and the United
 States Constitution: History, Interpretation, and Practice* (New York:
 Columbia University Press, 2003).

Gail Collins, *America's Women: 400 Years of Dolls, Drudges, Helpmates, and
 Heroines* (New York: William Morrow, 2003).

Kathleen M. Brown, "Women in Early Jamestown," Virtual Jamestown,
 http://www.virtualjamestown.org/essays/brown_essay.html (accessed
 June 29, 2016).

John Hope Franklin, *From Slavery to Freedom* (New York: Alfred A. Knopf,
 1967).

Benjamin Rush, "Thoughts upon Female Education, Accommodated to the
 Present State of Society, Manners, and Government, in the United
 States of America. Addressed to the Visitors of the Young Ladies
 Academy in Philadelphia, 28th July, 1787, at the Close of the Quarterly
 Examination." Quoted in "Benjamin Rush, from 'Thoughts upon Female

Education,'" ExplorePaHistory.com, http://explorepahistory.com /odocument.php?docId=1-4-15B (accessed June 27, 2016).

"About Oberlin: History," Oberlin College, https://new.oberlin.edu/about /history.dot (accessed June 27, 2016).

Marilyn Richardson, *Maria W. Stewart, America's First Black Woman Political Writer: Essays and Speeches* (Bloomington, IN: Indiana University Press, 1987).

General Association of Massachusetts, "Pastoral Letter of the General Association of Massachusetts, June 28, 1837," in *American Rhetorical Discourse*, 2nd ed., edited by Ronald F. Reid (Prospect Heights, IL: Waveland Press, 1995), 363–367. Available at http://users.wfu.edu /zulick/340/pastoralletter.html (accessed February 27, 2017).

Angelina Grimké, "An Appeal to the Christian Women of the South," 1836, in *Uncle Tom's Cabin & American Culture: A Multi-Media Archive*, University of Virginia, http://utc.iath.virginia.edu/abolitn/abesaegat .html (accessed July 7, 2016).

Sarah Grimké, "Letters on the Equality of the Sexes," 1837, National Humanities Center, http://nationalhumanitiescenter.org/ows /seminarsflvs/Grimke%20Letters.pdf (accessed July 7, 2016).

Carol Faulkner, *Lucretia Mott's Heresy: Abolition and Women's Rights in Nineteenth-Century America* (Philadelphia: University of Pennsylvania Press, 2011).

Ira V. Brown, "Am I Not a Woman and a Sister? The Anti-Slavery Convention of American Women, 1837–1839." *Pennsylvania History* 50, no. 1 (January 1983), https://journals.psu.edu/phj/article/view /24363/24132 (accessed August 22, 2016).

Sidebar:
Lucy Stone: A Woman of Courage

Sally G. McMillen, *Lucy Stone: An Unapologetic Life* (Oxford and New York: Oxford University Press, 2015).

Jean H. Baker, *Sisters: The Lives of America's Suffragists* (New York: Hill and Wang, 2005), 13–53.

Flexner, *Century of Struggle*, 69.

Elizabeth Cady Stanton, Susan B. Anthony, and Matilda Joslyn Gage, eds., *History of Woman Suffrage*, vol. 1, *1848–1861* (Rochester, NY: Charles Mann, 1889), 261.

Lucy Stone, "A Disappointed Woman," Primary Source Documents: 1850 to 1874, Facts On File, 2014. History Research Center Web (accessed May 31, 2016).

Alice Stone Blackwell, *Lucy Stone: Pioneer of Woman's Rights* (Charlottesville and London: University of Virginia, 1930).

Sidebar:
Lucretia Mott: Uncompromising Reformer

Faulkner, *Lucretia Mott's Heresy*.

Frederick Douglass, *The Life and Times of Frederick Douglass* (Boston: Dewolfe & Fisk, 1895).

Elizabeth Cady Stanton, "Eulogy at the Memorial Services Held in Washington by the National Woman Suffrage Association, January 19, 1881," in Stanton, Anthony, and Gage, eds., *History of Woman Suffrage*, vol. 1, 431–432.

Philip S. Foner, "The Rights of Women," in *Frederick Douglass: Selected Speeches and Writings* (Chicago: Lawrence Hill Books, 1999).

Section 2: The Awakening: A Declaration of Sentiments

Faulkner, *Lucretia Mott's Heresy*.

Flexner, *Century of Struggle*.

"Report of the Woman's Rights Convention," National Park Service, Women's Rights National Historical Park, https://www.nps.gov/wori /learn/historyculture/report-of-the-womans-rights-convention.htm (accessed July 3, 2016).

"Report of the Woman's Rights Convention, Held at Seneca Falls, N.Y., July 19th and 20th, 1848 (Rochester, 1848)," in Ann D. Gordon, ed., *The Selected Papers of Elizabeth Cady Stanton and Susan B. Anthony*, vol. 1, *In the School of Anti-Slavery, 1840 to 1866* (New Brunswick, NJ: Rutgers, The State University of New Jersey, 1997). Available at http://ecssba .rutgers.edu/docs/seneca.html (accessed July 3, 2016).

Sally G. McMillen, *Seneca Falls and the Origin of the Women's Rights Movement* (Oxford and New York: Oxford University Press, 2008).

"Signers of the Declaration of Sentiments," National Park Service, Women's Rights National Historical Park, https://www.nps.gov/wori /learn/historyculture/signers-of-the-declaration-of-sentiments.htm (accessed July 3, 2016).

"Quaker Influence," National Park Service, Women's Rights National Historical Park, https://www.nps.gov/wori/learn/historyculture /quaker-influence.htm (accessed July 4, 2016).

"Report of the Woman's Rights Convention, 1848," *University of Rochester Library Bulletin* 4, no. 1 (Autumn 1948), http://rbscp.lib.rochester .edu/2448 (accessed July 5, 2016).

Bradford Miller, *Returning to Seneca Falls: The First Woman's Rights Convention and Its Meaning for Men and Women Today* (Hudson, NY: Lindisfarne Press, 1995).

Lisa Tetrault, *The Myth of Seneca Falls: Memory and the Women's Suffrage Movement, 1848–1898* (Chapel Hill: University of North Carolina Press, 2014).

Judith Wellman, *The Road to Seneca Falls* (Urbana and Chicago: University of Illinois Press, 2004).

"From the Seneca Falls (N.Y) Courier, July 21. Women's Rights Convention," *Liberator*, August 25, 1848.

Stanton, Anthony, and Gage, *History of Woman Suffrage*, vol. 1.

Christopher Densmore, "Radical Quaker Women and the Early Women's Rights Movement," Bryn Mawr College, Quakers & Slavery, http://trilogy.brynmawr.edu/speccoll/quakersandslavery/commentary/themes/radical_quaker_women.php (accessed July 21, 2016).

Frederick Douglass, *Frederick Douglass on Women's Rights*, edited by Philip S. Foner (New York: Da Capo Press, 1992), 49–51.

Frederick Douglass Paper, July 28, 1848, Accessible Archives, http://www.accessible.com/accessible/print?AADocList=189&AADocStyle=STYLED&AAStyleFile=&AABeanName=toc1&AANextPage=/printFullDocFromXML.jsp&AACheck=1.8311.189.0.0 (accessed July 20, 2016).

Faulkner, *Lucretia Mott's Heresy*, 147.

"Josephine Sophia White Griffing: American Abolitionist and Suffragist," *Encyclopaedia Brittanica*, https://www.britannica.com/biography/Josephine-Sophia-White-Griffing (accessed July 7, 2016).

Sidebar:
Elizabeth Cady Stanton: The Mother of the Movement

Baker, *Sisters*.

Lori D. Ginzberg, *Elizabeth Cady Stanton: An American Life* (New York: Hill and Wang, 2009).

Stanton, Anthony, and Gage, *History of Woman Suffrage*, vol. 1, 420.

Tetrault, *Myth of Seneca Falls*, 10–12.

Elizabeth Cady Stanton, *Eighty Years and More: Reminiscences, 1815–1897* (1897), chapter 9, University of Pennsylvania, Penn Libraries, A Celebration of Women Writers, http://digital.library.upenn.edu/women/stanton/years/years.html#IX (accessed February 27, 2017). This online version is not paginated.

Section 3: The Early Conventions

"Paulina Kellogg Wright Davis," *American National Biography Online*, http://www.anb.org/articles/15/15-00166.html (accessed July 8, 2016).

"Woman's Rights Convention: Awful Combination of Socialism, Abolitionism, and Infidelity," *New York Herald*, October 25, 1850.

Frederick Douglass Paper, September 4, 1851, Accessible Archives, http://www.accessible.com/accessible/print?AADocList=1&AADocStyle=STYLED&AAStyleFile=&AABeanName=toc1&AANextPage=/printFullDocFromXML.jsp&AACheck=2.10.1.0.0 (accessed July 12, 2016).

Ida B. Husted Harper, *The Life and Work of Susan B. Anthony* (Indianapolis and Kansas City: Bowen-Merrill, 1899), 64.

Faulkner, *Lucretia Mott's Heresy*.

Proceedings of the Cleveland meeting were also printed and circulated. See *Proceedings of the National Woman's Rights Convention Held at Cleveland, Ohio* (Cleveland: Gray, Beardsley, Spear, 1854). An electronic facsimile is available at the Internet Archive, http://www.archive.org/stream/proceedingsnati08convgoog#page/n19/mode/2up (accessed February 27, 2017).

Sidebar:
Sojourner Truth: Powerful Orator

Gerda Lerner, *Black Women in White America: A Documentary History* (New York: Vintage Books, 1992).

Tetrault, *Myth of Seneca Falls*.

Nell Painter, *Sojourner Truth: A Life, A Symbol* (New York: W.W. Norton, 1996).

Lerner, *Black Women in White America*, 570.

Marius Robinson, "Women's Rights Convention: Sojourner Truth," *Anti-Slavery Bugle* (New Lisbon, OH), June 21, 1851. Available at Library of Congress, Chronicling America, http://chroniclingamerica.loc.gov/lccn/sn83035487/1851-06-21/ed-1/seq-4/ (accessed August 23, 2016).

Sidebar:
The Bloomer: "Dress Reform"

Flexner, *Century of Struggle*.

Harper, *Life and Work of Susan B. Anthony*.

Stanton, Anthony, and Gage, *History of Woman Suffrage*, vol. 1.

Blackwell, *Lucy Stone*, 103–105.

Lynn Sherr, *Failure Is Impossible: Susan B. Anthony in Her Own Words* (New York: Times Books / Random House, 1995), 192.

Ibid., 195.

"Woman," *Lily*, October 16, 1854, Accessible Archives, http://www.accessible

.com/accessible/print?AADocList=31&AADocStyle=STYLED&AAStyleFile
=&AABeanName=toc1&AANextPage=/printFullDocFromXML
.jsp&AACheck=1.96.31.0.0 (accessed July 15, 2016).

Sidebar:
The Temperance Movement

Flexner, *Century of Struggle*, 174.

Baker, *Sisters*.

"Roots of Prohibition," PBS, *Prohibition*, http://www.pbs.org/kenburns
/prohibition/roots-of-prohibition/ (accessed October
31, 2016).

"Temperance & Prohibition," Ohio State University, College of Arts and
Sciences, Anti-Saloon League, https://prohibition.osu.edu/anti
-saloon-league (accessed October 31, 2016).

"18th and 21st Amendments," History.com, http://www.history
.com/topics/18th-and-21st-amendments (accessed October
31, 2016).

Section 4: A Division

Franklin, *From Slavery to Freedom*.

Flexner, *Century of Struggle*.

Sherry H. Penney and James D. Livingston, *A Very Dangerous Woman:
Martha Wright and Women's Rights* (Amherst and Boston: University of
Massachusetts Press, 2004).

Harper, *Life and Work of Susan B. Anthony*, 212.

Sidebar:
The Party of Lincoln

Stephen B. Oates, *With Malice Toward None: The Life of Abraham Lincoln* (New
York and Scarborough, Ont.: New American Library, 1977), 122.

Heather Cox Richardson, *To Make Men Free: A History of the Republican Party*
(New York: Basic Books, 2014).

Karen Grigsby Bates, "Why Did Black Voters Flee the Republican Party in
the 1960s?" NPR, Code Switch, July 14, 2014, http://www.npr.org
/sections/codeswitch/2014/07/14/331298996/why-did-black
-voters-flee-the-republican-party-in-the-1960s (accessed
November 1, 2016).

"Republican Party Founded," History.com, This Day in History, http://
www.history.com/this-day-in-history/republican-party-founded
(accessed November 1, 2016).

"Free-Soil Party," Gilder Lehrman Institute of History, History by Era,
    Slavery and Anti-Slavery, http://www.gilderlehrman.org/history-by
    -era/slavery-and-anti-slavery/timeline-terms/free-soil-party
    (accessed October 31, 2016).

Harper, *Life and Work of Susan B. Anthony*, 226.
Elizabeth Cady Stanton, Susan B. Anthony, and Matilda Joslyn Gage, eds.,
    History of Woman Suffrage, vol. 2, *1861–1876* (Rochester: Susan B.
    Anthony, 1881).
McMillen, *Lucy Stone*.
"13th Amendment to the U.S. Constitution," Library of Congress, Primary
    Documents in American History (Virtual Programs and Services),
    https://www.loc.gov/rr/program/bib/ourdocs/13thamendment.html
    (accessed July 24, 2016).
Geoffrey C. Ward et al., *Not for Ourselves Alone: The Story of Elizabeth Cady
    Stanton and Susan B. Anthony* (New York: Alfred A. Knopf, 1999), 103.
Flexner, *Century of Struggle*, 142.
Tetrault, *Myth of Seneca Falls*.
Elizabeth Cady Stanton, December 24, 1868, Accessible Archives, http://www
    .accessible.com/accessible/print?AADocList=9&AADocStyle=
    STYLED&AAStyleFile=&AABeanName=toc1&AANextPage=
    /printFullDocFromXML.jsp&AACheck=5.223.9.0.0 (accessed July 25, 2016).
Garrett Epps, *Democracy Reborn: The Fourteenth Amendment and the Fight
    for Equal Rights in Post–Civil War America* (New York: A John Macrae
    Book / Henry Holt, 2006), 217.
Douglass, *Frederick Douglass on Women's Rights*.
Elizabeth Cady Stanton, May 27, 1868, Accessible Archives, http://www
    .accessible.com/accessible/print?AADocList=15&AADocStyle=
    STYLED&AAStyleFile=&AABeanName=toc1&AANextPage=
    /printFullDocFromXML.jsp&AACheck=2.353.15.0.0 (accessed July 27, 2016).
"The Revolution 1868–1872," Accessible Archives, http://www.accessible
    -archives.com/collections/the-revolution/ (accessed July 27, 2016).
McMillen, *Lucy Stone*, 169.
Tom Rea, "Right Choice, Wrong Reasons: Wyoming Women Win the Right to
    Vote," WyoHistory.org, http://www.wyohistory.org/essays/right
    -choice-wrong-reasons-wyoming-women-win-right-vote (accessed
    July 26, 2016).
"Partial Census Figures and Other Vital Data for Chinese Living in Wyoming
    from 1869–1890," Western Wyoming Community College, Wyoming
    History, http://www.wwcc.wy.edu/wyo_hist/Chinese_census_data
    .pdf (accessed November 2, 2016).

Sidebar:
Susan B. Anthony: The Drum Major for Suffrage

Alma Lutz, *Susan B. Anthony: Rebel, Crusader, Humanitarian* (Washington, D.C.: Zenger, 1959).

Stanton, Anthony, and Gage, *History of Woman Suffrage*, vol. 1.

Baker, *Sisters*, 60.

Flexner, *Century of Struggle*.

Harper, *Life and Work of Susan B. Anthony*.

"The Motts: Lydia and Abigail," Underground Railroad History Project, http://undergroundrailroadhistory.org/page_id46/page_id76/ (accessed July 16, 2016).

Abigail Mott. "Biographical Sketches and Interesting Anecdotes of Persons of Color. To Which Is Added a Selection of Pieces in Poetry," Priscilla Juvelis, http://www.juvelisbooks.com/pages/books/8292/abigail-mott/biographical-sketches-and-interesting-anecdotes-of-persons-of-color-to-which-is-added-a-selection#sthash.gXhNJsxV.dpuf (accessed July 16, 2016). (This web page is no longer available.)

Jacqueline Van Voris, *Carrie Chapman Catt: A Public Life* (New York: Feminist Press at the City University of New York, 1987), 45.

Paula Giddings, *When and Where I Enter: The Impact of Black Women on Race and Sex in America* (New York: Amistad, 2006).

Mary Church Terrell, "Susan B. Anthony, the Abolitionist," 1, Howard University, Moorland-Spingarn Collection, Mary Church Terrell Papers.

Mary Church Terrell, "Use the Franchise! An Appeal to the Colored Woman to Vote," 1946, Howard University, Moorland-Spingarn Collection, AfraAmerican / Mary Church Terrell Papers.

Neale McGoldrick, "Women's Suffrage and the Question of Color." National Council for the Social Studies, http://www.socialstudies.org/system/files/publications/se/5905/590503.html (accessed August 17, 2016).

Section 5: Are Women Persons?

Flexner, *Century of Struggle*.

Baker, *Sisters*.

Sherr, *Failure Is Impossible*.

Sidebar:
The Woodhull Scandal

Myra MacPherson, *The Scarlet Sisters: Sex, Suffrage, and Scandal in the Gilded Age* (New York: Twelve, 2014).

Victoria Woodhull, "Victoria Woodhull Address Before Congress," December

19, 1870, University of Massachusetts Lowell, An American Time Capsule: Three Centuries of Broadsides and Other Printed Ephemera, http:// faculty.uml.edu/sgallagher/Woodhullmemorial.htm (accessed July 29, 2016).

Jill Norgren, "Belva Lockwood: Blazing the Trail for Women in Law," *Prologue Magazine* 37, no. 1 (Spring 2005). Available at National Archives, http://www.archives.gov/publications/prologue/2005 /spring/belva-lockwood-1.html (accessed August 2, 2016).

New York Times, "The Claflin Family. Arrest of Victoria Woodhull, Tennie C. Claflin and Col. Blood—They are Charged with Publishing an Obscene Newspaper. Times Machine: November 3, 1872," http://timesmachine .nytimes.com/timesmachine/1872/11/03/79024263.html?pageNumber=1 (accessed July 29, 2016).

Susan B. Anthony, "Are Women Persons?" Primary Source Documents, 1850–1874, Facts on File, History Research Center Web.

An Account of the Proceedings on the Trial of Susan B. Anthony on the Charge of Illegal Voting at the Presidential Election in Nov., 1872, and on the Trial of Beverly W. Jones, Edwin T. Marsh and William B. Hall, the Inspectors of Election by Whom Her Vote Was Received (Rochester, NY: Daily Democrat and Chronicle Book Print, 1874).

"The Trial of Susan B. Anthony: A Short Narrative," Federal Judicial Center, History of the Federal Judiciary, http://www.fjc.gov/history /home.nsf/page/tu_anthony_narrative.html (accessed July 31, 2016).

Doug Linder, "The Trial of Susan B. Anthony for Illegal Voting," 2001, University of Missouri–Kansas City, Faculty Projects, http://law2 .umkc.edu/faculty/projects/ftrials/anthony/sbaaccount.html (accessed July 29, 2016).

Steve Cottrell, "Our History: A Champion of Women's Suffrage," *Nevada City Advocate*, http://nevadacityadvocate.com/ellen-clark (accessed July 31, 2016).

McMillen, *Lucy Stone*.

Henry W. Blair, J. E. Brown, J. N. Dolph, G. G. Vest, Geo. F. Hoar, Debate on Woman Suffrage in the Senate of the United States, 2d Session, 49th Congress, December 8, 1886, and January 25, 1887, The Project Gutenberg EBook, http://www.gutenberg.org/files/11114/11114 -h/11114-h.htm (accessed December 12, 2016).

"The Remonstrance (Boston), January, 1909," Library of Congress, American Memory Timeline, http://www.loc.gov/teachers/classroommaterials /presentationsandactivities/presentations/timeline/progress /suffrage/remonst.html (accessed November 4, 2016).

Giddings, *When and Where I Enter*.

Terrell, "Susan B. Anthony," 1.

Terrell, "Use the Franchise!"

McGoldrick, "Women's Suffrage and the Question of Color."

Sidebar:
Ida B. Wells-Barnett

Mia Bay, *To Tell the Truth Freely: The Life of Ida B. Wells* (New York: Hill and Wang, 2009).

New York Times, "Death of Fred Douglass," February 21, 1895, http://www .nytimes.com/learning/general/onthisday/bday/0207.html (accessed August 24, 2016).

Marjorie Spruill Wheeler, ed., *One Woman, One Vote: Rediscovering the Woman Suffrage Movement* (Troutdale, OR: NewSage Press, 1995).

Henry Louis Gates Jr. and Evelyn Brooks Higginbotham, eds., *African American National Biography* (Oxford and New York: Oxford University Press, 2008).

Mary Church Terrell, "The Progress of Colored Women," Sweet Briar College, Gifts of Speech, http://gos.sbc.edu/t/terrellmary.html (accessed August 2, 2016).

Ward et al., *Not for Ourselves Alone*, 185.

"Death of Fred Douglass."

New York Times, "Tributes of Two Races," February 25, 1895, http://query.nytimes.com/mem/archive-free/pdf?_r=2&res =990CE7D6123DE433A25755C2A9649C94649ED7CF (accessed August 23, 2011).

Sidebar:
Carrie Chapman Catt

Van Voris, *Carrie Chapman Catt*.

Van Voris, *Carrie Chapman Catt*, 44.

Section 6: How Long Must Women Wait?

Ida Husted Harper, ed., *History of Woman Suffrage*, vol. 5, *1900–1920* (Washington, D.C.: National American Woman Suffrage Association, 1922), 742.

Baker, *Sisters*, 204.

Jennifer L. Borda, "The Woman Suffrage Parades of 1910–1913: Possibilities and Limitations of an Early Feminist Rhetorical Strategy," *Western Journal of Communication* 66, no. 1 (Winter 2002), 25–52.

New York Times, "Great Advance of Suffrage Since Last Year's Parade," May 4, 1913, http://query.nytimes.com/mem/archive-free /pdf?res=9903E5D8173FE633A25757C0A9639C946296D6CF (accessed August 9, 2016).

James Glen Stovall, *Seeing Suffrage: The Washington Suffrage Parade of 1913, Its Pictures and Its Effect on the American Political Landscape* (Knoxville: University of Tennessee Press, 2013).

J. D. Zahniser and Amelia R. Fry, *Alice Paul: Claiming Power* (Oxford: Oxford University Press, 2014).

Sidebar:
Alice Paul

Baker, *Sisters*.
Flexner, *Century of Struggle*.

Van Voris, *Carrie Chapman Catt*.
Pamela Newkirk, *Letters from Black America* (New York: Farrar, Straus and Giroux, 2009), 124–125.
Beth A. Behn, "Woodrow Wilson's Conversion Experience: The President and the Federal Woman Suffrage Amendment," 2012, 34. Available from University of Massachusetts—Amherst, http://scholarworks .umass.edu/cgi/viewcontent.cgi?article=1503&context=open_access _dissertations (accessed November 7, 2016).
Wheeler, *One Woman, One Vote*.
Behn, "Woodrow Wilson's Conversion Experience," 21.
Flexner, *Century of Struggle*.
Jessica Bliss, "Alan LeQuire's Women Suffrage Monument to Be Unveiled in Centennial Park," *Tennessean*, August 24, 2016, http://www .tennessean.com/story/news/2016/08/24/alan-lequires-women -suffrage-monument-unveiled-centennial-park/87150580/ (accessed August 25, 2016).
Carol Lynn Yellin and Janann Sherman, *The Perfect 36: Tennessee Delivers Woman Suffrage* (Memphis, TN: Serviceberry Press, 1998).

Sidebar:
Equal Rights Amendment

Tabby Biddle, "Wait, Women Don't Have Equal Rights in the United States?" *Huffington Post*, January 3, 2015, http://www.huffingtonpost.com /tabby-biddle/wait-women-dont-have-equa_b_6098120.html (accessed November 9, 2016).

Baker, *Sisters*, 226.

Elizabeth Kolbert, "Firebrand: Phyllis Schlafly and the Conservative Revolution," *New Yorker*, November 7, 2005, http://www.newyorker .com/magazine/2005/11/07/firebrand (accessed November 9, 2016).

Zahniser and Fry, *Alice Paul*.

Carrie Chapman Catt and Nettie Rogers Shuler, *Woman Suffrage and Politics: The Inner Story of the Suffrage Movement* (New York: Charles Scribner's Sons, 1926), 107–108.

Sidebar:
The League of Women Voters

Van Voris, *Carrie Chapman Catt*.

"History," League of Women Voters, http://lwv.org/history (accessed November 8, 2016).

Annie Correal, "Pantsuit Nation, a 'Secret' Facebook Hub, Celebrates Clinton," *New York Times*, November 9, 2016, http://www.nytimes .com/216/11/09/us/politics/facebook-pantsuit-nation-clinton .html?smid=fb-nytimes&smtyp=cur (accessed November 9, 2016).

Alex Orlov, "More White Women Voted for Donald Trump Than for Hillary Clinton," Policy.Mic, November 9, 2016, https://mic.com /articles/158995/more-white-women-voted-for-donald-trump -than-for-hillary-clinton#.LYLBIo6IB (accessed November 9, 2016).

Mattie Kahn, "Let's Celebrate the Women Who Won Last Night: They Need You," *Elle*, November 9, 2016, http://www.elle.com/culture/career -politics/news/a40643/election-2016-women-winners/ (accessed November 9, 2016).

Appendix 1:
Congressional Women's Caucus

"Congressional Caucus for Women's Issues," Women's Policy, Inc., http:// www.womenspolicy.org/our-work/the-womens-caucus/ (accessed November 9, 2016).

Bibliography

An Account of the Proceedings on the Trial of Susan B. Anthony on the Charge of Illegal Voting at the Presidential Election in Nov., 1872, and on the Trial of Beverly W. Jones, Edwin T. Marsh and William B. Hall, the Inspectors of Elections by Whom Her Vote Was Received. Rochester, NY: Daily Democrat and Chronicle Book Print, 1874; e-book and Kindle editions.

Adams, Abigail. "Letter from Abigail Adams to John Adams, 31 March–5 April 1776." Massachusetts Historical Society. http://www.masshist .org/digitaladams/archive/doc?id=L17760331aa&bc=%2 Fdigitaladams%2Farchive%2Fbrowse%2Fletters_1774_1777.php (accessed June 22, 2016).

Akers, Charles W. *Abigail Adams: An American Woman.* Boston and Toronto: Little, Brown, 1980.

Anthony, Susan B. "Are Women Persons?" Primary Source Documents, 1850–1874, Facts on File, History Research Center Web. May 31, 2016.

"The Articles of Confederation." USConstitution.net. http://www.us constitution.net/articles.html (accessed October 25, 2016).

Associated Press. "Steady Crowd Marks Election Day at Susan B. Anthony's Grave" (accessed on Lexis-Nexis, November 9, 2016).

Baker, Jean H. *Sisters: The Lives of America's Suffragists.* New York: Hill and Wang, 2005.

Bates, Karen Grigsby. "Why Did Black Voters Flee the Republican Party in the 1960s?" NPR, Code Switch. July 14, 2014. http://www.npr.org /sections/codeswitch/2014/07/14/331298996/why-did-black-voters -flee-the-republican-party-in-the-1960s (accessed November 1, 2016).

Bay, Mia. *To Tell the Truth Freely: The Life of Ida B. Wells.* New York: Hill and Wang, 2009.

Behn, Beth A. "Woodrow Wilson's Conversion Experience: The President and the Federal Woman Suffrage Amendment," 2012. University of Massachusetts—Amherst. http://scholarworks.umass.edu/cgi /viewcontent.cgi?article=1503&context=open_access_dissertations (accessed November 7, 2016).

Biddle, Tabby. "Wait, Women Don't Have Equal Rights in the United States?" *Huffington Post*, January 3, 2015. http://www .huffingtonpost.com/tabby-biddle/wait-women-dont-have -equa_b_6098120.html (accessed November 9, 2016).

Blackstone, William. *Commentaries on the Laws of England*, book 1, chapter 15. University of Adelaide, Ebooks@Adelaide. https://ebooks .adelaide.edu.au/b/blackstone/william/comment/book1.15.html (accessed June 23, 2016).

Blackwell, Alice Stone. *Lucy Stone: Pioneer of Woman's Rights*. Charlottesville and London: University of Virginia, 1930.

Bliss, Jessica. "Alan LeQuire's Women Suffrage Monument to Be Unveiled in Centennial Park." *Tennessean*, August 24, 2016. http://www .tennessean.com/story/news/2016/08/24/alan-lequires-women -suffrage-monument-unveiled-centennial-park/87150580/ (accessed August 25, 2016).

Borda, Jennifer L. "The Woman Suffrage Parades of 1910–1913: Possibilities and Limitations of an Early Feminist Rhetorical Strategy." *Western Journal of Communication* 66, no. 1 (Winter 2002), 25–52.

Brown, Ira V. "Am I Not a Woman and a Sister? The Anti-Slavery Convention of American Women, 1837–1839." *Pennsylvania History: Journal of Mid-Atlantic Studies* 50, no. 1 (January 1983). https:// journals.psu.edu/phj/article/viewFile/24363/24132 (accessed August 22, 2016).

Brown, Kathleen M. "Women in Early Jamestown." Virtual Jamestown. http://www.virtualjamestown.org/essays/brown_essay.html (accessed June 29, 2016).

Butterfield, L. H., Marc Friedlaender, and Mary-Jo Kline. *The Book of Abigail and John: Selected Letters of the Adams Family, 1762–1784*. Cambridge, MA, and London: Harvard University Press, 1975.

Catt, Carrie Chapman, and Nettie Rogers Shuler. *Woman Suffrage and Politics: The Inner Story of the Suffrage Movement*. New York: Charles Scribner's Sons, 1926.

"CAWP Fact Sheet: Gender Differences in Voter Turnout," June 2005. Rutgers, the State University of New Jersey. Eagleton Institute of Politics. Center for American Women and Politics. http://www.cawp

.rutgers.edu/sites/default/files/resources/genderdiff.pdf (accessed August 18, 2016).

Chapin, Henry. *Address Delivered at the Unitarian Church, in Uxbridge, Mass., in 1864: With Further Statements, Not Made a Part of the Address, But Included in the Notes.* Worcester, MA: Press of Charles Hamilton, 1864. Available at https://books.google.com/books?id=ua-pgcKRY2QC&pg=PA172#v=onepage&q&f=false (accessed June 23, 2016).

Chernow, Ron. *Alexander Hamilton.* New York: Penguin, 2004.

Chisholm, Shirley. *The Good Fight.* New York: Harper & Row, 1973.

Collins, Gail. *America's Women: 400 Years of Dolls, Drudges, Helpmates, and Heroines.* New York: William Morrow, 2003.

Collinson, Stephen, Dan Merica, and Jeff Zeleny. "Hillary Clinton Delivers Painful Concession Speech." CNN Politics, November 9, 2016. http://www.cnn.com/2016/11/09/politics/clinton-to-offer-remarks-in-new-york-city/ (accessed November 9, 2016). An earlier version of this article was titled, "Clinton to Offer Remarks in New York City."

"Congressional Caucus for Women's Issues." Women's Policy, Inc. http://www.womenspolicy.org/our-work/the-womens-caucus/ (accessed November 9, 2016).

Correal, Annie. "Pantsuit Nation, a 'Secret' Facebook Hub, Celebrates Clinton." *New York Times*, November 9, 2016. http://www.nytimes.com/2016/11/09/us/politics/facebook-pantsuit-nation-clinton.html?smid=fb-nytimes&smtyp=cur (accessed November 9, 2016).

Cottrell, Steve. "Our History: A Champion of Women's Suffrage." *Nevada City Advocate.* http://nevadacityadvocate.com/ellen-clark (accessed July 31, 2016).

Densmore, Christopher. "Radical Quaker Women and the Early Women's Rights Movement." Bryn Mawr College. Quakers & Slavery. http://trilogy.brynmawr.edu/speccoll/quakersandslavery/commentary/themes/radical_quaker_women.php (accessed July 21, 2016).

Dodge, Arthur M. (Mrs.). "Mrs. Arthur M. Dodge Declares Suffrage Unnecessary." *Columbia Daily Spectator,* October 29, 1915. *Columbia Spectator* Archive. http://spectatorarchive.library.columbia.edu/cgi-bin/columbia?a=d&d=cs19151029-01.2.27 (accessed November 5, 2016).

Douglass, Frederick. *The Life and Times of Frederick Douglass.* Boston: Dewolfe & Fisk, 1895.

———. "The Rights of Women." In *Frederick Douglass: Selected Speeches and Writings,* edited by Philip S. Foner. Chicago: Lawrence Hill Books, 1999.

DuBois, Ellen. "Reconstruction and the Battle for Woman Suffrage."
    Gilder Lehrman Institute of American History. https://www
    .gilderlehrman.org/history-by-era/reconstruction/essays
    /reconstruction-and-battle-for-woman-suffrage (accessed July 27,
    2016).

Ellis, Joseph J. *American Creation: Triumph and Tragedies at the Founding of
    the Republic*. New York: Random House, 2007.

Epps, Garrett. *Democracy Reborn: The Fourteenth Amendment and the
    Fight for Equal Rights in Post–Civil War America*. New York: Henry
    Holt, 2006.

Faulkner, Carol. *Lucretia Mott's Heresy: Abolition and Women's Rights in
    Nineteenth-Century America*. Philadelphia: University of Pennsylvania
    Press, 2011.

Ferguson, David. "Angela Rye: Evangelical Voters 'Can't See Women as
    Head of a Household'—Let Alone the Country." *Raw Story*, November
    9, 2016. https://www.rawstory.com/2016/11/angela-rye-evangelical
    -voters-cant-see-women-as-head-of-a-household-let-alone-the
    -country/ (accessed November 9, 2016).

Flexner, Eleanor. *Century of Struggle: The Woman's Rights Movement in the
    United States*. Cambridge, MA: Belknap Press of Harvard University
    Press, 1966.

Foner, Philip S., ed. *Frederick Douglass on Women's Rights*. New York: Da
    Capo Press, 1992.

Franklin, John Hope. *From Slavery to Freedom*. New York: Alfred A. Knopf,
    1967.

Frederick Douglass Paper, July 14, 1848. Accessible Archives. http://www
    .accessible.com/accessible/print?AADocList=5&AADocStyle=
    STYLED&AAStyleFile=&AABeanName=toc1&AANextPage=
    /printFullDocFromXML.jsp&AACheck=3.3478.5.0.0 (accessed July 20,
    2016).

Frederick Douglass Paper, July 28, 1848. Accessible Archives. http://www
    .accessible.com/accessible/print?AADocList=189&AADocStyle=
    STYLED&AAStyleFile=&AABeanName=toc1&AANextPage=
    /printFullDocFromXML.jsp&AACheck=1.8311.189.0.0 (accessed July 20,
    2016).

Frederick Douglass Paper, September 4, 1851. Accessible Archives. http://
    www.accessible.com/accessible/print?AADocList=1&AADocStyle=
    STYLED&AAStyleFile=&AABeanName=toc1&AANextPage=/
    printFullDocFromXML.jsp&AACheck=2.10.1.0.0 (accessed July
    12, 2016).

"Free-Soil Party." Gilder Lehrman Institute of History. http://www

.gilderlehrman.org/history-by-era/slavery-and-anti-slavery/timeline
-terms/free-soil-party (accessed November 1, 2016).

Gates, Henry Louis Jr., and Evelyn Brooks Higginbotham, eds. *African
American National Biography*. Oxford and New York: Oxford University
Press, 2008.

Gelles, Edith B. *Abigail & John: Portrait of a Marriage*. New York: William
Morrow, 2009.

General Association of Massachusetts. "Pastoral Letter of the General
Association of Massachusetts, June 28, 1837." In *American Rhetorical
Discourse*, 2nd ed., edited by Ronald F. Reid (Prospect Heights, IL:
Waveland Press, 1995), 363–367. Available at http://users.wfu.edu
/zulick/340/pastoralletter.html (accessed February 27, 2017).

Giddings, Paula. *When and Where I Enter: The Impact of Black Women on
Race and Sex in America*. New York: Amistad, 2006.

Ginzberg, Lori D. *Elizabeth Cady Stanton: An American Life*. New York: Hill
and Wang, 2009.

Grimké, Angelina. "An Appeal to the Christian Women of the South,"
1836. In *Uncle Tom's Cabin & American Culture: A Multi-Media Archive*,
University of Virginia. http://utc.iath.virginia.edu/abolitn
/abesaegat.html (accessed July 7, 2016).

Grimké, Sarah. "Letters on the Equality of the Sexes," 1837. National
Humanities Center. http://nationalhumanitiescenter.org/ows
/seminarsflvs/Grimke%20Letters.pdf (accessed July 7, 2016).

Harper, Frances Ellen Watkins. "We Are All Bound Up Together," May
1, 1866. Iowa State University. Archives of Women's Political
Communication. http://www.womenspeecharchive.org/women
/profile/speech/index.cfm?ProfileID=185&SpeechID=675 (accessed
July 26, 2016).

Harper, Ida B. Husted. *History of Woman Suffrage*, vol. 5, *1900–1920*.
Washington, D.C.: National American Woman Suffrage Association, 1922.

———. *The Life and Work of Susan B. Anthony*. Indianapolis and Kansas
City: Bowen-Merrill, 1899.

Heritage Foundation. "New Jersey Recognizes the Right of Women to
Vote: February 22, 1797." First Principles Series. http://origin
.heritage.org/initiatives/first-principles/primary-sources/new-jersey
-recognizes-the-right-of-women-to-vote (accessed July 1, 2016).

History.com. "18th and 21st Amendments." http://www.history.com
/topics/18th-and-21st-amendments (accessed October 31, 2016).

———. "Republican Party Founded: March 20. 1854." This Day in History.
http://www.history.com/this-day-in-history/republican-party
-founded (accessed November 1, 2016).

"Josephine Sophia White Griffing: American Abolitionist and Suffragist."
    Encyclopaedia Brittanica. https://www.britannica.com/biography
    /Josephine-Sophia-White-Griffing (accessed July 7, 2016).

Kahn, Mattie. "Let's Celebrate the Women Who Won Last Night: They
    Need You." *Elle*, November 9, 2016. http://www.elle.com/culture
    /career-politics/news/a40643/election-2016-women-winners/
    (accessed November 9, 2016).

Klinghoffer, Judith Apter, and Lois Elkis. "'The Petticoat Electors':
    Women's Suffrage in New Jersey, 1776–1807." *Journal of the Early
    Republic* 12, no. 2 (Summer 1992), 159–193. http://www.jstor.org
    /stable/3124150 (accessed July 1, 2016).

Kolbert, Elizabeth. "Firebrand: Phyllis Schlafly and the Conservative Rev-
    olution." *New Yorker*, November 7, 2005. http://www.newyorker.com
    /magazine/2005/11/07/firebrand (accessed November 9, 2016).

League of Women Voters. "History." http://lwv.org/history (accessed
    November 8, 2016).

Lerner, Gerda. *Black Women in White America: A Documentary History.* New
    York: Vintage Books, 1992.

Liberator. "From the Seneca Falls (N.Y.) Courier, July 21. Women's Rights
    Convention." August 25, 1848.

Library of Congress. "13th Amendment to the U.S. Constitution." Primary
    Documents in American History (Virtual Programs and Services).
    https://www.loc.gov/rr/program/bib/ourdocs/13thamendment.html
    (accessed July 24, 2016).

———. "14th Amendment to the U.S. Constitution." Primary Documents
    in American History (Virtual Programs and Services). https://www
    .loc.gov/rr/program/bib/ourdocs/14thamendment.html (accessed July
    25, 2016).

———. "The Remonstrance (Boston), January, 1909." American Memory
    Timeline. http://www.loc.gov/teachers/classroommaterials
    /presentationsandactivities/presentations/timeline/progress
    /suffrage/remonst.html (accessed November 4, 2016).

Linder, Doug. "The Trial of Susan B. Anthony for Illegal Voting," 2001.
    University of Missouri–Kansas City, Faculty Projects. http://law2
    .umkc.edu/faculty/projects/ftrials/anthony/sbaaccount.html
    (accessed July 29, 2016).

Lowen, Linda. "Who's More Likely to Vote—Women or Men?" About
    .com. http://womensissues.about.com/od/thepoliticalarena/a
    /GenderVoting.htm (accessed August 18, 2016).

Lutz, Alma. *Susan B. Anthony: Rebel, Crusader, Humanitarian.* Washington,
    D.C.: Zenger, 1959.

MacPherson, Myra. *The Scarlet Sisters: Sex, Suffrage, and Scandal in the Gilded Age*. New York: Twelve, 2014.

Marcotte, Amanda. "Trying to Make America Male Again: Women Control the Ballot Box—and Angry, Sexist Trump Voters Can't Deal." *Salon*, August 9, 2016. http://www.salon.com/2016/08/09/trying-to-make -america-male-again-women-control-the-ballot-box-and-angry-sexist -trump-voters-cant-deal/ (accessed August 18, 2016).

McGoldrick, Neale. "Women's Suffrage and the Question of Color." National Council for the Social Studies. http://www.socialstudies.org/system /files/publications/se/5905/590503.html (accessed August 17, 2016).

McMillen, Sally G. *Lucy Stone: An Unapologetic Life*. Oxford and New York: Oxford University Press, 2015.

———. *Seneca Falls and the Origin of the Women's Rights Movement*. Oxford and New York: Oxford University Press, 2008.

Milbank, Dana. "A Thank-You for 18 Million Cracks in the Glass Ceiling." *Washington Post*, June 8, 2008. http://www.washingtonpost.com /wp-dyn/content/article/2008/06/07/AR2008060701879.html (accessed August 18, 2016).

Miller, Bradford. *Returning to Seneca Falls: The First Woman's Rights Convention and Its Meaning for Men and Women Today*. Hudson, NY: Lindisfarne Press, 1995.

Mott, Abigail. "Biographical Sketches and Interesting Anecdotes of Persons of Color. To Which Is Added a Selection of Pieces in Poetry." Priscilla Juvelis. http://www.juvelisbooks.com/pages/books/8292/ abigail-mott/biographical-sketches-and-interesting-anecdotes-of -persons-of-color-to-which-is-added-a-selection#sthash.gXhNJsxV .dpuf (accessed July 16, 2016).

"The Motts: Lydia and Abigail." Underground Railroad History Project. http://undergroundrailroadhistory.org/page_id46/page_id76/ (accessed July 16, 2016).

National Park Service. "Quaker Influence." Women's Rights National Historical Park. https://www.nps.gov/wori/learn/historyculture /quaker-influence.htm (accessed July 4, 2016).

———. "Report of the Woman's Rights Convention," 1848. Women's Rights National Historic Park. https://www.nps.gov/wori/learn /historyculture/report-of-the-womans-rights-convention.htm (accessed July 3, 2016).

———. "Signers of the Declaration of Sentiments," July 20, 1848. Women's Rights National Historical Park. https://www.nps.gov/wori /learn/historyculture/signers-of-the-declaration-of-sentiments.htm (accessed July 3, 2016).

"New Jersey State Constitution of 1776," Section IV. Official Website of the State of New Jersey. http://www.state.nj.us/njfacts/njdoc10a.htm (accessed June 23, 2016).

New York Times. "The Claflin Family. Times Machine: November 3, 1872." http://timesmachine.nytimes.com/timesmachine/1872/11/03/79024263.html?pageNumber=1 (accessed July 29, 2016).

———. "Death of Fred Douglass," February 21, 1895. http://www.nytimes.com/learning/general/onthisday/bday/0207.html (accessed August 24, 2016).

———. "Great Advance of Suffrage Since Last Year's Parade," May 4, 1913. http://query.nytimes.com/mem/archive-free/pdf?res=9903E5D8173FE633A25757C0A9639C946296D6CF (accessed August 9, 2016).

———. "Transcript: Hillary Clinton's Speech at the Democratic Convention," July 28, 2016. http://www.nytimes.com/2016/07/29/us/politics/hillary-clinton-dnc-transcript.html (accessed August 18, 2016).

———. "Tributes of Two Races," February 26, 1895. http://query.nytimes.com/mem/archive-free/pdf?_r=2&res=990CE7D6123DE433A25755C2A9649C94649ED7CF (accessed August 23, 2016).

Newkirk, Pamela. *Letters from Black America*. New York: Farrar, Straus and Giroux, 2009.

Norgren, Jill. "Belva Lockwood: Blazing the Trail for Women in Law." *Prologue Magazine* 37, no. 1 (Spring 2005). Available at National Archives. http://www.archives.gov/publications/prologue/2005/spring/belva-lockwood-1.html (accessed August 1, 2016).

Oates, Stephen B. *With Malice Toward None: The Life of Abraham Lincoln*. New York and Scarborough, Ont.: New American Library, 1977.

Oberlin College. "About Oberlin: History." https://new.oberlin.edu/about/history.dot (accessed June 27, 2016).

Orlov, Alex. "More White Women Voted for Donald Trump Than for Hillary Clinton." Policy.Mic, November 9, 2016. https://mic.com/articles/158995/more-white-women-voted-for-donald-trump-than-for-hillary-clinton#.LYLBIo6IB (accessed November 9, 2016).

Painter, Nell. *Sojourner Truth: A Life, A Symbol*. New York: W. W. Norton, 1996.

"Partial Census Figures and Other Vital Data for Chinese Living in Wyoming from 1869–1890." Western Wyoming Community College. Wyoming History. http://www.wwcc.wy.edu/wyo_hist/Chinese_census_data.pdf (accessed November 2, 2016).

"Paulina Kellogg Wright Davis." *American National Biography Online*. http://www.anb.org/articles/15/15-00166.html (accessed July 8, 2016).

Penney, Sherry H., and James D. Livingston. *A Very Dangerous Woman: Martha Wright and Women's Rights*. Amherst and Boston: University of Massachusetts Press, 2004.

Peterson, Merrill D. *Thomas Jefferson and the New Nation*. London, Oxford, and New York: Oxford University Press, 1970.

Rea, Tom. "Right Choice, Wrong Reasons: Wyoming Women Win the Right to Vote." WyoHistory.org. http://www.wyohistory.org/essays/right -choice-wrong-reasons-wyoming-women-win-right-vote (accessed July 26, 2016).

"Report of the Woman's Rights Convention, 1848." *University of Rochester Library Bulletin* 4, no. 1 (Autumn 1948). http://rbscp.lib.rochester. edu/2448 (accessed July 5, 2016).

"Report of the Woman's Rights Convention, Held at Seneca Falls, N.Y., July 19th and 20th, 1848 (Rochester, 1848)." In Ann D. Gordon, ed., *The Selected Papers of Elizabeth Cady Stanton and Susan B. Anthony*, vol. 1, *In the School of Anti-Slavery, 1840 to 1866*. New Brunswick, N.J., Rutgers, The State University of New Jersey, 1997. Available at http:// ecssba.rutgers.edu/docs/seneca.html (accessed July 3, 2016).

"The Revolution 1868–1872." Accessible Archives. http://www.accessible -archives.com/collections/the-revolution/ (accessed July 27, 2016).

Richardson, Heather Cox. *To Make Men Free*: *A History of the Republican Party* New York: Basic Books, 2014.

Richardson, Marilyn. *Maria W. Stewart, America's First Black Woman Political Writer: Essays and Speeches*. Bloomington, IN: Indiana University Press, 1987.

Robinson, Marius. "Women's Rights Convention: Sojourner Truth," *Anti-Slavery Bugle* (New Lisbon, Ohio), June 21, 1851. Available at Library of Congress, Chronicling America. http://chroniclingamerica .loc.gov/lccn/sn83035487/1851-06-21/ed-1/seq-4/ (accessed August 23, 2016).

Rochester, City of. "Office of the Mayor." http://www.cityofrochester.gov /article.aspx?id=8589934829 (accessed August 17, 2016).

Rodrique, Jessie M. "Why Worcester?" 2002. Worcester Women's History Project. http://www.wwhp.org/Resources/whyworcester.html (accessed July 12, 2016).

"Roots of Prohibition." PBS. *Prohibition*. http://www.pbs.org/kenburns /prohibition/roots-of-prohibition/ (accessed October 31, 2016).

Rush, Benjamin. "Thoughts upon Female Education, Accommodated to the Present State of Society, Manners, and Government, in the United States of America. Addressed to the Visitors of the Young Ladies Academy in Philadelphia, 28th July, 1787, at the Close of the Quarterly Examination." *Universal Asylum and The Columbian Magazine* (Philadelphia), April 1790, 209–213; May 1790, 288–292. Quoted in "Benjamin Rush, from 'Thoughts upon Female Education.'" ExplorePAhistory.com. http://explorepahistory.com/odocument. php?docId=1-4-15B (accessed June 27, 2016).

Salinger, Tobias. "Susan B. Anthony's Grave Decorated with 'Thank You' Sign Celebrating Hillary Clinton's Nomination." *New York Daily News*, July 28, 2016. http://www.nydailynews.com/news/politics/susan-b -anthony-grave-decorated-sign-article-1.2730071 (accessed August 16, 2016).

Schwarzenbach, Sibyl A. *Women and the United States Constitution: History, Interpretation, and Practice*. New York: Columbia University Press, 2003.

Sherr, Lynn. *Failure Is Impossible: Susan B. Anthony in Her Own Words*. New York: Times Books / Random House, 1995.

Smolkin, Rachel. "The Long Journey from Seneca Falls to Hillary 2016," June 8, 2016. CNN Politics. http://www.cnn.com/2016/06/08/politics /hillary -clinton-historic-nomination/index.html (accessed August 18, 2016).

Spencer, Samuel R. Jr. *Booker T. Washington and the Negro's Place in American Life*. Toronto: Little, Brown, 1955.

Stanton, Elizabeth Cady. December 24, 1868. Accessible Archives. http:// www.accessible.com/accessible/print?AADocList=9&AADocStyle= STYLED&AAStyleFile=&AABeanName=toc1&AANextPage=/printFull DocFromXML.jsp&AACheck=5.223.9.0.0 (accessed July 25, 2016).

———. May 27, 1868. Accessible Archives. http://www.accessible.com /accessible/print?AADocList=15&AADocStyle=STYLED&AAStyleFile= &AABeanName=toc1&AANextPage=/printFullDocFromXML .jsp&AACheck=2.353.15.0.0 (accessed July 27, 2016).

———. *Eighty Years and More: Reminiscences, 1815–1897*. New York: T. Fisher Unwin, 1898.

Stanton, Elizabeth Cady, Susan B. Anthony, and Matilda Joslyn Gage. *History of Woman Suffrage*, vol. 1, *1848–1861*. Rochester, NY: Charles Mann, 1889.

———. *History of Woman Suffrage*, vol. 2, *1861–1876*. Rochester: Susan B. Anthony, 1881.

Stone, Lucy. "A Disappointed Woman." Primary Source Documents, 1850 to 1874. Facts On File, 2014. History Research Center Web (accessed May 31, 2016).

Stovall, James Glen. *Seeing Suffrage: The Washington Suffrage Parade of 1913, Its Pictures and Its Effect on the American Political Landscape*. Knoxville: University of Tennessee Press, 2013.

"Temperance & Prohibition." Ohio State University. College of Arts and Sciences. Anti-Saloon League. https://prohibition.osu.edu/anti -saloon-league (accessed October 31, 2016).

Terborg-Penn, Rosalyn. *African American Women in the Struggle for the Vote, 1850–1920*. Bloomington: Indiana University Press, 1998.

Terrell, Mary Church. "The Progress of Colored Women." Sweet Briar College. Gifts of Speech. http://gos.sbc.edu/t/terrellmary.html (accessed August 2, 2016).

———. "Susan B. Anthony, the Abolitionist." Howard University, Moorland-Spingarn Collection, Mary Church Terrell Papers.

———. "Use the Franchise! An Appeal to the Colored Woman to Vote," 1946. Howard University. Moorland-Spingarn Collection. AfraAmerican / Mary Church Terrell Papers.

Tetrault, Lisa. *The Myth of Seneca Falls: Memory and the Women's Suffrage Movement, 1848–1898*. Chapel Hill: University of North Carolina Press, 2014.

"The Trial of Susan B. Anthony: A Short Narrative." Federal Judicial Center, History of the Federal Judiciary. http://www.fjc.gov/history /home.nsf/page/tu_anthony_narrative.html (accessed July 31, 2016).

University of Chicago Press. "Representation: John Adams to James Sullivan, May 26, 1776." *The Founders' Constitution*, vol. 1, chapter 13, document 10. http://press-pubs.uchicago.edu/founders/documents /v1ch13s10.html (accessed October 25, 2016).

"Upstate New York and the Women's Rights Movement." University of Rochester. River Campus Libraries. Rare Books, Special Collections and Preservation. http://rbscp.lib.rochester.edu/1800#seneca (accessed July 6, 2016).

Van Voris, Jacqueline. *Carrie Chapman Catt: A Public Life*. New York: Feminist Press at the City University of New York, 1987.

Ward, Geoffrey C. et al. *Not for Ourselves Alone: The Story of Elizabeth Cady Stanton and Susan B. Anthony*. New York: Alfred A. Knopf, 1999.

Wellman, Judith. *The Road to Seneca Falls*. Urbana and Chicago: University of Illinois Press, 2004.

Wharton, Martha L. "Maria W. Stewart." In *African American National Biography*, vol. 7. Edited by Henry Louis Gates Jr. and Evelyn Brooks Higginbotham. Oxford and New York: Oxford University Press, 2008.

Wheeler, Marjorie Spruill, ed. *One Woman, One Vote: Rediscovering the Woman Suffrage Movement*. Troutdale, OR: NewSage Press, 1995.

"Woman." *Lily*. October 16, 1854. Accessible Archives. http://www.accessible .com/accessible/print?AADocList=31&AADocStyle=STYLED&AAStyle

-File=&AABeanName=toc1&AANextPage=/printFullDocFromXML
.jsp&AACheck=1.96.31.0.0 (accessed July 15, 2016).

"Woman's Rights Convention: Awful Combination of Socialism, Abolitionism, and Infidelity." *New York Herald*, October 25, 1850. Available at Assumption College. U.S. Women's History Workshop. http://www1.assumption.edu/WHW/old/NY_HeraldI.html (accessed August 23, 2016).

Woodhull, Victoria. "Woodhull Address Before Congress." December 19, 1870. University of Massachusetts Lowell, An American Time Capsule: Three Centuries of Broadsides and Other Printed Ephemera. http://faculty.uml.edu/sgallagher/Woodhullmemorial.htm (accessed July 29, 2016).

Yellin, Carol Lynn, and Janann Sherman. *The Perfect 36: Tennessee Delivers Woman Suffrage*. Memphis, TN: Serviceberry Press, 1998.

Zahniser, J. D., and Amelia R. Fry. *Alice Paul: Claiming Power*. Oxford: Oxford University Press, 2014.

Index

Note: Italic page numbers refer to illustrations.